A LITTLE GOD TIME

FOR GIRLS

CAROL GARBORG

BroadStreet
KIDS

BroadStreet Publishing Group LLC
Racine, Wisconsin, USA
Broadstreetpublishing.com

A LITTLE GOD TIME FOR GIRLS

ISBN 978-1-4245-5391-4 (hardcover)
ISBN 978-1-4245-5392-1 (ebook)

Devotional entries written by Carol Garborg.

Design by Chris Garborg | garborgdesign.com
Editorial services by Michelle Winger.
Printed in China.

17   18   19   20   21   22   23   8   7   6   5   4   3   2

THIS IS THE DAY THAT
THE LORD HAS MADE.
LET US REJOICE AND
BE GLAD TODAY!

PSALM 118:24 NCV

INTRODUCTION

If you are looking for a great way to start off your day, you've come to the right place!

Be encouraged with truth and flooded with joy as you spend time with God, reflecting on these devotions, scriptures, and prayers. Let him show you that you are beautiful, you are loved, and you were created with a purpose. There is no one quite like you, and he is delighted to call you his daughter.

Let God's everlasting promises strengthen your heart, mind, and spirit as you spend a little time with him.

JANUARY

God chose us to belong to Christ
before the world was created. He
chose us to be holy and without
blame in his eyes. He loved us.

EPHESIANS 1:4 NIRV

A NEW YEAR AND A NEW BABY SISTER

Anyone who belongs to Christ has become a new person. The old life is gone; a new life has begun!
2 CORINTHIANS 5:17 NLT

Sophia looked down in her arms at her new baby sister. She was so beautiful! Soft, perfect skin. Tiny toes and little fingers that wrapped around her own finger. *And look at her little mouth when she yawns!* Sophia thought. Pretty soon she'd be cooing and belly laughing, crawling and blowing bubbles. Babies were just so much fun.

Babies are a reminder of new birth. New birth means a new beginning. Jesus said that if you believe in him, he promises to take away everything you've ever done wrong and give you new life. With that new life comes a new beginning. You can start over fresh and new.

There's nothing that would make Jesus happier than to have you believe in him and start this New Year with a new beginning.

Dear Jesus, I believe in you. Please forgive my sin and give me new life. Thank you that you don't hold anything against me or keep track of how I've messed up in the past. With you I have a new beginning. Amen.

STRESSING OUT AND BEING STILL

Be still and know that I am God.
I will be praised in all the nations;
I will be praised throughout the earth.
PSALM 46:10 NCV

Jessica could never sit still. She couldn't watch TV without wiggling her foot. She couldn't sit in class without bouncing her leg up and down. Her hands were always fidgeting or texting or twirling her hair. Being still was out of the question. She loved to be moving and doing.

Sometimes that's how we are on the inside. We can't "sit still" inside because we're busy thinking and stressing out…

about a stupid comment we made yesterday
about how to fix a broken friendship
about falling apart at dance tryouts

Maybe you're stressing out about all the bad news on TV and the violence and problems in the world. *It's so awful,* you think. *I'm starting to freak out.* God says in this verse, "Be quiet inside. Be still. I've got things covered and I'm in control."

So instead of stressing out, talk to God. Then just chill and be still, knowing that he is God.

God, sometimes I get worked up on the inside and get really stressed out. Remind me to quiet my heart and remember that you are a big, powerful God. Amen.

DO AND DON'T

Don't worry about anything; instead, pray about everything.
Tell God what you need, and thank him for all he has done.

PHILIPPIANS 4:6 NLT

Problems are like magnets. They attract all your attention. You think about them, talk about them, text about them, and journal about them. Most people worry about problems. All. The. Time.

God says, "Don't worry about anything." Which is good advice (we are, after all, talking about God's Word here), but he knew you needed a little more than a list of don'ts.

Don'ts can be discouraging because they tell you what you *can't* do.

- Don't forget to wash your hands.
- Don't go outside until you finish your homework.
- Don't worry.

Do's are empowering because they tell you how you *can* change the situation. In this verse, you find out what you can do to change the situation you're in.

- Pray about everything.
- Tell God what you need.
- Thank him, even though you haven't seen an answer yet. It's coming!

What would help you remember to pray and tell God about everything instead of worrying so much?

Lord, my mind gets stuck on problems like bees buzz around honey. Help me to focus on you instead of on my problems. When I'm tempted to worry, would you remind me to thank you that you've got things covered? Amen.

MESSING UP

*To him who is able to keep you from stumbling
and to present you before his glorious presence
without fault and with great joy.*

JUDE 24 NIV

Zoe and her dad were hiking down a steep road, carefully placing one foot in front of the other. Zoe's left foot hit loose gravel on the rocky road and she stumbled, tripped, and fell onto her back. Zoe's dad held out his hand and helped pull her up. She came away embarrassed and with a few bruises.

When the Bible talks about stumbling, it's talking about making mistakes and messing up. A thoughtless word. An angry look. The results can be a lot more serious than bruises and embarrassment. A quick, unkind word can ruin a friendship. An angry look can hurt feelings. When it's past, we feel terrible. We really do. But the damage sometimes has already been done.

The Lord is your helper. He can keep you from slipping, stumbling, and messing up. He can keep you from making mistakes you really don't mean, or want, to make and keep you standing. His specialty is taking failure and turning it into success.

Dear God, thanks for your patience with me. Thanks for continuing to work in my life even when I mess up. I want to let you have your way in me. Amen.

BEING BOLD

I am not ashamed of the gospel, because it is the power of God that brings salvation to everyone who believes.
ROMANS 1:16 NIV

There's an idea floating around these days that if you tell someone about God you're forcing your beliefs on them. But forcing your beliefs on someone has more to do with *how* you tell others about God than actually telling them about him.

Say you just got tickets to the next Taylor Swift concert. (Don't you wish.) You call your friend and say, "Guess what? I'm going to the Taylor Swift concert! I'm so excited!" That's not forcing your friend to be excited too. You're just sharing your joy.

Or say you found a new app you love. Wouldn't you tell all your girlfriends about it? You're not forcing the app on anyone. You just want them to use what you think is amazing.

The gospel—the news that Jesus Christ died on the cross and offers forgiveness and salvation to everyone—is good news! Share it without being apologetic or ashamed or pressured into thinking that you're doing something wrong.

Dear God, I don't want to be ashamed of your Word. It's the power of God and it brings salvation. Bring people my way who I can encourage to believe in you. Amen.

SNOWBALLS

*Fix your thoughts on what is true, and honorable,
and right, and pure, and lovely, and admirable.
Think about things that are excellent and worthy of praise.*
PHILIPPIANS 4:8 NLT

Every snowman starts with a little snowball. Scoop up cold, wet snow and pack it into a small ball. Drop that little snowball and then roll it around in a patch of snow or send it rolling down a sledding hill. With every roll, the ball picks up more snow and grows bigger and bigger until you've got an enormous snow "body."

Thoughts are like a snowball that start small and get bigger. Say you're on the way to art class. A few friends pass you in the hall without smiling. *I wonder why they didn't say anything to me*, you might think. *Maybe they're mad at me. But I didn't do anything wrong. I didn't do anything to deserve getting mad at. That's totally unfair!*

See what happens. Once a negative thought gets rolling, it's hard to stop it. Thinking things that are unkind, untrue, and impure is a great way to become worried, irritated, and angry. But once you get a good, true, encouraging thought rolling it can make your heart soar!

How do negative thoughts make you feel? How do good thoughts make you feel?

Dear God, sometimes my thoughts roll around like a snowball getting bigger and bigger with each roll. When I'm "on a roll," remind me to think about things that are true and lovely and right. Amen.

FEELING GOOD

We have thought on Your lovingkindness, O God.
PSALM 48:9 NASB

Jessica was the kind of person everyone loved to be around. She was fun and funny and kind. She always wore a smile and gave out hugs like they were Skittles. Being around Jessica just made people feel good.

If you've ever had a friend like that, you come away feeling encouraged and happy. Spending time with God does exactly the same thing. Thinking about who he is makes you feel loved and special. That's because he...

shows mercy,

is kind,

does not become angry quickly and

has great love. (Psalm 103:8 NCV)

In fact, his love reaches all the way up to heaven; his faithfulness stretches up to the sky (Psalm 33:5). Close your eyes, breathe in deep, and think about this: God's love for you doesn't fail. It will never stop but go on and on and on and on. How does that makes you feel?

Dear God, your love reaches to heaven. Your faithfulness stretches up to the sky. You never change. You never stop loving. Thank you for loving me. Amen.

DR. PEPPER AND SPRITE

We use our tongues to praise our Lord and Father, but then
we curse people, whom God made like himself. Praises and
curses come from the same mouth! My brothers and sisters,
this should not happen.... Can a fig tree make olives,
or can a grapevine make figs? No!

JAMES 3:9-12 NCV

Karissa sprinkled her fries with salt and then walked across the food court for a soda refill. She pressed the lever under the Dr. Pepper sign and bubbly white came out. *What?* She took a sip. It was Sprite. Weird. She pressed it again and the same thing happened. She pressed it a third time and foamy Dr. Pepper filled her cup. She walked away happy but puzzled. *That was strange*, she thought. *Really strange.*

Everyone knows that you can't get Dr. Pepper and Sprite from the same spigot. You can't pick pears from apple trees or blueberries from strawberry plants. It just doesn't make sense.

But that's what sometimes happens with our mouths. Praise songs pour out of our mouth in church on Sunday and a dirty joke spills out on the bus the next day. We say, "Hi, Gina. How's it going?" at volleyball practice and then, "Gina is such an idiot!" at a sleepover the next day. It doesn't make sense. More than that, it's just not right!

Dear Lord, help me guard my heart. I pray that what's inside my heart would be consistent with what I say and do. Amen.

14

DESIGNER LABEL

*We are God's masterpiece. He has created us anew
in Christ Jesus, so we can do the good things
he planned for us long ago.*
EPHESIANS 2:10 NLT

You can tell a real Coach purse from a knock-off by the label. That label tells you who made the purse—and that's where the real value is. Who made the purse makes all the difference. It tells you about the soft leather, the quality, the detail, and ultimately how much the purse is worth.

You were made by the Creator of heaven and earth. You're his masterpiece and you wear his label. That's where your value comes from. It doesn't come from what you have, do, or what people say about you any more than pasting a "Coach" label on a cheap purse turns it into the real thing. Your value never changes either.

You can make the dance team, or not.

You can have a swimming pool and a big house, or not.

You can be part of the "in" group, or not.

Someone can say hurtful things about you, or not.

And your value won't change—because who made you doesn't change. So if things get tough or someone questions your value by calling you names, remember who made you. Remember your value.

Dear God, I am your masterpiece: a priceless person in your eyes. Thank you for making me who I am. Not someone else. Not different. Just me. Amen.

VENDING MACHINE

Here is what we can be sure of when we come to God in prayer. If we ask anything in keeping with what he wants, he hears us.

1 JOHN 5:14 NIRV

"Okay, Lena. What'll it be?" asked her Dad. "Chips or pretzels? Or does a chocolate chip cookie sound better? And please do not let your mother know we're eating from a vending machine for dinner."

Sometimes we treat God like a vending machine. We go to him when we need something, and then expect him to deliver.

Step one: Insert prayer and a lot of faith.

Step two: Press your request.

Step three: Reach in to receive your delivered answer.

That's not of course how it works. Yes, God loves to answer your prayers. Yes, he likes to give you good things. But he's not a request-on-demand God. He's a real person with a big plan and reasons for why he says yes or no. Just like your mom. Just like your dad.

When you pray, expect God to listen—because he will. But trust him if the answer is different than what you wanted.

Dear God, thank you for hearing my prayers. I pray that I'd trust you no matter what the answer is. I know that you are good. Amen.

A NEW DRESS

Since God chose you to be the holy people he loves,
you must clothe yourselves with tenderhearted mercy,
kindness, humility.
COLOSSIANS 3:12 NLT

Finally! Molly held up the pale green dress and smiled. On Saturday she was going to be a bridesmaid in her cousin's wedding. After weeks of waiting, her dress was finally here.

Molly unzipped her jeans and left them in a puddle on the floor. She slipped the dress over her head then twirled around in front of the mirror. She felt layers of soft silky fabric swish around her. The dress was perfect!

One of the best things you can dress yourself with is humility and kindness. (Of course a perfect bridesmaid dress runs a close second.) You can choose how you treat people like you choose the clothes you wear. Being humble and kind looks good on you and it feels good. And it makes those around you feel good too.

Can you think of anyone who "dresses" with humility and someone who is always kind?

Dear Lord, when I get dressed every morning, remind me how beautiful humility and kindness looks to you. Amen.

HEALTHY BODY, HEALTHY BONES

Don't depend on your own wisdom.
Respect the Lord and refuse to do wrong.
Then your body will be healthy, and your bones will be strong.
PROVERBS 3:7-8 NCV

Push-ups. Sit-ups. Jumping jacks and jogging on the treadmill. Do all that and eat salads, fruits, veggies, and cut out sugars and fried foods and you'll be healthy, right? Sort of.

Physical fitness is what comes to mind when we think of having a healthy body. Things like food, exercise, vitamins, and a good night's sleep. But refusing to do what's wrong and fearing, or respecting, the Lord instead of relying on yourself brings health too.

God's Word and his commands protect us from what's harmful and what's wrong. They keep us healthy and strong. Worry, anger, and unforgiveness all have a serious negative effect on the body and on our stress levels. And these things—sin—also make God sad so he can't have his perfect way in our bodies. Think healthy, do healthy, and be healthy by fearing God and staying away from what's wrong.

Dear Lord, when I think about being healthy my mind jumps to working out, playing sports, eating healthy. But I don't want to forget the most important health component of all—obeying you and trusting in your Word. Thanks for your commands that protect my mind and heal my body. Amen.

TASTY BITES

The words of a gossip are like tasty bits of food.
People like to gobble them up.
PROVERBS 18:8 NCV

Melissa was propped on her bed doing homework when the phone rang. "Hey, Taylor," she said.

"You're never going to believe what I just heard? Jackson said Samantha isn't going to the party Saturday. She's grounded for something really serious."

"Really? I wonder what it is. Maybe it's...."

Gossiping can be fun. Who doesn't like handing out delicious bits of information that no one else knows? You become the center of attention as every ear turns—to you! It makes you feel important, the expert on a subject everyone else is clueless about.

Listening to gossip can also be fun. Eating up all that juicy information about *her* or *him* or *that* puts you in the know, inside the circle of people who understand what's *really* going on. And knowing what's really going on is important, right?

God says that in the end gossip stirs up trouble. It morphs into rumors and divides friends instead of bringing them together. It assumes things are true even when they're not. And gossip spills secrets that are best kept locked-up safe.

When you're in a conversation and someone starts to gossip, what could you do?

Dear Lord, I want to be the kind of friend who can be trusted—with secrets, with sticking up for others, with telling the absolute truth. If I start to say something I know doesn't need to be shared, please remind me to stop! Amen.

PICKING FRIENDS

The righteous choose their friends carefully,
but the way of the wicked leads them astray.
PROVERBS 12:26 NIV

Hmm, what should I wear? thought Harper as she stood in her closet. *Will it be the pink tunic with black leggings or the three-quarter sleeve tee with skinny jeans?* Big decision.

Choosing friends is a little like choosing clothes, only far more important of course. Actually being *careful* about picking friends isn't something we usually think about. After all, some friendships just happen.

Here are some questions to think about:

- Where are my friends headed? (And we're not talking about the mall here.) If I lived like they're living, how would I end up?
- What's important to my friends? Is it what I want to be important to me?
- What kinds of things do they encourage me to do?
- Do they make doing what's right easy or hard?
- Do my closest friends share my faith in Jesus?

The answers will empower you to decide if they're the best friends to have or if they're headed in a direction you'd rather not be going.

God, thank you for good friends. I don't know what I'd do without them. Help me to be careful choosing my friends. Amen.

OWIES

Whoever would foster love covers over an offense,
but whoever repeats the matter separates close friends.
PROVERBS 17:9 NIV

When Addison's brother was four, he fell off his trike onto the pavement and skinned his knee. He started to cry, and Addison wrapped him up in a hug and told him it was going to be okay. She took him inside to her mom who cleaned the owie and covered it up with a superhero Band-Aid.

After a few days her little brother's owie started to heal and a small scab covered the sensitive skin underneath. But being curious he pulled off the Band-aid and the scab, and the owie started to hurt again.

When someone hurts us with what they do or say, it's like we get an "owie" inside. What we do with that hurt can make it worse or help it heal. Reminding someone of what they did wrong and turning it over and over in our mind is like what Addison's brother did. It uncovers the hurt, makes it worse, and keeps it from healing. But choosing to forgive allows the hurt to heal. Forgiveness makes love grow.

Is there someone who has hurt you? Or do you know someone who's been hurt? How can you encourage them to let love grow?

Dear Lord, I don't feel like forgiving. What they did hurt. But you said forgiveness makes love grow, and that's what I want. So I let go of hurt and hug forgiveness. Amen.

GOOGLE IT

All Scripture is God-breathed and is useful for teaching, rebuking, correcting and training in righteousness.
2 TIMOTHY 3:16 NIV

Want to know what the number one selling cosmetic brand in America is? Google it.

Want to know how much a singer is worth? Google it.

With Google, Bing, Yahoo, or any search engine, you can access any information you want. If you need it, you can find it.

In some ways, God's Word, the Bible, is the ultimate search engine. It doesn't just pull together answers though; it has all the answers for life. Struggling with temptation? Want to know how to get along with others? Not sure what decision to make? God's Word will lead you to the answer. It's packed with true stories, principles, and truth that give you God-power and God-wisdom to live everyday life.

What's the first thing you'd like to "google" in God's Word?

Dear God, you've given me everything I need to know about you. The Bible isn't just a book. It's your Word, and it's life! Teach me how to learn your Word inside and out. Amen.

THE HIDDEN YOU

LORD, You have searched me and known me.
You know when I sit down and when I stand up;
You understand my thoughts from far away.
PSALM 139:1-2 HCSB

She had two strikes against her. First, she was a woman in a country where women weren't important. Second, she was a bad woman. She had done so many bad things no one wanted to be her friend, which is why she grabbed her bucket and walked past the chickens and sheep to get water at the village well—all alone.

Truth was, even though she seemed strong on the outside, she hurt on the inside. Because it hurt not to have people like you. But she brushed away that thought as she brushed the sweat from her forehead. *Boy, it is hot out here!*

At the well she met a man unlike any other person. His name was Jesus.

Jesus talked to her.

Jesus was kind to her.

Jesus knew all about her. He told her that he wanted to give her a gift, a gift of living water and of eternal life.

Just like Jesus knew that woman, he knows you. Even when you've done something bad, Jesus loves you. He knows all about you and he wants to give you the same gift he gave her—kindness, hope, and eternal life.

Dear Jesus, you're not like anyone who ever lived. You're God! You know everything about me and you came so that I would have life. Amen.

CHECK IT OUT: You can read the story of the woman at the well in John 4.

HOPE

Those who hope in the LORD will renew their strength.
They will soar on wings like eagles; they will run
and not grow weary, they will walk and not be faint.
ISAIAH 40:31 NIV

I hope I get Mrs. J. for my teacher.
I hope we can go camping.

Hope is that sparkle of excitement inside that keeps us going. There's always that possibility that even if today isn't that fun or exciting, something better will come along.

What happens when what you hope for doesn't happen? When you don't get Mrs. J. as your teacher and your dad says it won't work to go camping. Or worse, when the person you hoped would be your best friend says unkind things about you. Then what?

Everyone talks about hoping *for something*—a good grade or a spot on the softball team. The problem is that people and circumstances change. If that's where our hope is, we'll be disappointed—a lot.

Read the three words after "hope" in the verse above. It says to be hopeful *in someone*. God never changes. He's always good, always loving, always in control. Even when it doesn't seem like it. Even when bad things happen. Hope in God is never disappointed.

Dear God, I know that you've put desires in my heart, to do, go, and be different things. But things and people and places change. Help me to put my hope in you—the only thing that stays the same from day to day. Amen.

MIRROR, MIRROR ON THE WALL

Those who hear God's teaching and do nothing are like people who look at themselves in a mirror. They see their faces and then go away and quickly forget what they looked like.
JAMES 1:23-24 NCV

Leah was headed out the door for cheer practice. She stopped for a quick look in the hallway mirror and—*ack!* A little zit was poking out from the bottom of her chin. And was that PopTart filling on her shirt?

If you're walking out the door, glance in the mirror, and something's off, you fix it, right? If your zipper's undone, you zip it up. If your braid is loose, you tuck it in. If you've got a spot on your white shirt, you go and change. The point is you do something.

Listening to God's Word without doing what it says is like looking in a mirror and then walking away without doing a thing. It's like shrugging your shoulders and saying, "Oh well. No big deal."

All that good stuff you read in the Bible, all the sermons you listen to at church, all the amazing worship music you sing, don't just listen to it—do it. Don't just hear—act. The result? You'll be blessed! (Read James 1:25.)

Dear Lord, I hear a lot about you—at church, at home, through friends and family. I haven't always been good about putting what I hear into practice. If there's any area like that, please show me what it is. I want to put words into action—and be blessed! Amen.

IT ALL COUNTS

*Whatever you do, whether in word or deed,
do it all in the name of the Lord Jesus,
giving thanks to God the Father through him.*
COLOSSIANS 3:17 NIV

If you divided this list into two different sets, what would they be?

Apples, oranges, carrots, squash, pineapple, green beans, strawberries

Easy, right?

How about this list?

Reading your Bible, playing card games with your cousin, going to youth group, praying, going to the zoo

Most people, and you may or may not be one of them, put them into two categories: things that are spiritual and things that are not. Things that you do for God and things that you do just because.

Truth is, *anything* you do can be a beautiful act of worship to God. Unloading the dishwasher, vacuuming the living room, even picking up dog poop (well, maybe not). You can practice piano as if Jesus were sitting in the room, do your English assignment as if he were going to read it the next day. Not out of a sense of fear, like, *I have to get this perfect or God will be disappointed*—but out of joy, like, *I love the Lord and want to give him my best.*

What's something you never thought was a way to show your love to God? Would you change anything about how you did it?

Dear Lord, I want everything I do to show my love for you—because you deserve the best. Thank you that even the ordinary things in my day can praise you. Amen.

SUPER CREATIVE

"He has filled him with the Spirit of God, with wisdom, with understanding, with knowledge and with all kinds of skills—to make artistic designs for work in gold, silver and bronze, to cut and set stones, to work in wood."
EXODUS 35:30-33 NIV

Some jobs sure seem more important than others. Like being a nurse or doctor or a pilot. After all, doctors and nurses save lives. And hundreds of people rely on a pilot's skill. Or being a pastor. Pastors tell people about God, and what's more important than that?

God chose a guy named Bezalel to create works of gold, silver, bronze, stone, and wood for the tabernacle, a place of worship. Then God filled him up with the power and creativity of his very own Spirit. Not to preach, not to sing, but in order to build and make crafts.

God values creativity and beautiful things. As the one who's super creative, he can give you special gifts of creativity—like writing a poem or a song, or designing a hand-crafted card for a grandparent, or painting a portrait. And because it's special, he'll give you all that you need to do it well. You just have to ask.

Dear Father, thank you for the gift of your Spirit. It's amazing to think that you are inside of me, empowering me to do the jobs I have. Fill me up with your creativity and joy. Amen.

FREE!

We have freedom now, because Christ made us free.
So stand strong.
GALATIANS 5:1 NCV

Chloe, her mom, and her best friend Layla stood just inside the mall's entrance. Chloe's mom handed her a twenty-dollar bill.

"You're free to do whatever you like," Chloe's mom said. "Just meet me back here in an hour."

Free to do whatever I want, thought Chloe. "Hello, Yummy Yogurt shop," Chloe said. "Come on, Layla. Let's go."

Nowhere in the back of Chloe's mind did she think "free to do whatever" meant she could shoplift or trash the food court. She knew what her mom meant.

Freedom isn't something you use to do whatever you want. Real freedom means being free from what's wrong so you can do what's good. Freedom is being free to stand up for others. Free to speak truth. Free to learn. Free to worship God. Free to be strong and do what's right.

How would your life be different if you *weren't* free?

Dear God, thank you that I'm free—free to pray, have friends, and do things I love. Thank you mostly that you freed me from sin. Show me how to use that freedom to serve and love you with all my heart. Amen.

PAY BACK?

The LORD your God has….watched over your journey through this vast wilderness. These forty years the LORD your God has been with you, and you have not lacked anything.

DEUTERONOMY 2:7 NIV

For forty years the people of Israel wandered around in the desert. No swimming pools. No air-conditioning. No glasses of iced tea. No houses, just tents and a lot of dust and sweltering heat. And yet…their clothes never wore out, they didn't get blisters on their feet, they never went thirsty or hungry—even though the reason they were in the desert was their own fault. They had messed up and God grounded them for forty years.

When it comes to his children, and that includes you, God isn't into payback or getting revenge for something you've done wrong. God does correct. He does discipline, but it's with a real goal—to turn your heart back to him and get you on a path that's good.

Dear God, thank you that you love me enough to correct me. Thank you that your love doesn't go away. You always care for and watch over your people, and that includes me. Help me be quick to listen, so I can get on a path that's good. Amen.

SUPER SLOW

You are a forgiving God, gracious and compassionate,
slow to anger and rich in faithful love.
NEHEMIAH 9:17 HCSB

Have you ever turned the honey jar upside down and waited and waited for the honey to slide slowly down the side of the jar and dribble onto your toast? Or whacked the bottom of a ketchup bottle hoping just a little would sloooowly make its way down and plop onto your hot dog?

In a different kind of way, God is really slow too—slow to get angry. It takes forever to make him angry. He's gracious and full of compassion and extremely patient with you. He's not in a hurry to get angry because he loves you.

When you love someone, you believe in that person. You give them not just one chance but two, three, four, five because deep inside you know they're going to get it right. That how God sees you. "From everlasting to everlasting the LORD's love is with those who fear him" (Psalm 103:17).

How would you explain God's snail-slow anger to someone else?

Dear Father, thank you for being slow to anger and patient with me. Thank you for believing in me and giving me more than just one chance. Amen.

KEEPING TRACK

Love...keeps no record of being wronged.
1 CORINTHIANS 13:4-5 NLT

Once upon a time a man owed his king 10,000 bags of gold. He didn't have the money, so the king ordered that the man, his wife and kids, and everything he had be sold to pay the debt.

"Be *patient* with me," the man begged the king. "Please give me more time!"

The king not only was *patient*—he cancelled the debt. The man didn't owe a thing!

The man was ecstatic! He went out and found someone who owed him 100 silver coins, grabbed him by the neck, and said, "Pay up—now!"

The second man fell to knees. "Please, be *patient* with me. Please give me more time!"

But the first man said "Absolutely not!" and he... (Read what happened in Matthew 18:21-35).

The king didn't keep track of the first man's debt. He said, "You don't owe me anything" and let him go free. God doesn't keep track of everything you've done wrong.

When you confess your sin, he completely forgives you and says, "You are forgiven and free!" Remembering that can help when others... start a rumor about you, dump you for another best friend, or even borrow your sweater and then lose it.

Being patient with others is like forgiving a 100-coin debt when God has forgiven your debt of 100,000 bags of gold.

Dear God, when I run into people who are difficult to be patient with and hard to forgive, remind me how patient and forgiving you are with me. Amen.

DEAR DIARY

Hatred stirs up conflict,
but love covers over all wrongs.
PROVERBS 10:12 NIV

Dear Diary,

I think I'm going to be sick. She has that effect on me. It's bad enough that she brags about their family's new cars and vacation homes and how her mom works for the NFL. As if anyone cares about football. Seriously. Then today she tried to steal Mackenzie's crush. She was totally gushing over him, "Oh, Michael, you're so funny!" and then she laughs this fake laugh and puts her hand on his arm. Like he's her pet or something. Argh!

Alaina

You can hardly avoid conflict. It happens to everyone. A classmate says something mean. A friend does something hurtful. Someone tries to take away your friend's crush.

But you can keep that conflict from turning into something worse. An angry remark or a sharp look stirs up conflict and makes it more intense. Showing kindness and forgiveness, even if you don't feel like they deserve it, erases conflict. Love makes up for what's wrong.

What is it about love that makes things better?

Dear God, I get frustrated when people are mean, especially when it hurts those I love. I know getting mad only makes things worse. Help me support my friends and forgive and love those who aren't being nice. Amen.

I WAS MADE TO LIVE FOR YOU

Since God has shown us great mercy,
I beg you to offer your lives as a living sacrifice to him.
Your offering must be only for God and pleasing to him.

ROMANS 12:1 NCV

There once was a blind man who sat by the side of the road asking for money. He did this all day. Every day. It was what he could do. He couldn't hold down a job. Who would hire him? So he held out his hand and asked for a few bucks from those who passed by.

One day Jesus passed by. He gave that man who was born blind his sight. But better than that Jesus gave the man purpose, a reason to get up every day—live for God!

You were made to live for Jesus. He gives your life purpose. Whether you're babysitting or washing dishes or hanging out at the mall, every day is filled with a reason to live—getting to know him and praising him in everything you do, think, or say.

How has Jesus given your life meaning?

Dear God, thank you for giving my life purpose. No matter what I'm doing remind me that I live for you. Amen.

CHECK IT OUT: You can read the whole story about how Jesus gave the blind man purpose in John 9.

THE MUNCHIES

You satisfy me more than the richest feast.
I will praise you with songs of joy.
PSALM 63:5 NLT

Cheesy pizza. Walking tacos. Juicy steaks with mashed potatoes. Stir-fry with noodles or a huge taco salad. If you've got a case of the munchies, what would you want to eat?

Whether it's an all-you-can-eat buffet or hamburger and potato salad feast, munchies are a part of every sleepover, youth retreat, and birthday party. Salty, sour, gooey, sweet. They tease your tongue in a way that begs for more.

Knowing God, who he is and what he likes, satisfies more than the biggest and best feast. Not in a "my-stomach-is-full" kind of way but in a "you-put-a-smile-on-my-face" way. Like the way you feel after you've had your favorite meal, kind of happy and content. Out of that happiness bubbles up songs of joy.

How is it that God satisfies you?

Dear God, people say that spending time with you satisfies in a way that nothing else can. I want to experience that. To slow down, really listen, and get to know you the same way you know me. Amen.

BEST FRIENDS

A friend is always loyal.
PROVERBS 17:17 NCV

Sigh. A whole weekend with my besties, Shelley thought. *I could just die I'm so happy.* Nothing could ruin her day except...well if it just weren't for Diana. Diana could start the meanest rumors. And they *were* rumors. There's no way she, Shelley Williams, would EVER cheat on a test. Never.

Best friends are for fun times like sleepovers and parties. Best friends are for sad times like bad grades and tough news. The best friends, though, are always loyal, and always stick up for you even when no one else does.

How do you think your friends would describe you? Would loyal make the list?

Dear God, thank you for my friends. I don't know what I'd do without them. Please give me friends that love at all times. And help me be that kind of friend to them. Amen.

RAGING OCEAN

If any of you needs wisdom, you should ask God for it.
He is generous to everyone....But when you ask God,
you must believe and not doubt. Anyone who doubts is
like a wave in the sea, blown up and down by the wind.
JAMES 1:5-6 NCV

Should I or shouldn't I?
What if I don't? What if I do?
How will it work out? What if it doesn't work out?
Ack, what do I do?!

If you've got a choice to make, some of these thoughts
might be tearing around inside your brain, threatening to
make your head explode. Who do you ask over for a birthday
party, what do you say to the boy you really like, or should you
try out for the volleyball team? Whether it seems like a big
decision to anyone else, to *you* it really is a big deal. So what
do you do?

First, just ask God for wisdom. Easy, right? But then,
believe that he'll answer. God loves to give out wisdom. God
doesn't reluctantly say, "Well, I'm not sure I'll give *her* any of
my wisdom." No, he's generous! So ask boldly, knowing he'll
answer. Because he wants to!

Then decide. Go ahead, choose. Don't second guess
yourself. Don't doubt. Don't wonder, *Did I do the right
thing?* Just do it. When you doubt or are indecisive, you're
like a wave on the sea that's blown around and doesn't go
anywhere.

Dear God, I haven't always thought of you as generous. I'm sorry.
Please give me wisdom for the choice I need to make.
Thank you that you will. Amen.

FEELINGS

We live by what we believe, not by what we can see.
2 CORINTHIANS 5:7 NCV

Angry. Frustrated. Sad. Confused. Disappointed. Inferior. These are all feelings that can bubble up inside us and threaten to spill over. We want to act on how we feel. Angry? It's tempting to slam a door or yell or pout. Sad? It's tempting to hole up in a room with music cranked up loud or call a friend and talk over how miserable we feel.

The problem is feelings are undependable and unreliable. They're like the wind. They change, they shift, they come, and they go. Trying to live your life on feelings is like trying to walk on a floor that moves.

If you belong to Jesus, you can live by what you know, not by how you feel. When you're feeling disappointed, frustrated, sad, angry, plop down on your bed and pull out the Bible. God's Word is steady, true, and always reliable, unlike your feelings. Read what God says about your situation and act on that. Live by what you know to be true, what you believe in the Bible to be true, not by the circumstances you see.

Dear God, sometimes feelings overwhelm me. I feel so mixed up that I don't know what to do. Show me how to live by your Word that never changes instead of by my feelings. Amen.

FEBRUARY

In ourselves we are not able
to claim anything for ourselves.
The power to do what
we do comes from God.

2 CORINTHIANS 3:5 NIRV

A SNUGGLE

The LORD is close to all who call on him,
yes, to all who call on him in truth.
PSALM 145:18 NLT

"Taryn?"

Taryn looked up from her journal to see three-year-old Jessica standing in the doorway. Her blankie was in one hand and a raggedy teddy bear in the other.

"Taryn, I need a snuggle."

And how could she say no to that. Sometimes you just had to love little sisters.

Whether you're talking about a three-year-old or a thirteen-year-old, sometimes you just want to snuggle—with a mom or a grandpa or a chocolate lab. Being close to someone you love makes you feel loved, special, and safe. Just being with them makes whatever you're going through easier to handle and maybe even a little more distant now that someone else is near.

The Lord is near when you call. Whether you're feeling excited, scared, miserable, or lonely, when you call he draws near. His presence surrounds you. He might not say anything at all but you can know you're safe and understood.

Dear God, I just need to know you're close and that you care. Thanks for answering when I call. Be close, God. Be near. Amen.

39

FATHER TIME

Daniel…went home to his upstairs room where the windows opened toward Jerusalem. Three times a day he got down on his knees and prayed, giving thanks to his God, just as he had done before.

DANIEL 6:10 NIV

Even though Daniel was a slave, he was one of the most powerful men in the kingdom. The king had given him power over all Babylon. Daniel was responsible for a lot of people, so he had a busy schedule. But still Daniel went to his room three times a day, got down on his knees, and prayed. That very important man knew what was most important in his day—spending time with God.

Life gets busy with swimming practice, homework, birthdays, and church events. And still, there's nothing more important—and amazing—than getting to spend time with our Heavenly Father who just happens to be the creator of the whole universe.

Here are a few things you can do to spend time with God:

- Praise—Praise God for who he is. (You are so forgiving, God!)
- Thank—Thank him. (Thank you for helping me with my science homework yesterday.)
- Confess—Confess anything you've done wrong. (God, I got impatient with my mom tonight. Please forgive me.) (Mom, I'm sorry I was impatient and disrespectful.)
- Read—Read a chapter of the Bible or one psalm or proverb a day.
- Ask—Ask God to speak to you through his Word. Tell God what you need. Pray for others.
- Listen—Be quiet in his presence, away from your smartphone or music.

Dear Lord, thank you for taking time to meet with me—anywhere, anytime, about anything. I'm excited to spend time with you and to get to know you. Amen.

A CASE OF THE SILLIES

A cheerful heart is good medicine,
but a crushed spirit dries up the bones.
PROVERBS 17:22 NIV

Have you ever been with a group of friends and had a giggle inside that you couldn't keep quiet? The more you try, the more you start to sputter until you burst out laughing. And because giggles are contagious, one person giggles and then another until pretty soon everyone is laughing. Even when you're all giggled out, it's hard not to keep a big smile from tugging at the corners of your mouth.

Getting someone else to laugh or giggle can make that person feel better. One of the best things you can do for a friend is to make them smile. What's one thing you could do today to make your mom smile? What would make your sister or brother smile? How about your friend?

Dear God, I'm glad you gave us giggles and laughter. They make life silly and fun. Give me the gift of giggles and help me to cheer others up by making them laugh and smile. Amen.

DOWNRIGHT SMART

Yes, I have more insight than my teachers,
for I am always thinking of your laws.
PSALM 119:99 NLT

Don't drop out of school yet!

This verse isn't saying you know more than your math teacher or more French than your French teacher or more about tennis than your tennis coach. That's totally not what this verse is talking about.

God gives wisdom and insight so you're able to understand people and situations spot-on. If you're filling your hard-drive brain with God's truth, it's not surprising that he'd show you things from his perspective, things that others might miss. *That* gives you an edge. It happened with Daniel and his three friends. (Read Daniel 1:17.)

Your teachers can offer information that's helpful for living. When you meditate and learn God's Word, though, you'll be able to understand people and situations in a way that you never could on your own. That kind of insight only comes from God.

So get smart and plug in to his Word.

Dear God, when I think about being smart, I think of the kind of smart that comes from studying hard and knowing a lot. But remind me to meditate on your Word and fill my brain with your truth and insight. Amen.

CHEW ON IT

Oh, how I love your law!
I meditate on it all day long.
PSALM 119:97 NIV

What's your absolute favorite food? Chinese food? Pasta? Let's say it's a candy bar—chewy, gooey, and filled with stringy caramel. When someone hands you a candy bar, do you just look at it or do you chew it over and over and let all that chocolatey goodness melt in your mouth?

One of the best parts of eating is tasting and enjoying it. That means breaking it down into smaller pieces so all that wonderful goodness can get inside you. Meditation is a lot like chewing. It's thinking about something over and over again. It is *not* emptying your mind of everything and just being open. Instead it's filling your mind with God's true Word and chewing on it over and over.

What's one verse you could meditate on today and tomorrow?

Here are a couple suggestions:

"I keep my eyes always on the LORD" (Psalm 16:8).

"Trust in the LORD with all your heart" (Proverbs 3:5).

Dear God, thank you for giving me your Word, the Bible. Thank you for all the promises in your Word and the love I see. Amen.

THUMBS-UP

"The LORD bless you and keep you;
the LORD make his face shine on you and be gracious to you;
the LORD turn his face toward you and give you peace."
NUMBERS 6:24-26 NIV

Miranda was shaking she was so nervous. How would the judge at the meet score her vault? What would he think? The minutes passed slowly and then—a 14.75!

Some people's approval matters more than others. God wanted his people to know that he approved of them, so he told the priest to bless them. The blessing was a message that said, "God loves you. God is with you. God is for you."

God's plan was to surround you with people who would affirm you and let you know that he's for you, not against you. Sometimes he gives you a mom or a dad who does that. Other times it's a grandparent or a youth pastor. Maybe no one has ever blessed you. If that's the case, read this blessing out loud as your own.

God blesses and keeps and cares for you.
God makes his face shine on you. God is gracious to you.
God turns his face toward, not away, from you.
He gives you peace, not worry, not frustration, just peace.

When you crawl into bed tonight and pull the sheets under your chin, take a minute to remember—God gives you a thumbs-up.

Dear God, thank you for your blessing. Thank you that you're for me. Please take away any doubts I have about your love and care. Amen.

SODA CAN AND SELF-CONTROL

A gentle answer will calm a person's anger,
but an unkind answer will cause more anger.

PROVERBS 15:1 NCV

Do you have a can of soda nearby? If you do, *and* if it's okay with your mom or dad, take it outside and shake it up real good. Do it again. Now pop the top. What happens? Depending on how hard you shook the can, the soda will bubble all over your hands and down onto the floor.

That's what happens when someone is angry and you speak angry words back.

Your friend says, "What were you thinking? That was a stupid thing to do!"

And you snap back, "What do you mean stupid? You're the one who's always getting us into trouble!"

Take that approach and it's like shaking a soda can. Keep it up and your friend may just explode.

But if you give them a gentle answer, it might just calm them down.

Your friend says, "What were you thinking? That was a stupid thing to do!"

You say, "It wasn't the best decision. I'm sorry."

It might not work right away. But give it some time.

Before you snap back at someone, ask yourself, "Is what I'm about to say going to make the problem worse or better?"

Dear God, I am tempted to snap back when other people say something angry or hurtful. Remind me to answer anger with gentleness and kind words. Amen.

45

BUT, MOM!

Honor your father and your mother,
as the Lord your God has commanded you,
so that you may live long and so that you may prosper.
DEUTERONOMY 5:16 HCSB

"But, but...why?!"

That was a question a man called Naaman couldn't figure out. He had traveled all the way to the prophet Elisha's house, hoping Elisha would heal him of a nasty skin disease. But Elisha hadn't even bothered coming to the door!

Instead he sent a servant who said, "You're supposed to wash in the Jordan River seven times."

"But why?" Naaman complained. *Wash in the muddy Jordan River?* But someone convinced him he should at least give it a try. Six times he dipped into the river, and on his seventh time up his disease was completely gone. He did what Elisha told him to do and *then* he understood why.

Understanding why we have to do something often gets in the way of doing it. Before we do something, we want to understand, right?

Sometimes you won't understand why you can't go on a missions trip, invite a friend over, or watch a certain movie. Honoring your parents, though, means doing it whether you understand it or not. Later, and sometimes much later, you'll understand why.

Dear God, even when I don't understand why, help me to do it anyway. Amen.

A 21ST CENTURY PRINCESS

"I will be a father to you, and you shall be sons and daughters to Me," says the Lord Almighty.
2 CORINTHIANS 6:18 NASB

Twenty-nine year old Siriwannawari is a fashion designer. But she's also a real princess who lives in Thailand. With the title of princess, Her Royal Highness has privileges and prestige. She's very important, after all. Her grandfather was the King of Thailand.

Wouldn't it be cool to be a princess, just for a day at least? To be driven around in a big limousine and wear real diamonds and gold. To know that you were important enough to pick up the phone and dial a king.

If you've put your faith in Jesus, you are the daughter of a King. He's adopted you into his family and called you his own. No, you don't have a castle, a crown, or a butler to serve you tea. But...

You have status.

You have value.

You have an important name.

Your heavenly Father is King of the universe and you have access to him any hour of the day.

Hold your head up high and act like the royalty you are.

Dear God, you're a perfect Father—and you're a King. Thank you for adopting me into your family and calling me your daughter. I'm totally in awe that you'd do such a thing. Remind me of who I am in you. Amen.

CAVED IN

Truthful lips endure forever,
but a lying tongue, only a moment.
PROVERBS 12:19 HCSB

"Now what are we going to do?" Daniella asked. Ahead of their car the road was caved in.

"It has to be from all the rain we've gotten," her dad commented. "It's eroded the foundation of dirt from under the road. Looks like we'll have to back up and go the other way around."

Daniella groaned. She wanted in the worst way to see Mount Rushmore. But it didn't look like that wasn't going to happen any time soon. Her vacation was a total washout.

Caved in and washed out is what happens when we don't tell the truth. Speaking what's true is like building a road on a foundation of rock. Rain can pour down and that road won't be washed out.

Lying is like building a road on sand. Rain pours down and the road washes out. The road doesn't last and neither does a lie. Someone will always find out the truth. Someone who does what Jesus says and tells the truth is like the house that lasts. The truth lasts forever.

Whether you tell just a little bit of untruth or a full-blown lie, a lying tongue will always be found out. Truthful lips last forever.

Dear God, if I'm ever tempted to lie, help me remember that in the end the truth is what is going to last. Keep me from everything untrue. Amen.

SOMEONE YOU CAN COUNT ON

Whoever can be trusted with a little can also be trusted with a lot, and whoever is dishonest with a little is dishonest with a lot.
LUKE 16:10 NCV

Madelyn and her parents lived in a small apartment. They had a few pieces of used furniture, including an old dining room table and six rickety chairs. One night Maddie's parents invited a family over for dinner. Their teenage son sat down on one of the old chairs. All during dinner, Maddie kept wondering if that chair would hold him up or not. In the middle of chocolate cake and ice cream, Maddie heard a *crack*! And then *splat*! The wobbly chair broke and the guy crashed to the ground. He wasn't hurt. But Maddie was really embarrassed.

Some people are unreliable just like that chair. You don't know if you can trust them or not to be solid and secure. You ask them to do something—and they forget. They promise they'll give you something—and they don't. They keep a secret—sometimes, but you never know when they will and when they won't. They're totally unreliable.

Being the kind of person people can count on, even in the very little things, is practice for learning how to be reliable for bigger things.

Do you think other people describe you as dependable or not?

Dear God, I want to be the kind of person that other people can count on, not like a wobbly chair. When I'm tempted to avoid my small responsibilities, remind me that little things often lead to bigger things. Amen.

49

WORRY WARS

*"You cannot add any time to your life
by worrying about it."*
MATTHEW 6:27 NCV

Emma was a worrier. She worried about her homework and about her grades. She worried what people would think of her. She worried that bad things *would* happen. She worried that good things *wouldn't* happen. Sometimes she was so worried she couldn't sleep at night. All Emma's worrying didn't make anything better; it just made her feel worse. So why did she worry?

People worry because it gives them the illusion they're accomplishing something. Spending time and energy on whatever they're worrying about gives them the false impression that they're more in control. Actually what needs controlling aren't circumstances so much as what's going on in their heads.

Emma found out that the more she thought about God and good things, the less time she had to worry about other things. That's how she fought her worry war, by squeezing out the worry thoughts with thankful, God-filled thoughts.

Have you ever been in a worry war? Can you think of some good things to think on that would help in that fight?

Dear God, sometimes I worry about things that I can't control as if worrying can help me get a handle on what's happening. But I can't. Thank you that you are always in control. Help me to focus on you and what's good and true and right. Amen.

ORDINARY

*Don't you know that you are God's temple
and that God's Spirit lives in you?*
1 CORINTHIANS 3:16 NCV

Lucia and her friends had a front row seat at the pep rally for the Homecoming coronation (okay, it was sitting on the gym floor, but whatever). It was *so* exciting!

I can't wait to find out if Jasmine is crowned queen. Jasmine was her older sister and everyone said she was bee-oou-tiful. She had long flowing black hair, long legs, and a smile that made you feel good inside.

No chance I'll ever get to be homecoming queen, Lucia thought. Not that it bothered her much. She wasn't ugly. It wasn't like people covered their eyes and screamed "Eww!" when she walked by. She was just…well, ordinary.

Average. Regular. Ordinary. That describes most people. They don't stick out; they just blend in and no one really notices they're there or not.

Which might describe how you feel sometimes, like you're so ordinary that you disappear and no one knows you're really there. There's someone who gets that. The Bible says there was nothing about Jesus that made people give him a second glance (Isaiah 53:2). Not a thing. Yet he was the Son of God.

You might be ordinary, but if you believe in Jesus, God's Spirit lives in you. You and others who have faith in him are God's holy temple.

Dear Jesus, thank you for coming to earth and living like any other normal kid. Thank you that you understand what it's like to be powerful but just plain ordinary. Amen.

WHAT LOVE ISN'T

Love…is not jealous, it does not brag,
and it is not proud. Love is not rude,
is not selfish, and does not get upset with others.
1 CORINTHIANS 13:4-5 NCV

I *love* chocolate.
I *love* going to the mall.
I *love* my new puppy.
I *love* her clothes!

We use the word "love" a lot but sometimes we forget
what it means. We *like* all of the things above. After all, who
doesn't like chocolate? Going to the mall *is* fun, especially
with friends. Puppies are so cute, cuddly, and adorable. And
clothes, well, who doesn't appreciate some trendy clothes,
right? But…

Real love isn't liking something a lot

Real love isn't even liking *someone* a lot.

Real love isn't a feeling.

Real love doesn't get jealous or walk around bragging
around what they've done.

Real love doesn't get upset with others.

Real love isn't happy when something bad happens to
someone who isn't nice.

Real love is so much more. So what *IS* love? Read on to the
next page.

**Dear God, you gave me so many things to enjoy—chocolate,
puppies, new clothes, places to go. I like them a lot! But I LOVE
you. Please show me how to love others like you love me. Amen.**

WHAT LOVE IS

Love never fails.
1 CORINTHIANS 13:8 NCV

If you want to know what real love *isn't* you can check out the previous page. But if you want to know what real love *is,* you're at the right place.

Real love comes from God. God is love!

Real love is a relationship between people.

Real love is a choice. Feelings change depending on your mood. You can choose to love someone even if you don't feel like it and even if that person isn't acting very lovable.

Real love is a forever commitment. That commitment shows itself by being patient, kind, and believing the best of someone else, even in hard times.

Someone who loves helps those in need (1 John 3:17).

Someone who loves forgives (1 Peter 4:8).

Someone who loves prays for their enemies (Matthew 5:44).

The greatest love of all, though, is giving up everything for a friend (John 15:3). That's what real love is!

Dear God, thank you for showing me what real love is.
Giving up your life shows me the greatest love of all. Amen.

53

GREAT EXPECTATIONS

"Be merciful, even as your Father is merciful."
LUKE 6:36 ESV

"I don't know why Catalina didn't give me a Valentine this year. We give each other Valentines every year. Ever since we were kids," said Eleanor to her mom.

"I wouldn't worry about it too much," suggested Eleanor's mom. "Maybe something came up."

"Yeah, or maybe she's got more important friends to think about," Eleanor said glumly.

We all walk into relationships with expectations—how we think we should be treated, what we think we should get, what we think someone else should do. When someone doesn't meet those expectations, our mind starts racing. *They don't like me. They don't want to be friends with me anymore. They're trying to ignore me.*

The truth might be something completely different. Maybe they want to be your friend but aren't sure you want to be theirs. Maybe they just forgot your birthday or can't figure out what to get you. Maybe they didn't ignore you when you passed in the hallway; they were worried about something else.

The real reason behind any situation can be a whole lot different than you think. So don't jump to conclusions. Think the best; don't assume the worst.

Dear God, help me to assume the best about people not the worst. Help me keep my thoughts in check. Show me how to be merciful, just like you show mercy to me. Amen.

LOVING THE UNLOVABLE

*The Holy Spirit produces this kind of fruit in our lives:
love, joy, peace, patience, kindness, goodness,
faithfulness, gentleness, and self-control.*
GALATIANS 5:22-23 NLT

Abby makes me so mad! Sadie thought as she walked out the door. *She's always talking about herself. Always thinks she knows everything. Well, she doesn't!*

Sound familiar? Some people are really hard to love. You know you're supposed to be patient with them. You know you're supposed to be kind. But it's hard! How do you love someone obnoxious? How do you love someone who's irritating just to be around?

You can't. Yep, that's right—you can't love them. You won't be able to be patient and kind and loving and gentle on your own. But God's Spirit in you can. Read the verse above. It's the Holy Spirit's job to produce patience, self-control, and kindness in you. It's your job to make sure there's nothing in your life that would keep his Spirit from working in and through you.

Dear God, I've been trying to love someone difficult, but I just can't on my own. Thank you for the gift of your Spirit inside of me. Show me anything in my life that would keep your Spirit of love from working through me. Amen.

55

BEAUTY THAT LASTS

Beauty does not last;
but a woman who fears the LORD
will be greatly praised.
PROVERBS 31:30 NLT

"I cannot believe I have to wear my sister Jenae's hand-me-downs," Valeria moaned. "They're two years old! Everyone knows those old jeans and tops are *so* out of style!"

Whether you're talking about smartphones or the latest fashion, neither of them last. Beauty isn't much different. God makes each of us beautiful—in a way that lasts.

Sure you might have a beautiful smile or deep brown eyes or a cute dimple in your cheek. That kind of beauty, while it's definitely nice to have, will someday fade. What doesn't fade is a woman—that would be you!—who fears, or respects, God. That's a different kind of beauty that lasts on and on.

Dear God, thank you for the different ways beauty shows up in different people around me—in deep brown eyes and long eyelashes and curly hair and straight hair. Thank you too for those people who are an example of beauty that lasts. That's the kind of beauty I want to have! Amen.

SHINE!

"Let your light shine before others, that they may see your good deeds and glorify your Father in heaven."
MATTHEW 5:16 NIV

It's a Friday night and you're at a friend's house for a movie and sleepover. The electricity goes out and everyone giggles and screams because it's both scary and fun. But after a few minutes of sitting in total darkness, it starts to get eerie and you're like "Someone get a flashlight, a candle, anything!"

When you help your mom make the beds, or write your grandma a thank-you note, or offer to play with the little neighborhood kids so their mom can have a break, or you tell someone about Jesus, you're like a flashlight. You're being a light that shines and shows other people who God is. The point of doing good deeds isn't to show people how wonderful you are; it's to show others what God is like and who he is. It's pointing them to him.

What are some good deeds that would show someone what God is like?

Dear God, thank you that I can praise you by doing good things. Thank you that I can show your light by doing what is good. Please give me creative ideas on how to do good for others. Amen.

BLAME GAME

Humble yourselves under the mighty power of God,
and at the right time he will lift you up in honor.
1 PETER 5:6 NLT

"It wasn't my fault," Adam complained, pointing at Eve. "She's the one who told me to do it."

"Don't blame me. It's his fault!" Eve countered and pointed at the serpent.

God looked from one to the other and shook his head unimpressed. Neither of them wanted to own the problem.

God had told Adam and Eve they could eat from any tree in the garden—except the fruit from one tree. They didn't pay any attention, and now they were playing the blame game.

When we justify what we did or point to someone else, that's blame. Owning up means humbling ourselves and taking credit for the part of the problem that was ours.

Even though it's not easy, humbling yourself is the first step toward being lifted up to a place of honor.

Dear God, it's hard for me to ask this, but is there anything that I need to own? Is there anything I'm blaming on someone else that I should be taking responsibility for myself? Amen.

READ THE ORIGINAL BLAME GAME: Check out Genesis 3:1-13.

JUST WANT TO JUMP

He jumped to his feet and began to walk.
Then he went with them into the temple courts,
walking and jumping, and praising God.

ACTS 3:8 NIV

"I did it!" Annabelle jumped up from off the bed and spun around.

"You did what? What did you do?" asked her cousin Jocelyn.

"I got the lead in the school play!" *Squeal.* Annabelle started jumping up and down and threw her arms around Jocelyn. "Hello, world, here I come!"

Sometimes you just gotta jump. One man in the book of Acts had more reason than most of us to jump. He'd been sitting by the side of the road like he did every day. All day. Begging for money since his crippled feet kept him from holding down a job.

When two followers of Jesus walked by, they said, "In the name of Jesus Christ of Nazareth, walk." God poured strength into the man's ankles and feet, and he jumped to his feet and started to walk. He couldn't believe it. He started jumping and praising God!

Have you ever felt like that? Like God's done something so amazing you've just got to jump up and down?

What's something God has done for you that makes you want to dance?

Move it. Shake it. Get up and praise the Lord!

Dear God, sometimes I'm so happy I could explode. Thank you for all you do. Thank you for listening and caring and answering prayer. I love you more than anything. Amen.

KEEP ON KEEPING ON

We also have joy with our troubles, because we know that these troubles produce patience. And patience produces character, and character produces hope.

ROMANS 5:3-4 NCV

When Joni was seventeen, she went swimming with her friends. She had a terrible diving accident and was paralyzed from her neck down. What would happen? What was she going to do?

During all that trouble, Joni found joy. Not joy because it happened, but joy in what happened. She learned to be patient and draw and paint by holding a paintbrush in her mouth. She started thinking about others and started a huge organization that helps people with disabilities. She has the hope of Jesus inside of her and shares that hope with others.

Trouble can lead to patience, then character, then hope. See how it works?

Whether your trouble is a nasty episode of asthma or a family member going through sickness, God can take that trouble and turn it into good. That doesn't mean what happened is good—it's not. But God can use what happened for good in your life.

Dear God, I don't like it when hard things happen. Next time they come, though, and I know they will, I'll thank you for the chance to learn patience, to hang in there, and to make me more like you— strong, steady, and hopeful even when things are hard. Amen.

CHECK IT OUT: Read about Joni in her book,
Joni: An Unforgettable Story.

JUST BEING THERE

Praise be to the Lord, to God our Savior,
who daily bears our burdens.
PSALM 68:19 NIV

Sometimes when Laura's mom came in to say goodnight, she'd sit on the edge of her bed and Laura would talk. She'd talk about how the girls on the cheer squad burst into giggles after goofing up a cheer. She'd talk about how she missed her tumble at practice or how she forgot the formula for her math test. Laura's mom usually didn't say anything. She just listened.

Sometimes we don't need anyone to fix our problems. All we need is a friend who listens and understands and says, "It'll be okay." That makes the problem seem a little smaller and not so overwhelming.

That's what God does. He doesn't always rescue us from problems; sometimes he walks along with us in them. He "daily bears our burdens" and is with us, carrying us along in whatever we're going through.

Dear God, I know I can talk to you and you listen. Not because you have to but because you care. You're my best friend. Amen.

61

I'VE GOT THIS!

The Spirit God gave us does not make us timid,
but gives us power, love and self-discipline.
So do not be ashamed of the testimony about our Lord.
2 TIMOTHY 1:7-8 NIV

If there was one thing Andrea admired about her mom, it was her confidence. She could stand up in front of executives from around the world and give a presentation. She could make anyone anywhere feel comfortable. Andrea, on the other hand, wasn't at all like her mom. She hated to stand up in class. She dreaded making new friends and even asking the teacher a question.

Confidence comes easily for some people. Other people hold back. They spend more time thinking than doing. It takes them awhile to make friends. They're not always sure what to do or how to do it or what they think.

God created all personality types—both outgoing and shy. In both cases, though, you can be confident. Confidence isn't being rude, outgoing, or in people's faces. Confidence comes from knowing.

Confidence comes...

when you *know* who you are—a daughter of God,

when you *know* who made you—the Creator of the entire universe,

when you *know* what you're created to do—love God and tell others about him,

when you *know* who is with you—an "always with you" God!

So be kind. Be loving. But also be bold and be strong!

Dear God, thank you for who you are. Thank you for making me, me. When I'm tempted to be afraid or timid, give me confidence and remind me of what I know. Amen.

PRACTICE MAKES PERFECT?

"Be perfect, therefore, as your heavenly Father is perfect."
MATTHEW 5:48 NIV

"Again, again!" demanded Brittany's piano teacher. "Watch your phrasing and ease into the *pianissimo* section. Remember, practice makes perfect."

"Practice makes perfect" is an expression you've probably heard a million times. Practice piano, and you'll nail your recital. Practice gymnastics, and you'll stick your landing. Practice math problems, and you'll ace your algebra test.

Aiming to do well is great, and there's nothing wrong with practice. The problem comes when the goal to do better turns into pressure.

Pressure to get it right.

Pressure not to mess up.

Pressure to be the best.

Have you ever felt like that? The perfection God talks about in the verse above is different. This kind of perfection doesn't stress you out or look over your shoulder waiting for you to make a mistake. It's an invitation and a command from God to be like him. "Be holy as I am holy" or "be like me because I'm everything that is good, right, and wonderful." Instead of a punishment, it becomes a privilege. It's imitating God.

When you feel overwhelmed, remember that drive for perfection probably isn't coming from God.

Dear God, if I look at the sun, moon, and stars, I feel kind of small. Yet you love me so much that you invite me to be like you. When I'm tempted to stress out, remind me that the audience I'm playing to is you. Amen.

JUST SAY NO

The grace of God...teaches us to say "No" to ungodliness and worldly passions, and to live self-controlled, upright and godly lives.

TITUS 2:11-12 NIV

"Do you want to read a book, Peyton?" asked Kylie.

Two-year-old Peyton screwed up his face. "No."

"Okay, how about we build a tower. Let's build a huge tower with your blocks."

"Mmm, no!"

Kylie loved to babysit Peyton. Tonight, though, Peyton was a challenge. His parents had said that "no" was his favorite new word. Now she understood why.

No is a small but powerful word!

Saying no can be the best thing to say when it comes to sin. When you're tempted to cheat on your history test, to gossip about the odd girl at school, or to hide the whole truth from your dad, sometimes you have to tell yourself, "Nope. I'm not going to do that."

The pressure to say yes can be huge. Here are a few things that make it easier to say no:

- Talking to a parent or adult you trust. Most adults will understand how you feel and want to help.
- Practicing ahead of time. What scenarios have your friends been faced with? Imagine yourself in those situations and practice what you'll say.
- Saying it out loud. Instead of trying to think your way out of a bad situation, make your intentions clear. "No, I'm not interested in _____."
- Remembering that no is always a yes. When you say no to losing your temper, you're saying yes to self-control. When you say no to lying, you say yes to the truth.

What's something else that would help make saying no easier?

Dear God, give me the courage and strength to say no, especially when people around me are saying yes to what's wrong. Thank you. Amen.

RUN!

Run away from the evil desires of youth.
2 TIMOTHY 2:22 NCV

Sometimes you just have to run. No, we're not talking about running to get to class on time or running to catch the bus or running during soccer practice. We're talking about running away when someone is planning to do something wrong. When you're tempted to go to the mall with girls you know are going to spray graffiti on the bathroom wall...

DON'T:
Don't bother talking to them, trying to reason with them, or explaining your point of view.
Don't go along to make sure they won't get in trouble.
Don't try to cover for them.

DO:
Get out of there!
Sometimes the smartest thing to do is run.

Have you ever been in a situation where you've had to run?

Dear God, will you let me know when I'm in a situation where I just need to leave? Give me wisdom to know when to get out of there and when to stay. Amen.

AUTHENTICITY

*"These people show honor to me with words,
but their hearts are far from me."*

MARK 7:6 NCV

If there was one thing Jesus absolutely hated it was hypocrisy. He called out the Pharisees more than one time on their proud, I'm-better-than-you attitude. Their religious rules and pretend holiness made him angry. Two-faced. That's what they were.

The difference between a hypocrite and an authentic person is the difference between a Gucci and a knock-off. One is a fake and the other the real deal.

People can be real or they can be fake. How can you tell the difference?

Real people mean what they say; fake people say what people want to hear.

Real people admit their faults; fake people act like they have it all together.

Real people aren't afraid to be who they really are; fake people are worried about making an impression.

Real people do what they say; fake people say one thing and do another.

How would you describe yourself, as real, or fake? How would others describe you?

Dear God, you see who I am and know what I'm thinking, but sometimes I pretend. Give me a group a people that I can be real with. Help me to be on the outside who I am on the inside. I don't want to try to fool you or anyone else. Amen.

MARCH

God's power has given us everything
we need to lead a godly life. All of
this has come to us because we know
the God who chose us. He chose
us because of his own glory and
goodness.

2 PETER 1:3-4 NIRV

BABY STEPS

*The LORD makes firm the steps
of the one who delights in him.*
PSALM 37:23 NIV

Emma and her family were in Guatemala on a missions trip. After five days of painting and cleaning a small village school, they took a vacation day and went to the beach. Only it wasn't like any beach Emma had ever seen.

The sand was covered with freshly hatched sea turtles. The turtles were small enough to fit into the palm of Emma's hand. They took tiny steps and slowly inched their way across the sand to the ocean. One. Step. At a time.

Life is made of small steps.

- Changing a bad habit, like chewing your fingernails or teasing your little sister, means deciding and then practicing a day at a time to be different.
- Buying the new phone you want means saving your money, week by week, birthday through Christmas.
- Forgiving someone means choosing to let go of hurt feelings every time those feelings come back.

Baby steps can lead to big things.

Dear God, I don't always feel like I'm making progress or getting the change I want. Remind me that small steps do equal big things if I'm patient and living to please you. Amen.

THE PERFECT FIND

"You will seek Me and find Me when you search for Me with all your heart."
JEREMIAH 29:13 NASB

Marie was out shopping with her mom looking for new hockey skates. The first store didn't have Marie's size. The second store had Marie's size but only in pink, and she wanted black. Marie thought the ice skates at the third store were perfect! But Marie's mom didn't think the price was perfect. They looked all afternoon and finally found a pair of black skates that fit just right.

Looking for God isn't nearly as hard as looking for a pair hockey skates. God isn't hiding. He isn't thinking, "Do I have to spend time with her?" God wants to be found; he wants to spend time with you. He promises that if you look for him, you won't be disappointed.

Maybe you're seeking God for an answer to a problem you have. Or maybe you're seeking God because, well, you're not sure he exists. He promises that if you seek him with all your heart, you'll be happy you did.

Dear God, I want to search for you with all my heart. Thank you for your promise to "be found." Amen.

69

BETTER THAN GOOD

You satisfy me more than the richest feast.
I will praise you with songs of joy.
PSALM 63:5 NLT

There's nothing like a chocolate malt, crispy fries, and a juicy cheeseburger. Or maybe you're a slice of ooey-gooey-cheesy-pizza kind of person, or you prefer stabbing your fork into a heaping salad with fresh veggies and lettuce. Any way you put it, these foods taste good—real good. Satisfaction!

Of course in a couple of hours you'll be hungry. And then the cycle starts over again. Not even the satisfaction of a Snickers bar will last.

God filled each of us with desires—the desire for good food, for friendship, for closeness, for fun. And, he loves giving us things to fulfill those desires. They give us a hint of the deeper, forever-satisfaction that comes from spending time with Jesus—and we're talking about more than just "doing devotions." Reading about him, learning about what kind of person he is, and talking with him like he is your best friend satisfies deep places of your soul. But you've got to do it.

If you're up for a challenge, determine to set aside five minutes a day for the next four days. Set your timer, turn off your phone, put your computer to sleep, unplug your ear buds and open up and talk to God. Tell him your favorite color. Tell him what makes you happy. Tell him about your favorite part of the day. Then just be still and listen.

You will be satisfied!

Dear God, you bring deep satisfaction like nothing else. I want to quiet myself, my hands, and my mind to spend time with you. Amen.

ANYWHERE, EVERYWHERE

I can never escape from your Spirit! I can never get away from your presence! If I ride the wings of the morning, if I dwell by the farthest oceans, even there your hand will guide me, and your strength will support me.

PSALM 139:7, 9-10 NLT

Mariana flopped into the hammock and began to swing. Back here in the yard, behind the tool shed, next to the daisies, under the oak tree was her favorite spot to get away and talk to God.

When it comes to spending time with God (some people call it doing devotions, but it's really just meeting up with God), there's nowhere we can go where he is not. Everywhere we go, God will be there with us.

You can meet God—going on a bike ride early in the morning, climbing a tree and telling him about your day, pulling the covers over your head late at night and using a flashlight to read your Bible, going for a run around the school track, praying for your family while you're on the treadmill, or swinging in a hammock and praising him for all the amazing creation you see.

Where and how do you enjoy meeting with God? How creative can you get?

Dear God, you are everywhere and that's amazing! If I can spend time with my friends at the mall, in my living room, or at a park, I can do the same with you. You are my friend. Amen.

WHEN DAD AND MOM ARE WRONG

*Have confidence in your leaders
and submit to their authority,
because they keep watch over you
as those who must give an account.*
HEBREWS 13:17 NIV

Parents aren't perfect. You probably knew that already. They make mistakes. They make decisions that don't always turn out. They sin (*gasp*).

Everyone is accountable to God for what they do. Here's the deal though. You're not accountable for what your mom does. You're not responsible for what your dad does or doesn't do. You're just responsible for you. So while you may be tempted to point out your parent's mistakes, let God take care of your mom or dad.

Do what they say and you'll make their work easier. Then pray for your mom and dad; they've got a huge responsibility. They will give an account for themselves and for you.

Dear God, thanks for giving me someone to watch over me. I know it's a lot of responsibility. Help them as they make decisions. Help me support them as they do. Amen.

PUZZLE PIECES

*Oh, how great are God's riches and wisdom and knowledge!
How impossible it is for us to understand his decisions
and his ways!*

ROMANS 11:33 NLT

A thousand puzzle pieces are scattered across the kitchen table, a jumble of yellow, pink, brown, and light blue pieces. Somewhere in there is a picture of four chocolate cupcakes covered with pastel-colored frosting. At least that's what the picture on the front of the puzzle box says.

Every day of your life is a puzzle piece. Sometimes you look at what happens and how it happens and think, *What?! That doesn't make sense,* or *What's going on? Why, God, why? Why was my dad in an accident? Why didn't I make the team?*

If you love God with all your heart, you can be sure God is working on the puzzle. He's standing over your life and bringing everything together to make a big beautiful picture.

Trust God to make sense of it all.

Dear God, you are big. You're so wise it's over my head! Help me to trust that you know what you're doing—because you do. Amen.

POWERHOUSE

Go to the ant, you slacker!
Observe its ways and become wise.
Without leader, administrator, or ruler,
it prepares its provisions in summer;
it gathers its food during harvest.
PROVERBS 6:6-8 HCSB

"Thanks for doing the dishes, Amelia. And clearing the table." Amelia's mom gave her a smooch on the cheek. "That was sweet."

"No big deal, Mom," Amelia said, but inwardly she was glad her mom noticed. It felt good.

Taking initiative and working hard are ways to impress not only your parents, but God too. God's Word points to the ant as an example of diligence. It's small—but it's mighty! It works, plans, organizes, and hustles. No leader lords it over this tiny hard-working powerhouse, yet it puts out work for something ten times its size.

Diligence won't just get the job done; it'll make you feel great.

Dear God, sometimes I don't feel like doing what I know I'm supposed to do. It's too much work, too much bother, and I give up—easily. I'm sorry I've been lazy sometimes. Forgive me, and teach me to work hard. Amen.

THAT HURTS!

God is the Father who is full of mercy and all comfort.
He comforts us every time we have trouble,
so when others have trouble, we can comfort them
with the same comfort God gives us.
2 CORINTHIANS 1:3-4 NCV

"Ow, that hurts!"

Whether it's a stubbed toe, a sprained wrist, or a broken ankle, your body has a tremendous capacity—to hurt! Some hurts go deeper than others. They're the ones inside that no one sees. Hurt feelings from someone's careless or angry words. Embarrassment from a mistake you made. Shame from what someone did to you, something that's not your fault. Confusion about a divorce. Hurts like those can seem almost too big for words.

With God, you don't have to say anything; he just understands. He is full of mercy and full of comfort. Just being near him can take some of the hurt away.

He also comforts by using others who have been through the same thing. Talk to them and ask, "How did God comfort you when you were hurting?"

Dear God, I hurt. Sometimes I hurt so much it's hard to talk. You see inside me. Wrap your arms around me. I need to know you're near. Amen.

75

MY OWN FAULT

Sing for joy. For the Lord has comforted his people and will have compassion on them in their suffering.
ISAIAH 49:13 NLT

"I'm sorry, Lila. I know you want to go to Anna's party, but you've got an assignment due tomorrow."

"But, Mom, that's not fair! Everyone is going to be there," argued Lila.

"I'm sorry, but I reminded you several times this week. You put it off then, so that means staying home now."

Many times the people of Israel decided to do what they wanted when they wanted. As a result, they landed in a lot of trouble. Still God loved them even though the mess they were in was their own fault.

Sometimes the mistakes we make have consequences that hurt. Then we wonder, *How can I ask God for help when I brought this on myself?* While he can't undo what's done, God still has compassion. He'll come alongside you just like he came alongside his people.

How have you seen God or your parents have compassion on you when you've made a mistake or done something wrong?

Dear God, thanks for your compassion. I got myself in a mess and it hurts. I know I don't deserve it, but please come and help me. Thanks for listening. Amen.

FAITH IN ACTION

*If a brother or sister is without clothes and lacks daily food
and one of you says to them, "Go in peace, keep warm,
and eat well," but you don't give them what the body needs,
what good is it? In the same way faith, if it doesn't have works,
is dead by itself.*

JAMES 2:15-17 HCSB

Some people see a need and talk about it. Others like Harriet Tubman do something about it. A freed slave herself, Harriet risked her life to make trips into the South to free other slaves. She traveled by night. She traveled undercover. A reward was posted for her capture. But danger didn't intimidate Harriet; she saw the bigger danger of slavery. How could she walk around free when so many others weren't?

To believe in God is to show it. Anyone can talk; action carries power. You show your faith by what you do. How will people know you believe unless you pair it with good deeds?

Faith requires action!

What are some practical ways you can show someone that your faith is real? (Check out the verse above for some ideas.)

Dear God, I don't want to be happy with simply believing. I want my faith to show! I may not be a Harriet Tubman, but show me what I can do to help those who are in need. Amen.

DIGNITY

A good name is more desirable than great riches;
to be esteemed is better than silver or gold.
PROVERBS 22:1 NIV

You've probably been told a million times, "Don't worry about what people think," right? That's mostly true, but not always. What people think of you does count, and your reputation matters.

Which of these do you think would give someone a good name?

- opening the door for her grandma
- wearing shorts that show too much
- interrupting someone when they're talking
- doing something she promised

How you act, how you dress, what you say, how you treat others are all associated with your name. Losing a good reputation is like getting a really bad grade; it takes time to pull it back up. If you want a good name, do and say good things.

Write down a few of the things you're known for. Put a star by those that'll give you a good name. Put a line through those that won't.

Dear God, remind me to consider how what I do impacts my name. I want the name you've given me to be associated with good things. I know it reflects on you too. Amen.

A GOOD NAME

Never let loyalty and kindness leave you!
Write them deep within your heart.
Then you will find favor with both God and people,
and you will earn a good reputation.
PROVERBS 3:3-4 NLT

Don't you just love to read about celebrities? Finding out who they're in love with or seeing what they wear? Reading about their latest album or where they went on vacation (can you believe some famous people own their own island?) fascinates us.

Celebrities are loaded with money and influence. They've definitely got a famous name. But do they have a *good* name?

Loyalty and kindness, rather than money and influence, gives people a good name. Not just with people but with God as well. And, because being loyal and kind is something everyone can do, everyone has the possibility of having a good name, including you.

What is a good name worth to you?

Dear God, I want to have a good reputation with other people and with you. You're the one who matters most. Amen.

WHEN IT'S OK TO GET ANGRY

He has told you what he wants from you:
to do what is right to other people,
love being kind to others, and live humbly,
obeying your God.

MICAH 6:8 NCV

Sometimes anger is a good thing. Really. After God gave Moses the Ten Commandments, Moses walked down the mountain and saw the Israelites dancing around a golden calf, treating it like a god. What they were doing was wrong, and Moses got angry. (Read Exodus 32:19.)

If you see a classroom bully making fun of your best friend, or read about warlords stealing food meant for poor children in Africa and you get angry, that's a *good* kind of angry. It's okay to be angry with what's wrong.

How you show that anger and what you do with it, though, can make the situation better or worse. You could slap the bully in the face. (Hmm, maybe not.) Or, you write to your senator and ask them to look in to the matter. (Good idea.)

Taking out anger on someone and being bitter just makes you like the one who's doing wrong. Working to make wrongs right and praying for those who suffer injustice is a great thing to do!

What's a wrong that you'd like to see made right?

Dear God, you're a righteous God who is in favor of what's right and totally saddened by what's wrong. Show me how I can help bring about what's right in a good way. Amen.

FEELING THE WAY I DO

When I am afraid,
I put my trust in you.
PSALM 56:3 NIV

"Come on now. Don't be afraid. It's not that bad. In fact, it'll be fun."

"But, Dad," said Alex, looking down at the zipline's forty-foot drop, "I *am* afraid."

People mean well. They really do. But when they say things like "don't be afraid" or "don't be down" or "don't be discouraged," it's like telling us to stop feeling the way we do. The problem is, we *are* down, we *are* afraid, or we might be feeling very discouraged.

God gets this, which is why the psalms are packed with emotions like fear, frustration, and anger. The psalmist doesn't hide his feelings from God; he tells it like it is.

Feeling fear isn't abnormal or something to be ashamed of. So instead of stuffing fear feelings into a corner of your heart or trying to ignore them, go to God when you are afraid. Even if someone has told you not to be afraid. Even if it's something you don't think you should be afraid of.

God won't dismiss you and say, "Well, just get over it." Instead he says, "Trust in me."

Dear God, I'm afraid. I'm afraid of many things, really.
But I put my trust in you. Amen.

ME FIRST?

Be devoted to one another in love.
Honor one another above yourselves.
ROMANS 12:10 NIV

Adalyn looked down at the plate of lasagna between her and her sister. She was hungry for seconds. Two hours of soccer practice would do that to you. But there was only one small piece of lasagna left, and her sister wanted it too. What should she do?

A woman in the Bible faced a similar dilemma. When she was down to her last meal, the prophet Elijah asked her for something to eat. If she gave it to Elijah, she would go hungry. If she kept it for herself, he would go hungry. What was she going to do?

We're all pretty good at looking out for ourselves. After all, if we don't who will, right? Yet if we're followers of Jesus, standing up for others instead of ourselves is the way to go. The woman in the Bible did what Elijah asked and gave him the meal. God rewarded her big time. For the next few years, she never ran out of food.

That's how it is when we do what God asks. We take care of trusting and obeying, and he takes care of the rest.

Dear Lord, help me to trust that when you ask me to put others first, you will provide for me. Amen.

CHECK IT OUT: Read the whole true story in 1 Kings 17:1-15.

BAND TRIP

They will tell about the amazing things you do,
and I will tell how great you are.
PSALM 145:6 NCV

"So, Courtney. What are your plans for the summer?" Mrs. Jasper asked as they picked up the nursery after church.

"I'm not sure. I need to earn money for our band trip next year, so I'll probably be babysitting a lot—a whole lot." *It's going to take a lot of babysitting to earn what I need.* Courtney thought.

"I know how you feel," said Mrs. Jasper. "During college, I wanted to spend a semester in Germany. I worked all summer but I had no idea how I'd earn all the money. The month before I was supposed to leave, someone gave me a gift to cover the difference."

"Thank you!" Courtney said and gave Mrs. Jasper a hug. "I needed to hear that!"

God promises to lead us on the best pathway for our life (Psalm 32:8). So many times he uses people to do that. Grandparents, teachers, pastors, parents encourage us and give us advice when we're wondering what path to take. Hearing what God has done for them can build up our own faith. So take time to listen and develop relationships with those you admire and respect.

Dear God, would you please put people in my life who encourage me and teach me what ways are best? Show me who they are, and teach me to listen. Amen.

BEING STRONG

In repentance and rest you will be saved,
In quietness and trust is your strength.
ISAIAH 30:15 NASB

If you were asked to describe a strong woman, what qualities would she have?

A woman who…

☐ makes things happen
☐ is good at figuring things out
☐ is self-reliant
☐ is self-confident

Nothing is wrong with being confident and capable, but those qualities put a serious weight on you—what you can make happen, what you can figure out, how you come across.

The Bible describes a different kind of strong. This strength replaces your efforts to make things happen with a complete dependence on God. Instead of being self-confident and self-reliant, you're God-confident and God-reliant. You realize you can't go it alone, you need to lean one hundred percent on God.

Be strong, but be strong in the Lord. That's where real strength is.

How can being quiet and trusting God make someone strong?

Dear Lord, I usually focus on doing as much as I can and pulling myself together to be strong. Instead, help me to be still inside and trust you. Amen.

SPRINKLE IT WITH SALT

Let your conversation be always full of grace, seasoned with salt, so that you may know how to answer everyone.
COLOSSIANS 4:6 NIV

Whether you're talking about French fries or scrambled eggs, salt makes everything taste better. It makes ketchup taste more "ketchupy" and chocolate taste more "chocolatey." Salt tingles our tongue and makes everything taste like—more!

Grace-filled words can be like salt sprinkled on a conversation—they make people want more. When our words are gracious, people want to sit down and hang out with us a little longer. When our words are spoken with kindness, people want to listen and then share what's going on inside. Most importantly, grace-filled words open the door to talking to people about Jesus.

If you're not sure what to say, kind, grace-filled words will always come in handy and never let you down.

Listen to what you say today. Are your words sprinkled with grace or something else?

Dear Lord, I've never thought about the power of my words. Help me to speak with grace. Amen.

GOD'S MASTERPIECE

We are God's masterpiece.
He has created us anew in Christ Jesus,
so we can do the good things
he planned for us long ago.
EPHESIANS 2:10 NLT

Apples are made for things like bag lunches or after-school snacks or applesauce or apple pie. Strawberries are made for strawberry shortcake and strawberry ice cream and strawberry jam. Bananas are made for smoothies and banana splits.

You are God's masterpiece and you were made to do good works. From the beginning, God planned good things for you to do. Like cheering for your little brother at his soccer game or saying thank you to your bus driver or praying for your teacher whose kid is at home with a fever.

When you do good things, you're stepping into God's game plan for your life. You're perfecting the routine he's created for your day.

What are two things you could do today that would show someone God is good?

Dear God, I want to do good things for other people. That way they'll see how good you are through me. Help me pay attention to opportunities for doing good. Amen.

SHADOWS

Every good and perfect gift is from above,
coming down from the Father of the heavenly lights,
who does not change like shifting shadows.
JAMES 1:17 NIV

On the short walk back from the bus stop, Mari caught a glance of her shadow walking alongside her. She was only four foot five but her "shadow" legs looked like they belonged on a giraffe.

Shadows move and change. They stretch skinny and then wide, depending on the time of day. Unlike shadows, God never changes. He's a good Father. He isn't two-faced, moody, or unpredictable. He doesn't say one thing and then later change his mind. God is faithful and trustworthy—always.

Sometimes things happen that might make you think God has changed. Bad things, sad things, scary things. But they're just like shadows. The real person—God—hasn't changed at all. The God you know, you can always trust.

Dear God, you aren't like a human being. You never lie or change your mind. What you say, you do. What you promise, you keep. You are always loving, just, and righteous. Amen.

EMILY ELIZABETH

He said to me..."When you are weak,
my power is made perfect in you."
2 CORINTHIANS 12:9 NCV

Nine-year-old Emily Elizabeth had long brown hair, a bright smile, and shiny brown eyes to match. She loved to read, run, and play with her brother and sister. But then Emily Elizabeth was diagnosed with a serious disease, and slowly everything changed. Today, thirteen years later, Emily seldom leaves her bed.

People who don't know Emily define her by what she can't do—she can't talk, walk, or even dress or feed herself. God, though, sees what she can do—she can love him, pray, learn about him and listen to him. And she does! Like the clouds that stretch across the sky, Emily speaks of God's glory louder than many who can talk. Though she's weak on the outside, God's power inside her shines to everyone around.

Even the weakest people can be strong. Not because of anything they do, but because God in them is strong. Sometimes we feel like we need to do great things for God. That he'll use us the most when we're popular or influential. But we don't need to do great things for God. We just need to let him be God in us.

Let God shine in and through you like he shines through Emily.

Dear God, sometimes I'm so busy "doing" that I forget about just "being" with you. I want to spend more time with you. Amen.

SPRING GARDEN

Humbly accept the word planted in you, which can save you.
JAMES 1:21 NIV

Every spring Camila and her mom planted a garden. They dropped bright yellow kernels into the soil to create rows of corn that would someday be used for grilled corn on the cob. They planted jalapeño peppers and cumin plants that would be used for her mom's famous tamales.

Around the edge of the garden was a patch of hard, rocky ground where they'd given up planting. It wasn't soft enough to plant any seeds. Nothing would grow there.

Listening and accepting what God says is like letting him plant a seed that grows into something big and beautiful. Ignoring what he says is like hardening your heart and refusing to let that seed grow.

For example, you might hear what God wants at church, from your grandmother, or from reading the Bible. Accepting it means agreeing with it and doing it—even if that means admitting you were wrong. Agreeing and obeying become more important than the need to be right.

That kind of humility throws the door wide open for God to bless!

Dear God, sometimes accepting what you and others say means admitting I'm wrong. That's tough for me to do. Still, Lord, I want to humble myself. If I start to get defensive or proud, please remind me to humbly accept what you say. Amen.

A BROKEN ELBOW

*Those who know the L*ORD *trust him,*
because he will not leave those who come to him.
PSALM 9:10 NCV

On the day after Easter, Ainsley had been jumping on her new trampoline. She did a front flip and came down hard on her elbow. *Snap.* It didn't look or feel so good. After a trip to the emergency room, the doctors said she needed more than a cast. She needed surgery. *But surgery means no summer job at horse camp!* she thought. In the end, though, she didn't have a choice.

Now after surgery and four months of intense physical therapy, Ainsley found herself back in the doctor's office.

"I'm sorry," the doctor said. "Your elbow hasn't healed the way we had hoped. The only option for improvement is to operate again."

Surgery? Again? This is just too much! I just want it to be over.

In this hard-to-understand situation, Ainsley is learning to trust God. She's trusting God to heal her; she's trusting God to work things out. Sometimes when she feels discouraged, her mom sits on Ainsley's bed and they talk things through. Sometimes her dad just listens and then prays with her.

If you're going through something that's hard to figure out…

- Trust God. He's famous for never leaving those who come to him.
- Find people who love God who can pray with you.

Dear God, I don't know what's going on and I can't figure it out, but I trust you. Give me friends who will help me through this time. Amen.

IF YOU HAD A CHOICE

Of all the people on earth, the Lord your God has chosen you to be his own special treasure. The Lord did not set his heart on you and choose you because you were more numerous than other nations, for you were the smallest of all nations!

DEUTERONOMY 7:6-7 NLT

If you had a choice would you…
- ☐ design your own clothing line,
- ☐ manage the company that made the new clothing line,
- ☐ help other girls dress for success, or
- ☐ model the new clothes.

If you chose a, you probably value creativity and imagination. If you chose b, you might be into leading and seeing things organized and run well. If you chose c, you enjoy helping people succeed. If you chose d, being the center of attention is where it's at.

What you choose says a lot about you. Who God chooses says a lot about God. He didn't choose the biggest, strongest, or the most influential nation as his people. He chose the one he loved, even though they were the smallest.

You don't need to impress God with how important you are, how much you know, or what job your mom or dad has. He chooses you because he loves you, not because you've earned his approval. God is love, and his love is just because.

Dear God, thank you for choosing me to be in your family. I don't deserve it but I am so thankful. Amen.

I CAN'T WAIT!

In the morning, Lord, you hear my voice;
in the morning I lay my requests before you
and wait expectantly.
PSALM 5:3 NIV

"I can't wait!" Madison said to her BFF Ava. She grabbed a plate of mac and cheese from the cafeteria line. "Just three more days and we leave for spring break in California! It's going to be amazing!"

"Well, I can wait," replied Ava as she grabbed a slice of pepperoni pizza. "I, on the other hand, have freezing temperatures and a cup of hot cocoa to look forward to. Bring me back some sunshine, will you?"

To pray is to have an *I can't wait!* attitude. That's because praying is more than mouthing words, hoping someone will listen, wishing you'll get an answer. It's knowing that you will.

With God, you don't have to…

Wait hopelessly – *I don't even know why I'm praying. God's never going to answer.*

Wait impatiently – *This is insane! What's taking so long anyway?*

You can wait expectantly, knowing absolutely positively that God *will* answer.

Dear God, sometimes when I pray I wait impatiently. Or I don't really even wait at all because there's a part of me that doesn't expect you to answer. Change my heart to wait expectantly, knowing you do hear and you do answer. Amen.

92

JUST HIT REFRESH

"For in six days the Lord made heaven and earth, but on the seventh day he stopped working and was refreshed."
EXODUS 31:17 NLT

"I don't get it. I updated our business homepage but it doesn't make the change. Argh!"

Harper's dad was brilliant when it came to performing eye surgery. He was one of the top surgeons in the state. But when it came to computers? Not so much.

"Just hit refresh," suggested Harper. "That refreshes the page's memory to show the latest update."

That's why God created the Sabbath. It's a day to hit refresh. That day of rest isn't a suggestion but a definite must, as in, without-this-things-won't-work-like-they-should and why-did-I-ever-think-this-wasn't-a-good idea? Mostly it's a time to stop, rest, reflect, and remember.

- Stop—Stop doing what you normally do. Don't think about school, homework, practice, and chores.
- Rest—Take a break, get outside, and do whatever you think is relaxing.
- Reflect—Look back on your week. What went well? What could have gone better? What would you do differently?
- Remember—Remember what your life is really about—knowing God more every day and living for him.

When was the last time you hit refresh?

Dear Lord, you made the heavens and earth and then you rested. Help me to stop, rest, reflect, and remember. Amen.

ELEPHANT IN THE ROOM

He stores up success for honest people.
He is like a shield to those who live without blame.
PROVERBS 2:7 NIRV

What if there really were an elephant in your room? After showing it off to all your friends, you'd have to walk *around* the elephant to get to the closet or *under* the elephant to get to your desk or *over* it to reach your top dresser drawer. Or maybe your room is so small you could only squeeze half an elephant inside.

Some people argue when there's a problem. Others completely avoid the topic, and that's what it means when people say there's an elephant in the room. Everyone knows something is going on, but no one wants to talk about it. They talk around, under, or over the topic. It's awkward.

Strong families don't let elephants sit in the room. They don't pretend something isn't there when it is. Instead they're honest and they get that elephant out!

Dear God, I want our family to be open and honest. Show me how to be a part of doing that. Teach me to do it in a way that's kind and considerate of others. Make our family strong. Amen.

FREE TO BE

God created human beings in his own likeness. He created them to be like himself. He created them as male and female.
GENESIS 1:27 NLT

When you were younger and people asked, "What do you want to be when you grow up?" what did you say? A teacher? A veterinarian? A mom? A professional athlete?

God created you to be like him. How that shows up in each person looks different; it can be expressed in different ways—in a way that's uniquely you. God created you to be free.

- Free to be who God meant you to be not who he created the girl in your class or the girl across the street to be.
- Free not to be who everyone else thinks you should be.
- Free to explore different likes and dislikes and try on different interests so you can find something you love and something that fits.

Whatever classes you take, activities you join, school you attend, or career you end up in, just remember to be free to be you.

Dear God, you created me in your image. Help me to be the best me I can be just because you made me this way! Thank you! Amen.

SEASHELLS

Thank you for making me so wonderfully complex!
Your workmanship is marvelous—how well I know it.
PSALM 139:14 NLT

Vacations on Sanibel Island were the best! Mandie loved visiting her grandparents. They would spend hours together biking and exploring. After heading to the ocean for a swim, they'd walk along the beach shelling. Mandie would scoop up bright pink and pale purple shells, clam shells and tulip shells, sand dollars and sometimes even an empty conch shell.

They're all so different, Mandie thought. *And they're all so beautiful!*

Whether you're talking about seashells or people, God created many different kinds of beautiful. People with black hair, blue eyes, freckly skin. Tall people, tiny people. People who love to laugh. People who love to think. People who love to talk, and people who love just to listen. God's creative genius shows up in everyone, including you.

Thinking of people as God's creation is the first step to treating them that way. Take a minute and think of one person. Anyone. How do you see God's uniqueness in them? Just like God finds you beautiful, he finds them beautiful too.

Dear God, thanks for making me wonderful and complex. When I look around at all the different people and cultures you've created, I'm blown away. Teach me to think of and treat others as beautiful. Amen.

RIGHT WHERE YOU ARE

A father is tender and kind to his children.
In the same way, the LORD is tender and kind
to those who have respect for him.
PSALM 103:13 NIRV

Isabelle had two sisters. Victoria had been reading since she was four, and she was in the gifted English class at school. Valentina stumbled over words and sentences, so she was in remedial reading classes. And Isabelle, well, she was in the regular class. Three sisters. Three different levels. And yet the school met them where they were to help each grow and learn.

God meets each person where they are. You aren't like your brother. Your brother isn't like your dad. Your neighbor isn't like your teacher. Each person is a bundle of hopes and dreams, abilities and needs. You're each at different places in your lives and God takes it all into account.

God meets us where we are so we can turn around and meet others where they are. That releases them of expectations to be like us, to be like someone else, to be better or more perfect. They're just them.

Are you trying to change anyone? Having any luck? Consider meeting them where they are.

Dear God, sometimes I'm wrapped up in what I know, what I need, and what I like. Help me to step out of my world just like you did and meet people where they are. Amen.

BRAIN BATTLE

*You will keep in perfect peace all who trust in you,
all whose thoughts are fixed on you!*
Isaiah 26:3 NLT

Katie flopped on the sofa and grabbed the remote. *I just need a break,* she thought. All day long it was… go to school, walk the dog, bake treats for student council, finish homework. Her mind was on spin cycle.

Katie turned on the TV and the news came on. An office bombing. People crying. People hurt. If Katie's brain was spinning on high it was on hyper speed now. *What if something like that happened here?* And her mind took off again.

When you focus your thoughts on God, the result is peace. When you zero in on your to-do lists, problems, the news, the result is a whole lot of worry and fear. If you're struggling with either one, you might want to ask yourself, *What have I been thinking about?* Changing how you think will invite peace in and keep the rest out.

Dear God, I've been thinking about things that make me feel frustrated, worried, or anger. Help me pick up my thoughts and put them on you. Amen.

APRIL

The Lord directs the steps of the godly.

He delights in every detail of their lives.

Though they stumble, they will never fall,

for the Lord holds them by the hand.

PSALM 37:23–24 NLT

THUNDERSTORMS

God is our refuge and strength,
an ever-present help in trouble.
Therefore we will not fear though the earth give way
and the mountains fall into the heart of the sea,
though its waters roar and foam
and the mountains quake with their surging.

PSALM 46:1-3 NIV

Thunder boomed and lightning cracked. The wind howled and the house seemed to shake. Kaylie watched the trees outside her window bending low in the strong gusts—and she wasn't even a little bit afraid.

When Kaylie was little, during a thunderstorm she and her dad would sit in the living room and watch it together. Just knowing her dad was near and being able to talk about the storm made her feel safe.

We sometimes think that when something bad happens, a good God isn't around. Even when earthquakes tremble, mountains crumble, oceans roar and foam, God says he is always close. Not even the most awful thing can drive God away. In the middle of a hurricane, a tornado, a flood or even a volcanic eruption, God won't leave you for a second. He's always present and forever near.

Dear God, no matter what happens, you never stop being near. Help me focus on you, instead of on the things that cause fear. Amen.

HOW TO DECIDE

No matter what happens, tell God about everything.
Ask and pray, and give thanks to him.
PHILIPPIANS 4:6 NIRV

It's the last day for softball camp signup. The computer at home is broken so you can't register online. You're going to drop off a registration form and a deposit at the school office on your lunch break. When you get to the office, no one is around. The bell for class is starting to ring. What do you do?

☐ Text your mom and let her handle it.
☐ Call the activities office and leave a message.
☐ Don't do anything; it's too hard to decide.
☐ Other?

At times life gets confusing. Two plus two might equal four but the answers to everyday situations are more complicated. You have so many scenarios to choose from. What do you do?

- Breathe. Take a deep breath and step back from the situation. Sometimes we panic because we imagine the worst case scenario.
- Tell God about the situation. All of it.
- Ask God for wisdom and thank him for the answer.

Nothing, absolutely nothing, is too small to "bother" God with.

Dear Lord, when I'm faced with a tough situation, help me take a step back, breathe, and pray. I trust you to work things out. Amen.

JUST LIKE JESUS

Walk in the way of love,
just as Christ loved us
and gave himself up for us.
EPHESIANS 5:2 NIV

"You know what I like about Coach?" Isabelle said as she flopped on the grass next to Lydia. "He doesn't just tell you what to do; he shows you how."

"Yeah," said Lydia. "Then he coaches you and helps you do it. Like how to jump a hurdle or set up your sprint."

Anybody can talk. Talk is easy. Jesus lived what he said. He said "love others." Then he showed us how—by accepting people, forgiving them, giving his life for them. Finally, he gave us his Holy Spirit who coaches us and gives us the power to live that way.

Could you do the same for someone else? Share the good news of Jesus and tell them to love. Show them what loving looks like by your own life. Then encourage them as they learn to love too. Just like Jesus.

Dear Jesus, thank you for giving me everything I need to be like you. Thank you for the gift of your Spirit. Please show me who I can encourage in your ways. Amen.

SWEET TOOTH

How sweet your words taste to me;
they are sweeter than honey.
Your commandments give me understanding;
no wonder I hate every false way of life.
PSALM 119:103-104 NLT

According to her mom, Meghan had a sweet tooth. She'd choose licorice over potato chips and ice cream over pretzels any day. If she could, Meghan would eat dessert before dinner or just have dessert for dinner. She could never get enough.

The psalmist who wrote Psalm 119—the longest psalm with a whopping 176 verses—had a sweet tooth when it came to God's Word. He couldn't get enough of it. The more he "tasted," the more he wanted.

What God says, his words, give you joy, comfort, and wise advice. And if that's not enough, living by them brings purity. People may try to talk you into believing that the Bible is just a book: black and white words on a page. But in reality they're life!

Why do you think the psalmist described commands as *sweet?*

Dear Lord, I want to get to the point where I want more and more of your Word. Put that desire in me. Thank you for your Word! Amen.

EASTER RESURRECTION

Then the angel spoke to the women. "Don't be afraid!" he said. "I know you are looking for Jesus, who was crucified. He isn't here! He is risen from the dead, just as he said would happen."
MATTHEW 28:5-6 NCV

Looking down the store aisles at Easter, you'd think that the holiday was mostly about jellybeans, chocolate bunnies, candy eggs, and pastel-colored Easter dresses. Nothing, of course, is wrong with an Easter filled with all those goodies. But at the center of Easter is Jesus.

Most people know that Easter celebrates the day Jesus rose from the dead. But not many understand why that's such a big deal. Why is it so important that Jesus rose from the dead? If he hadn't…

- He wouldn't be alive; he'd still be dead. Dead people can't see, hear, or move. So praying to him wouldn't do you much good.
- You wouldn't have salvation. How could someone save you if he couldn't save himself?
- Jesus wouldn't be different from anyone else who dies. The resurrection was proof that Jesus was God and had power, even over death.
- You'd miss out on the promise of a resurrection. How could Jesus resurrect anyone if he hadn't risen himself?

What happened on Easter changes everything! You can pray to someone who is alive! You can have salvation and forgiveness from sin. You can worship a powerful God who not even death could defeat! And you can hope for a resurrection in the future. That's the real story of Easter.

Dear God, thank you that Jesus really did rise from the dead. Jesus is alive! Amen.

A RUNAWAY

*She gave this name to the L*ORD *who spoke to her:*
"You are the God who sees me."

GENESIS 16:13 NIV

She slipped away in the middle of the day when everyone was busy. *No one will see me,* she thought as she ran. *No one will miss me. No one will care where I am.* Past the tents, past the people, into the desert she went.

Out where it was quiet and still, dusty and hot, where she thought no one would see her. That's when she heard his voice, "Hagar, slave of Sarai, where have you come from, and where are you going?" God saw Hagar and he knew her name. He saw her and knew all that she was running from.

God knows everything and sees everyone. And that includes you… and your family, your best friend, and your teacher. He sees and cares about everything and everyone. Nothing misses his attention.

Where are you right now? What would you like God to know? Guess what... he already does!

Dear God, thanks for seeing me. You're the God who knows all things, yet you still care about me. Here's what's on my mind... Amen.

SPRING CLEANING

Let's take a good look at the way we're living.
Let's return to the LORD.
LAMENTATIONS 3:40 NIRV

Shoes on the bed and clothes on the floor. Books piled high on the desk and a pair of cleats draped over the door. Stuffed animals and craft supplies falling out of the closet. It's definitely time for spring-cleaning. Well, at least that's what your mom said.

Every once in a while you've got to go through your room, pull everything out, sort, throw, organize, and give away. The same is true with life. Every once in a while you've got to examine what you're doing, how you're doing it, and sort it all out. Take out a sheet of paper and make a column for each question. Before you start, ask God to give you wisdom.

- What are my priorities?
- What should be most important?
- What's least important to me?
- What am I spending the most time on?
- What am I doing well?
- Where can I do better?

Of course, the most important priority of all is spending time, not just reading a devotional, but reading the Word of God. It's packed with wisdom and truth for everyday living.

Take a good look at what you're doing. Is there anything you'd change?

Dear God, help me take a hard look at what I'm doing and why I'm doing it. Help me to make my top priority my relationship with you. Amen.

ARE WE THERE YET?

If we look forward to something we don't yet have,
we must wait patiently and confidently.

ROMANS 8:25 NLT

"Mom, are we there yet?"

"Kaitlyn, we just left home an hour ago. No, we aren't there yet."

The 600 mile trip from Indianapolis to Washington D.C. was taking forever. Kaitlyn had one thing on her mind—exploring the National Air and Space museum. For this future pilot, the air and space museum was a must. Only eight more hours to go.

A lot of life is about doing... but a whole lot more is about waiting. Waiting in lines. Waiting to get a grade back. Waiting to get permission from your dad. Waiting for an answer to prayer. So what can you do while you wait?

- Remember what you're waiting for. It's worth it! Recalling your goal will help when you feel like giving up.
- Do something else! Don't let all that waiting time become wasted time. Distraction can be a good thing! Read a book. Learn a craft. The time will go a lot more quickly.
- Encourage someone else who's waiting. Strike up a conversation and cheer them on! Share and compare each other's waiting stories.

What are some other things that help you wait?

Dear God, I don't particularly like to wait, but I know it's part of life. Instead of complaining, help me make the best of the times when I have to wait. Amen.

JACK AND THE BEANSTALK

"I am the vine; you are the branches.
If you remain in me and I in you,
you will bear much fruit;
apart from me you can do nothing."
JOHN 15:5 NIV

Once upon a time in a land far away lived a boy named Jack and his mother. They were quite poor, so one day Jack's mother sent him to the market to sell their sheep. Instead of bringing home the money, Jack used the money to buy magic beans. His mother was furious, threw the beans on the ground, and sent him to bed.

A magical beanstalk sprouted that night, reaching into the sky. At the top was all Jack and his mother would need for the rest of their lives—a goose that laid golden eggs. The end. That's not quite the end, but the point is this: It all started when the seeds hit the ground since the soil is where seeds grow.

Jesus is like rich soil to a seed. He said what makes you grow and become all that he created you to be is staying close to him. Pull any plant out of the ground and it will start to droop. Pull away from God and the same will happen. But when you're listening to his Word and grounded in his truth, that's when you start to sprout, grow, and reach high!

Read the verse above. How does the picture of a vine and a branch help you understand your relationship with God?

Dear God, I want to stay close to you. Without you, I'm not anything. With you, I have everything. Amen.

JUST BECAUSE

God is so rich in mercy, and he loved us so much, that even though we were dead because of our sins, he gave us life when he raised Christ from the dead.

EPHESIANS 2:4-5 NLT

"Just because" gifts are the best. They're little sprinkles of happiness in the middle of ordinary life. They happen, not because it's Christmas or a birthday or because you begged and begged—"Please, will you buy it for me?" They happen just because someone loves you.

God's "just because" gift to us is new life through Jesus. This is more than little sprinkles. It's a game changer! Better than Disneyland Fast Passes! Better than ten puppies!

We are sinners who intentionally disobey God. We're spiritually "dead." Still God loved us so much that he made it possible for us to have new life. When we confess our sins and believe in Jesus, God gives us this new life. We haven't done anything to deserve it. We can't earn it. It's just because. Because he loves us.

Dear God, I don't deserve your love but you love me anyhow. Thank you for your "just because" gift. I ask you to forgive my sins and cleanse me from all wrong. Amen.

GOD SHARES HIS RICHES

My God will meet all your needs
according to the riches of his glory
in Christ Jesus.
PHILIPPIANS 4:19 NIV

Avril had just come down the stairs for a before-bed bowl of cereal when she overheard her parents.

"I just don't know what we're going to do," Avril's dad was saying. "How are we going to pay all those bills?" And that got Avril worrying.

God is good. He takes care of your needs *out of his riches*, not out of his throw-away pile, his give-away bin, or his second hand storage closet. In other words, he's not stingy or Grinch-like. He's big-hearted and generous. You can never out-ask what God can give.

What do you need? Take a minute to write it down. Now write a second list: What do you need today? God promises to give us our daily needs, not necessarily enough for us to stockpile for another day. Now write down what you want, and ask God about those things too. Just as a parent loves to give gifts to their kids, God loves giving gifts to his children.

Dear God, the whole earth is yours and everything in it. Providing for my needs isn't a big deal for you, and yet sometimes I doubt that you can. Help me to believe in your riches. Amen.

RICH

The Lord is gracious and compassionate,
slow to anger and rich in love.
PSALM 145:8 NIV

How can you tell if someone is rich? Depending on who you ask, you'll get a list of stuff. Fancy cars and designer clothes, swimming pools and high-end electronics, fairy-tale vacations to far off places. That's definitely one way to tell if someone is rich.

God is rich; he owns everything in heaven and everything on earth. What's best about him is he's also well-off in the love category. His love never runs out; he has an endless supply. He can never give it all away. His love for you is an ocean that never runs dry.

When a God who's powerful, mighty, *and* loving loves you, you've got everything you need and want. *Rich in love* means no need will ever be overlooked. It means no need will ever be forgotten. It means you'll have plenty of leftover love to give to others.

Who comes to mind when you hear the phrase "rich in love"?

Dear God, thanks for loving me so very much. Fill my heart with more of you, so I can love others in the same rich way too. Amen.

TRY IT OUT: Survey an adult and then someone your own age. Ask them how you can tell if someone is rich? Compare their answers. Did either one mention anything about love?

DO-OVER

"When you offer your gift to God at the altar, and you remember that your brother or sister has something against you, leave your gift there at the altar. Go and make peace with that person, and then come and offer your gift."
MATTHEW 5:23-24 NCV

Sometimes you just need a do-over. You said something stupid and it hurt your friend's feelings. You slammed the door in your mom's face. You teased your sister until she cried. And you're sorry. You're feeling just as bad as they did when you said what you said or did what you did.

Jesus knew this, which is why he talks about do-overs in the book of Matthew. He said that if you remember someone has something against you, go and make peace with them.

You can't take back what you did any more than you can put toothpaste you've squeezed out of the tube back inside. Once it's out, that's it. But you can make things right. Tell God how sorry you are. Then go to the other person and make things right.

They may or may not accept your apology, but chances are pretty good they will. What matters is that you took a step to making the relationship right.

Dear God, I need a do-ever. I did something that was wrong, and I'm sorry. Please forgive me. It was a dumb thing to do. Please give me the courage and the words to make it right. Amen.

LOST IN TRANSLATION

I can do everything through Christ, who gives me strength.
PHILIPPIANS 4:13 NLT

"I can do all things through Christ who gives me strength."

How many times have you heard that verse? Most people read it, started nodding their head, and say, "Totally. Jesus makes me strong, so I'm gonna do great things for God!"

Right?

God does give us strength to do great things and to do what's right, but that's not what the verse is talking about. Here's what the whole thing says. See if you can figure out the right translation.

I have learned the secret of being content in any and every situation, whether well fed or hungry, whether living in plenty or in want. I can do all this through him who gives me strength.

God gives you strength—to be content. Whether you've had three pieces of pizza for dinner or one, whether you have new cleats for the start of the soccer season or need to use the old ones, whether you've got a friend to hang out with or they're all busy, God gives you strength!

What situation are you in now where you need to say, "God, I need some strength to be content right now"?

Dear God, thank you that you give me strength to do great things. You also give me the strength to be content—always, anywhere, with anything I have or don't. Give me a content heart. Amen.

WHEN IT'S DARK OUTSIDE

"You are the light of the world—like a city on a hilltop that cannot be hidden. No one lights a lamp and then puts it under a basket. Instead, a lamp is placed on a stand, where it gives light to everyone in the house."
MATTHEW 5:14-15 NLT

Lights shine best in the darkness. Turn the light switch on in the middle of the day, and you'll hardly notice. But light a campfire against the backdrop of a midnight sky and you'll see that fire from miles around.

If you're living for Jesus, you're like a light to the world. Don't huddle around where there's a lot of light already. In other words, don't spend all your time with Christians and at church. Get to know people who don't realize how much God loves them.

- Write an I-hope-you're-having-a-great-day note to someone in your class.
- Offer to return someone's cart at the grocery store.
- Sign up for a sport with kids you don't know.
- Join an after-school club.

Then tell and show the people you meet about Jesus.

Dear Jesus, you are the light of the world. Because you live inside me, I can be the light to the world too. Show me different ways to spread your light to those who don't know you. Amen.

STICKING CLOSE

The LORD is my light and my salvation—
so why should I be afraid?
The LORD is my fortress, protecting me from danger,
so why should I tremble?
PSALM 27:1 NLT

Aubrey had gone camping in the Boundary Waters since she was a kid. Every day was filled with fishing and canoeing and exploring the rivers until they made camp for the night. It was dark at night—no electricity, no cars, no cell phones, just deep, dark wilderness. And Aubrey loved it.

One night her dad went down to the lake to make sure the canoes were still secured. He took the flashlight with him and Aubrey followed close behind. As long as she was by that light, she knew where she was going.

Staying close to that light is like staying close to God. When you walk close to him, you can see where you're going and what to do. You don't need to be afraid because he protects you and shows you where to go.

What's a good way to know if you're staying close to God?

Dear God, help me to know—not just in my head but my heart—that you are near. You are my light; you are my salvation. I don't have to be afraid. Amen.

WHAT I LIKE ABOUT YOU

*Let all that I am praise the LORD
may I never forget the good things he does for me.*
PSALM 103:2 NLT

"So why do you like to hang out with Evelyn?" Jessie asked her older brother, Caden.

"Well, she's nice and funny and she's really good at playing tennis. She can cook—okay, she makes brownies and caramel popcorn, but they're still good. That's why."

Nice. Funny. Tennis player. Cook. Those were just some of the reasons Caden liked Evelyn and wanted to hang out with her.

When we tell God what we like about him, that's called praise. It's telling God what makes him so amazing! Psalm 103 lists a ton of reasons why God deserves praise. Can you circle three or four of them?

Let all that I am praise the LORD; may I never forget the good things he does for me. He forgives all my sins and heals all my diseases. He redeems me from death and crowns me with love and tender mercies. He fills my life with good things. My youth is renewed like the eagle's. The LORD gives righteousness and justice to all who are treated unfairly. Psalm 103:2-6

What's something that makes you want to praise God?

Dear God, I praise you because you are so good to me. Thank you. Amen.

I AM

Then God said to Moses, "I AM WHO I AM.
When you go to the people of Israel, tell them,
'I AM sent me to you.'"

EXODUS 3:14 NCV

When you think of God, what do you imagine he's like?
Some people think God is like:

- A Santa Claus who smiles a lot and gives them what they want.
- A judge who waits for them to do something wrong to pronounce them, "Guilty!"
- A too-strict parent who taps their foot, crosses their arms, and waits for them to shape up.

Trying to describe God is like trying to put a rainbow's beauty in a box, or a bird's song in a bottle, or a flower's fragrance in a glass. It can't be done. God is too big, beautiful, and holy! Which is why he is called I Am.

Need a friend? God says "I Am."
Need a healer? God says, "I Am."
Need a helper? God says, "I Am."
Need a Savior? God says, "I Am."

Everything you need for all of your life, he is.

Dear God, you are the great I Am! There isn't anything good or beautiful or holy that you are not. Everything I need is in you. I pray that every day I'll know you more and more. Amen.

THE BIG FAT LIE

The snake was the most clever of all the wild animals the LORD God had made. One day the snake said to the woman, "Did God really say that you must not eat fruit from any tree in the garden?"

GENESIS 3:1 NCV

Eve was chillaxing on a summer day, surrounded by olive trees and fragrant flowers with just a bit of a breeze. It was a perfect day—until a serpent slithered up. He didn't bite her; he didn't even threaten her. All he did was ask a question.

"Did God *really* say...?"

The serpent knew exactly what God had told Eve. So why did he ask the question? Wasn't he sure? Or could it be that he wanted to introduce a little bit of doubt into Eve's mind and break up her tight relationship with God?

Our enemy, the devil, still asks questions that make us doubt what God said and who he is.

- Does God really love me?
- Is God's Word really true?
- Does God really give good gifts?
- Does God really answer prayer?

Don't fall for it. Do what Eve should've done and tell those lies to get lost!

Dear God, I want to believe in you! I want to believe what's true! When I'm tempted to question who you are and what you've done, remind me to focus on what's true. Amen.

PROMISES, PROMISES

The LORD is trustworthy in all he promises
and faithful in all he does.

PSALM 145:13 NIV

"Sarah is going to have a baby," God said.

When Sarah heard that she just laughed. *Ha!* There was no way she was having a baby. She was wrinkled and gray and ninety years old. But a year later her baby boy was born. Sarah named him "Isaac" which means laughter. She had laughed at God's promise but instead God had turned her laughter into joy.

God's Word is packed with more promises than a traffic jam. And all of them are true. All the promises you read in the Bible? Well, they're there for you. You can trust God to keep his promises. He always does what he says. Rest safe, rest secure. He won't let you down.

Dear God, I can count on what you say. There's no one better to trust. You don't change your mind. You don't make promises you can't keep or don't intend to keep. Amen.

BIG THINGS ARE GOING DOWN

*"God even knows how many hairs are on your head.
So don't be afraid."*

MATTHEW 10:30-31 NCV

Cut it, curl it, straighten it, spray it, highlight it, color it—red, blue, blonde, black, or brilliant pink—foil it, or style it. We spend a lot of time, and money, on our hair. But in the big picture of things, like school, family, politics, persecution, and world hunger, how big of a deal is hair anyway?

In this chapter of Matthew, Jesus tells his disciples that some pretty big stuff is going down—persecution, war, imprisonment. We're talking big! But then he says this: God is keeping tally on the hairs of your head, the very littlest things. How much more is he keeping track of the big things in life?

When you brush your hair in the morning, God sees how many float to the floor or slip into the bathroom sink. Nothing escapes him. He sees everything and pays close attention. So if you hear of scary things, don't be afraid. The one who pays attention to the littlest things is absolutely keeping track of the big stuff too.

What's some of the big stuff in the world right now? What are some of the little ways you've seen God work?

Dear God, you count every hair on my head. Details don't escape you because you care—about small things like hair, but even about bigger things. Amen.

UNASHAMED

"Whoever acknowledges me before others, I will also acknowledge before my Father in heaven."
MATTHEW 10:32 NIV

Imagine if Carrie Underwood walked into your school and you got to meet her. Wouldn't that be awesome? Better yet what if she walked right up to you, gave you a high five, then turned to your friends and said, "This is my friend. Isn't she amazing?" Wouldn't your chest just swell with pride? *Carrie Underwood is calling me her friend!*

When those who believe in Jesus get to heaven, Jesus will be the center of attention. Heaven will be full of his glory! And guess what? He'll name drop. He'll say, "I know you." But he'll do more than acknowledge you exist. He'll stand up for you. "She's a close friend. We love to hang out together!"

On the flip side, have you ever met those who make fun of Jesus and his followers? Who laugh at Jesus and belittle what he's done? The Bible says that Jesus won't stand up for them.

Acknowledging Jesus means being unashamed to let others know you belong to him. What do you imagine it'll feel like to have Jesus stand up for you before the Father in heaven?

Dear Jesus, thank you for loving me and not being ashamed of me. Sometimes I'm shy about being a Christian. Help me to be bold and brave and unashamed. Amen.

THE FAMILY NAME

*"All those who stand before others
and say they believe in me, I, the Son of Man,
will say before the angels of God that they belong to me."*
LUKE 12:8 NCV

"Table for four for Swift, please," Mrs. Swift told the hostess.

"Swift, huh," commented the hostess. "You aren't by any chance related to Taylor Swift, are you?"

"I am! She's my daughter." Mrs. Swift responded.

Your last name tells people what family you belong to, sometimes what country your ancestors came from, and even what place your family has in society. Some of you might have a name that's associated with good things. People might say, "That's the Miller girl. The Millers are all so smart." Or maybe you have a name that's associated with not-so-good things. People might say, "Oh, that's the Roberts girl. Those Roberts are always getting into trouble."

When you believe in Jesus Christ, you become a part of his family and belong to him. You take on his name and become a *Christ*ian. He calls you his own and writes your name in his book of life. From that point on, what you say and do reflects his family name. When you're faithful to that family name, he'll say in front of all the angels in heaven, "This is my child. She belongs to me!"

Dear Jesus, thank you for adopting me into your family. I'm so happy I belong to you. I pray that everything I do and say would make you proud. Amen.

HELP, PLEASE?

Our help is in the name of the LORD,
the Maker of heaven and earth.
PSALM 124:8 NIV

"Honey, can you help me in with the groceries?"
"Would you help set the table?"
"Would you help your brother with his homework?"

When people ask for our help, we expect to assist them with something that's mostly their responsibility. We're just helping, after all.

God is our help. But that doesn't mean he's our assistant. He doesn't stand next to us doing whatever it is we ask him to do. That's a different kind of help.

God is the same kind of help you'd need if you were sinking in the ocean and couldn't swim. God is the same kind of help you'd need if you suddenly lost your eyesight and couldn't get around. Without him you can't exist because he is your help! He gives you air to breathe, makes the sun rise, calms the ocean, and keeps the clouds in the sky. God is your help!

Dear God, you are my help. Without you, well, I don't know what I'd do. I depend on you completely. And right now I need help. Amen.

LOVING LIKE THAT

Dear friends, let us continue to love one another, for love comes from God. Anyone who loves is a child of God and knows God. But anyone who does not love does not know God, for God is love.

1 JOHN 4:7-8 NLT

Everyone likes to be loved differently. Some people like to be told, "I love you" or, "You're really good at that." Other people like to be given a high-five or a hug. Or, maybe you're the person who likes to get gifts, like a Starbucks gift card or a new sweatshirt. Maybe you like it when someone shows love by spending time with you—watching a movie together or going to the beach.

If you could pick two of your favorite ways to be shown love, what would they be?

God is love, and he loves deeply. He speaks loving things, "You are my child and I love you." He shows you love by giving you good gifts, like food and clothing. He shows you love by inviting you to spend time with him or by sending someone to give you a hug or a smile when you need it most. Bottom line: He loves you—perfectly!

How can you love others the same way God loves you? Can you think of two different people and two different ways you could show them love?

Dear God, thank you for loving me and pouring your own love inside me. Show me how I can love people in a way that they'll appreciate. Amen.

OH BROTHER

"I tell you the truth, anything you did for even the least of my people here, you also did for me."

MATTHEW 25:40 NCV

Lily was in her room listening to music when her five-year-old brother walked in.

"Do you know where my nerf gun is?" he asked.

"No idea."

"But I *neeed* it," he insisted.

"I'm busy right now. Mom!"

"Lily, help your brother out," Mom yelled from the laundry.

Oh man! Serious eye roll.

"Mom, Lily rolled her eyes at me."

"I did not!"

You know how it goes. Back and forth. Around and around. Siblings are great but sometimes, just sometimes, they can be a little annoying.

Just for kicks pretend that Jesus was the one who walked in the room and asked Lily for the nerf gun. (Yeah, wouldn't you like to see Jesus with a nerf gun!) The likelihood of Lily answering with an eye roll? Zero.

What you don't do for others, you don't do for Jesus. But what you do for them—give them a hug, look for that nerf gun—it's as if you're doing it for Jesus. So the next time you're tempted to "oh brother!" picture Jesus there and treat others like you would him.

Dear Jesus, I like my siblings, but sometime I get irritated with them. Help me treat them like I'd treat you. Amen.

JUST DELETE

*If we confess our sins, He is faithful
and righteous to forgive us our sins
and to cleanse us from all unrighteousness.*
1 JOHN 1:9 NLT

Three days ago, Fernanda's mom was all smiles. "Okay, everyone," she'd said. "Everybody say 'cheese.' Perfect."

Today, she was confused.

"Where did my pictures go?" she said, flipping through her cell phone pictures. "I can't find my pictures. Fernanda, I can't find my pictures!"

"Let me see, Mom" and Fernanda took the phone from her. "Hmm. Looks like you hit delete. They're here in your trash bin."

Deleting is sometimes a bad thing. But sometimes deleting is a good thing. Because of the blood of Jesus, God deletes all our sins. When we admit we're wrong and want to do what's right, he hits that delete key and they are gone for good (not even saved in the trash bin). Erased forever. Un-retrievable. Un-recoverable. Never to be seen again.

Dear Jesus, thank you for dying on the cross. Please forgive my sins and hit delete. Amen.

TULIP MANIA

"Look at how the lilies in the field grow.
They don't work or make clothes for themselves.
But I tell you that even Solomon with his riches was
not dressed as beautifully as one of these flowers."
MATTHEW 6:28 NCV

Each spring, visitors pour into Holland to see gorgeous tulips. Splashes of red, yellow, orange, and pink cover fields and gardens. Tulips are so famous in Holland that you can find tulip tours, a tulip festival, tulip flower markets, and even a tulip museum. Travelers can buy tulip bulbs in the Holland airport.

Tulips, like lilies or roses or daisies, never shop for clothes or read up on the latest fashions. Yet there's nothing in the world dressed as beautifully as a flower. Jesus said that not even King Solomon, one of the richest kings in history, was dressed as beautifully as a simple lily.

If God takes care of the smallest flower, if he dresses it with absolute "wow!" he'll take care of you.

What's on your mind these days? Looking out the window at the birds and the flowers and all God has made helps put things into perspective.

Dear God, thank you for taking care of me and my family. When I start to worry and wonder how things will work out, remind me to take a look outside at your creation. Amen.

CALLING IT WHAT IT IS

Everyone has sinned; we all fall short of God's glorious standard. Yet God, in his grace, freely makes us right in his sight. He did this through Christ Jesus.
ROMANS 3:23-24 NLT

If you look at any magazine cover, you'll see perfect-looking people. Shiny hair, straight teeth, flawless skin. Never mind that in real life they're no different from anyone else. You just don't notice because they've been altered digitally to cover up imperfections.

No one's perfect even though they'd like you to think they are. They're not perfect on the outside; they're not perfect on the inside. When it comes to perfection, only God is perfect. He's holy, perfect in love, kindness, and goodness. No one else is like him.

When you do what's wrong, your imperfection is showing. If you own up to that sin, God shares his perfection with you. He makes you right in his sight when you call sin what it is—wrong. And he doesn't just cover it up like they do in magazines. Through Jesus, he makes us completely right. Holy and acceptable.

When you call sin what it is, God gives grace!

Dear God, I want to call it like it is. No pretending, disguising, or ignoring. If there's something in my life that makes you sad and keeps me from having the best relationship possible with you, please show me what it is. So I can call it what it is and ask for your forgiveness. Amen.

PELICANS

*Teach me your way, Lord, that I may rely on your faithfulness;
give me an undivided heart, that I may fear your name.*
PSALM 86:11 NIV

Louisiana is called the Pelican State. Across its coast, brown pelicans dive headfirst into the ocean and use their large pouch-like beaks to scoop up fresh fish for dinner.

Seagulls like fish too, though, and instead of catching their own, they sit on a pelican's head and distract it by pecking its head. *Peck, peck, peck.* That distraction can cost the pelican a tasty lunch if the seagull snatches the fish away.

Distractions can cost you too. Distracted during a class? It could mean missing directions important for a good grade. Distracted while a friend is talking about her very bad day? It could mean she gets upset and says you don't care. Distracted by your phone while doing homework? It could mean homework takes two hours instead of one.

The biggest distraction to avoid is when other things become more important than loving God with all your heart. Distractions might be tempting, but they take away a better reward.

Dear God, sometimes it's hard for me to focus because I don't feel like it or because something else seems more interesting. Teach me to give everything I've got to whatever I'm doing. Amen.

MAY

We know that in all things God works
for the good of those who love him.
He appointed them to be saved in
keeping with his purpose.

ROMANS 8:28 NIRV

TXTSPK

Give all your worries to him, because he cares about you.
1 PETER 5:7 NCV

Hi,

How R U? Thought I'd check in J4F but saw UR :(
R U OK? Can I help?
JSYK ILY.
LMK if U want some F2F.
PTB coz I care. 4EAE.

God

Dear God, I'm really worried about some things, and am having a hard time thinking about anything else. Here. Could you take them for me and take care of everything please?
Thanks for caring for me. Amen.

WHEN IT'S HARD TO FORGIVE

"Now Joseph will show his anger and pay us back for all the wrong we did to him," they said.
GENESIS 50:15 NLT

If anyone had a reason to be angry with his brothers, Joseph did. If anyone had a great excuse to get revenge, Joseph did. Their sibling rivalry went way beyond teasing, hitting, and bullying. Joseph's brothers stole from Joseph, sold him as a slave, and then covered it up by lying. "He was killed by a wild animal," they told their dad.

Years later, Joseph had a chance to pay them back big time. He could have thrown them into jail. Instead he said, "Don't be afraid of me….Am I God, that I can punish you? You intended to harm me, but God intended it all for good" (Genesis 50:19-20).

Forgiving someone doesn't mean
- you feel just fine and don't hurt inside.
- you're saying what the person did to you wasn't wrong.

Forgiving someone does mean
- letting go of the right to be angry.
- letting God deal with them, instead of paying them back.
- asking God to use what happened for good.

Is there someone you need to forgive?

Dear God, what that person did really hurt, but I let go of my right to be angry. Help me to forgive. Use what happened for good in my own heart. Amen.

PRAYING FLOWERS?

The heavens declare the glory of God;
the skies proclaim the work of his hands.
They have no speech, they use no words;
no sound is heard from them.
Yet their voice goes out into all the earth,
their words to the ends of the world.

PSALM 19:1, 3-4 NIV

If you hiked through the desert you probably wouldn't come across a talking cactus or praying flowers. If you walked through the jungle, you wouldn't come across trees that preach.

The sun doesn't sing, the moon doesn't journal, and the stars don't shout, "Hallelujah!" But they still manage to praise God—not with words, but through their beauty. Without a word or sound, the stars and sky talk about God's glory and say, "God is amazing!"

Pink roses and prickly cactus praise him.

Smelly skunks and mooing cows praise him.

Streaking comets and lightning strikes praise him.

Everything in all creation praises him.

What in creation just makes you want to praise him?

Dear God, your creation is amazing! I love seeing and hearing your wonderful works. They praise you and I want to praise you too! Amen.

133

ROBIN'S NEST

A little sleep, a little slumber,
a little folding of the hands to rest.
PROVERBS 24:33 NIV

In the tree branch just outside Xiang's window, a robin was building a nest. For the last three days, Xiang watched as the robin brought a small twig or a piece of grass in her beak. Bit by bit a nest was starting to take shape. The little "bits" the robin brought were adding up to a whole lot.

Hard work happens bit by bit. You write an essay word-by-word and sentence by sentence. You memorize Scripture verse by verse. You put away your clothes piece by piece. You save up for something special dollar by dollar. Not all of it is easy or even fun, but together the hard work adds up to a lot.

Of course the opposite happens too. A little sleep, a little rest, a little "Maybe later, I don't feel like it now," can turn into a late assignment, a messy room, or a wasted opportunity. So be on your guard and remember the payoff. A little can add up to a lot!

How many different ways can you think of applying the "bit by bit" example?

Dear God, help me work hard at the little things. When I don't feel like doing what I'm supposed to be doing, remind me to be disciplined. Thank you for the results that'll happen in the end. Amen.

THE ONE THING

*"Martha, Martha, you are worried and upset about many
things. Only one thing is important. Mary has chosen the
better thing, and it will never be taken away from her."*
LUKE 10:41-42 NCV

"I am so tired of this! I'm doing all the work and she's just
sitting there! Why doesn't she help me out?"

Company was coming and Martha was trying to get ready.
Her sister Mary wasn't helping out. Instead she was just sitting
and listening to Jesus, like there was nothing else in the world
to do. Frustrating!

"Jesus, tell her to give me a hand. I mean, I'm going it
alone here."

And that's when Jesus answered with the verse at the top
of this page.

What do you think the "one thing" is that Jesus was talking
about?

Life sure is packed—with sports, church, camp, school,
homework, and music lessons. It's easy to get worried and
stressed out over everything. We have so much to do! But only
one thing really matters—spending time with God and getting
to know him, inviting him in the ordinary moments of our day.

**Dear God, sometimes I get so busy I forget just to listen. Help me
take time to welcome you into every activity of my life. I want you
to be the number one person in my life. Amen.**

SPOTS

Gray hair is like a crown of honor;
it is earned by living a good life.
PROVERBS 16:31 NCV

True story.

"Michelle, would you mind talking to Mr. Anderson for a while," said Michelle's uncle. "He just came over for a visit, but I have to take this call."

Honestly, Michelle did mind, but she really didn't have a choice. She glanced at Mr. Anderson. He looked old. His hair was gray, and he had brown spots on his hands.

The conversation began clumsily. Michelle figured they wouldn't have anything in common. But they did! Michelle loved to read books and write. Mr. Anderson was a writing teacher. The next forty-five minutes flew by. And when Michelle's uncle came back, Michelle didn't want to stop talking. As Mr. Anderson walked away, she forgot about his gray hair and spots. She saw him for who he was.

When you look at someone older, what do you see? Do you really see them? Ask them a question. Find out their story. Really see them, like Jesus does.

Here are a few things you can ask:

What did you want to be when you grew up? What did you end up doing? What was your favorite childhood memory? What's the coolest thing you've ever done?

What's their story?

Dear God, when I look at gray hair, I see someone who is old. When you look at gray hair, you see someone you love and someone who has a lot of experience. Help me to do the same. Amen.

THE OVAL OFFICE

Let us come boldly to the throne of our gracious God.
There we will receive his mercy, and we will find grace
to help us when we need it most.
HEBREWS 4:16 NLT

Nearly every time a new president moves into the White House, the Oval Office gets a makeover—rugs, curtains, paint, everything. President Obama had a light beige rug and red-orange drapes. President George Bush had a light blue rug with blue drapes. No matter what color the walls or curtains or rugs are, the Oval Office represents power and authority. It's a place where important decisions are made because the president works there.

Presidents and leaders from around the world have met in the Oval Office. The only people allowed to go see the president are invited in and go through strict security clearance.

When you need to talk to God and need help—right away!—you can go right into the seat of power. You don't need to check in with the Secret Service, go through a metal detector, or wait for an invitation. You can go straight to God, without any appointment, and talk to him. He's always there to give you grace.

How does that make you feel?

Dear God, you are my help. Even though you're Lord of the earth and your throne is in heaven, I can come to you for help. Thank you! Amen.

VOICES

The LORD says, "Don't be afraid of what you have heard.
Don't be frightened by the words the servants
of the king of Assyria have spoken against me."
ISAIAH 37:6 NCV

Things were not looking good for King Hezekiah. The king, his people, and the whole city were surrounded. They were trapped, and they knew it. To make matters worse, the enemy started to shake them up: "Don't listen to your king. God will never save you. You can't count on God. You're going down!"

Do you ever hear those voices? Whether they're in your mind or the voices of other people, they try to make you doubt what you've been told and what you know to be true: *Never mind what your parents say. God isn't listening. He'll never answer. You can't count on him. You're going down!*

If that's how you feel or that describes the thoughts swirling around in your head, God says to you what he said to the king of Israel. "Don't be afraid. Trust me. I have a plan. Listen to me."

When you trust God no matter what, people aren't going to like it. They might try to make you second-guess your commitment to him.

So what voice will you listen to? The one that says, "Freak out!" or the one that says, "Do not fear?"

Dear God, I sometimes feel confused. People and circumstances seem to scream different messages to me about what to think or what to do. I want to shut out all those voices and just listen to you saying, "Do not fear!" Amen.

LOVING AND LIKING

"Love your enemies, do good to them."
LUKE 6:35 NIV

You don't have to like someone to love them. Yep, you read that right. Liking is not the same as loving. Liking someone means you can't wait to call your girlfriend and tell her you're going to Mexico for Christmas! Liking someone means you have sleepovers and do puzzles together and laugh at the same things.

Loving means treating someone the way Jesus would treat them, even if they don't treat you that way back.

Fiction: When you love someone, you have to feel all warm and fuzzy and happy inside toward someone. If you don't feel all warm and fuzzy inside, well, then you don't love them. Fact: Love is choosing to do what's right even if the feelings aren't there. Loving your enemies means praying for them, doing good to them, lending to them without expecting to get anything back.

That's loving! Does knowing the difference between loving and liking make it easier to love your enemies?

Dear God, some people are hard for me to love. Thank you that I don't have to feel all loving inside to really love them. I can choose to treat them well. Remind me to pray for those who treat me badly and do good to them whether I feel like it or not. Amen.

WHAT GOD SEES IN YOU

*The angel of the LORD appeared to Gideon and said,
"The LORD is with you, mighty warrior!"*

JUDGES 6:12 NCV

Gideon had a little bit of a problem. For years, the enemies of his people ruined their food, stole their animals, and trampled their crops. Gideon had to hide to grind flour for making bread!

While he was working, an angel showed up. "The Lord is with you, mighty warrior!"

"Excuse me? Mighty warrior?" Gideon asked. "You mean me?"

In spite of Gideon's lack of confidence, God used him to set the people of Israel free. Gideon wasn't so sure about things at first. He started timidly and then became bolder and braver as his faith grew. Read the whole story in Judges 6 & 7. It's pretty amazing!

When God looks at you, he doesn't see problem he sees possibility! He sees the potential of what he can do through you. What he wants is a simple, "Yes! I'll do what you want, Lord." The possibilities are limitless because God is all-powerful!

Dear God, thank you for seeing the potential in me. Help me to trust you and obey you with all my heart so you can do what you want in and through me. Amen.

140

SEA ANEMONES

Two people are better off than one, for they can help each other succeed. If one person falls, the other can reach out and help. But someone who falls alone is in real trouble.

ECCLESIASTES 4:9-10 NLT

If you swam along the ocean floor or next to a coral formation, you might see the long tentacles of a sea anemone waving back and forth in the salty water. As beautiful as they are, the red, yellow, orange and different-colored tentacles are poisonous.

A clownfish, though, is a sea creature that isn't bothered by the anemone's stinging tentacles. The sea anemone helps the clownfish by giving it protection from predators. When a predator comes near, the clownfish ducks into the tentacles and hides until the predator passes by. The clownfish helps the sea anemone by providing it with food scraps.

Together the sea anemone and the clownfish are a great team.

Good friends can be a great team too. When one friend is down, the other can cheer them up. When one friend has a problem, the other can help find an answer. Friends make good teammates.

How do you like to be helped? How do you like to help others?

Dear God, I want to be the kind of friend who helps, supports, and stands by others. Will you give me a friend who will do the same? Thank you! Amen.

141

STOP AND GO, QUICK AND SLOW

My dear brothers and sisters, take note of this:
Everyone should be quick to listen,
slow to speak and slow to become angry.
JAMES 1:19 NIV

It always seems like a bonus to be fast. Fast food. Fast service. You might be fast at track or quick at solving a math equation. Fast answers (after all, isn't that what the internet is for). Fast results. Everyone wants to be fast. But are you quick to listen?

Slow on the other hand is for losers. Who wants to be slow to understand? The last one to get a joke? Stand in a slow line or be sitting in slow-moving traffic? No one. But are you slow to get angry? Are you slow to give an answer?

God's Word pairs up words that we don't often see together. Instead of reacting in anger quickly, be slow to get angry. Instead of being quick to pipe in with your opinion, be slow to speak.

Dear God, I usually lead with my mouth and am slow to listen. Teach me to stop, wait, listen, and then answer and respond. Amen.

DUMB STUFF

Human anger doesn't produce the holy life God wants.
So get rid of everything that is sinful.

JAMES 1:20-21 NIRV

"Ethan! I told you not to use my laptop," Katherine said closing the laptop on her brother's fingers. "This is my laptop for my homework. Now get lost!"

"Sisters are just dumb," muttered Ethan as he walked out the door.

"I heard that, Ethan," Katherine said.

When we're angry we can say and do stupid things. Slam the door, yell, stop talking to someone, say things that later we wish we could take back, but we never, ever can!

Acting out when we're angry is just plain dumb. Nothing good comes of it. Can you think of one good thing that comes out of showing anger? Okay, we might feel a little better for a teensy moment when we first let the bad feelings out. Once they're all out, though, there's no taking them back.

Just because an angry feeling bubbles up inside, you don't need to act on out. Try this: Pick one thing to do every time you start to feel angry—get a drink of water, wash your hands, put your hands in your pockets, etc. While you're doing this, train yourself to use those few moments to ask God for help dealing with the anger.

God's Spirit in you can control anger; anger doesn't have to control you.

Dear God, I know that when I act on my anger, I do dumb stuff that can hurt other people. Teach me to get in the habit of going to you. Amen.

SECRET WEAPON

A secret gift will calm an angry person.
PROVERBS 21:14 NCV

Sixty years ago a storm blew through the country of Holland. Wind howled and lightning flashed and thunder shook the ground. As rain poured down, the ocean swelled and waves grew bigger and bigger.

A fifteen-foot wall of water crashed against a dam that protected the province of Zeeland. Water pressure built up and the dam burst. Waves crashed over the area. Over 1500 people died that night because of a break in the dam.

Anger can build up inside people like the waves built up against the dam, pressuring it until it threatened to burst. They're frustrated, they're furious, they're mad—at you!—even though you may not have done anything wrong. What do you do?

King Solomon, famous for his wisdom and wealth, offered this secret—quietly give them a gift. A gift can soothe a frustrated temper and calm someone who is furious. Being nice can defuse a tense situation. Giving a simple gift like a smile, a card, a kind word, their favorite kind of cookie, can make them feel a little less angry.

Dear God, when someone around me is angry, I sometimes don't know what to do. Instead of being angry back, remind me that being kind and giving a gift can calm and soothe. Amen.

THE POWER OF A NAME

"In his name the nations will put their hope."
MATTHEW 12:21 NIV

When someone says these words what do you think of? Golden arches. A swoosh. Apple.

What comes to mind is more than what the word means but everything that word has come to represent. Golden arches means crispy fries and fast food. Apple means a multinational company that specializes in making technology friendly for everyday people. And what would Nike be without its swoosh?

The same thing is true for the name of Jesus. That name means more than a name like Jacob or Sam or Peter. It stands for everything Jesus is and everything he has done. So when you end your prayer with "in Jesus' name" you're saying:

- Jesus the Son of God,
- Jesus who rose from the dead,
- Jesus who forgives sin and has power over death.

Of course that's a lot to say at the end of each prayer, so we shorten it to "in Jesus' name". Jesus' name has power. Calling on that name and praying in that name makes things happen.

Dear God, thank you that I can come to you because of everything Jesus did. Show me how to pray boldly. In Jesus' name! Amen.

LOST AT SEA

*I pray that you and all God's holy people
will have the power to understand
the greatness of Christ's love—
how wide and how long and how high
and how deep that love is.*

EPHESIANS 3:18 NCV

In September 2015, Rickson and Chris left their village in Papua New Guinea and hopped on a boat. They expected to be back later that day, but the boat engine sputtered and stopped. They drifted across the Pacific Ocean—for six weeks! They were rescued six hundred miles from where they first left shore.

If God's love were an ocean, you'd get lost in its bigness. It stretches wider than the sea and deeper than it too. It's too great to understand on your own. You'd need God's power to understand how high, wide, and deep his love is.

Do you have any idea how much God loves you?

Dear God, show me how wide, deep, and high your love is for me, for my family, and for those around me. Amen.

GOOD GIFTS

"If you then, being evil, know how to give good gifts to your children, how much more will your Father who is in heaven give what is good to those who ask Him!"

MATTHEW 7:11 NASB

If you walked in the door for lunch and asked for a PB&J sandwich, would your mom hand you a rock to eat? Or if you asked your grandma for an after-school snack, would she feed you a live snake instead?

Of course not. It sounds ridiculous, but that's often how we picture God. We're afraid that when we ask him for something we want, he'll hand us something not-so-good instead. Something we really don't want. Something that's "good for us" but not something we'll like.

If your parents know how to give good gifts, though, imagine how much more God knows how to give good gifts. And *wants* to give good gifts! He's a good Father, a perfect Father. When you ask, you can expect God to answer. It might not always be what you expect, but it will be good.

For the record, God loves answering prayers!

Dear God, you're a good Father who gives good gifts, not bad ones. When I ask for something and I get something different, remind me that you give out of your goodness. You love me and give me what's perfect and good and best. Amen.

CAREER DAY

*"Go everywhere in the world,
and tell the Good News to everyone."*
MARK 16:15 NCV

Jonah looked around him at the sea of strangers. This was *not* what he had in mind when they talked about prophets at Career Day. Being a prophet, a messenger of God, was supposed to be exciting and glamorous.

Instead God had sent Jonah to Ninevah where everyone hated God. So Jonah went. (Okay it was after he tried to run away, got thrown overboard in a storm and then was swallowed up and spit out by a huge fish.) He wasn't happy about it but he was here.

For the next three days, he told the people of Ninevah about God. And something beautiful happened—they all decided they wanted to follow God. All because Jonah went.

There may be kids at your school or in your neighborhood who are the last people you want to reach out to. They're not your type. It's inconvenient. You're not sure what to say. You wonder what they'll think of you. But God loves them!

Dear God, telling people about you isn't something that comes easily to me. But I want to share the good news about your love with those who need it most. Remind me that it's more important than anything, and fill me up with your love for others. Amen.

CHECK IT OUT: Read the whole story in the book of Jonah, chapters 1-4.

SPIRIT WEEK

Clap your hands, all you people.
Shout to God with joy.
The Lord Most High is wonderful.
He is the great King over all the earth!
PSALM 47:1-2 NCV

We got spirit! Yes we do!
We got spirit! How 'bout you?

After a week of crazy hair day, wacky-tacky day, and PJ and slipper day, it's time for the big football game, complete of course with nachos, hot dogs, and popcorn. Cheerleaders are shaking pom-poms, the pep band is playing, and you and everyone else packed in the stands are cheering (aka screaming) and celebrating.

Shout. Dance. Clap. Celebrate.

Those words might describe a scene out of Spirit Week, but they also describe what the people of Israel did "in church." They were so filled up with joy they had to celebrate.

When you realize how big, awesome, wonderful, good, and powerful God is, you can't help but celebrate too. He's better than all the things in Spirit Week combined.

Close the door, pump up the music, and with no one else around sing, dance, and praise the Lord!

What makes you want to praise the Lord?

Dear God, you are amazing! I praise you because you are God over all the earth. There's nothing you can't do. Praise you! Amen.

TAKE YOUR PARENTS TO WORK DAY

The Word became human and made his home among us.
He was full of unfailing love and faithfulness.
JOHN 1:14 NLT

Yep, you read that right. You've probably heard of Take Your Daughter and Son to Work Day, but what if it were the other way around? What if millions of parents flooded school hallways to see what their kids' lives were like every day?

Can you imagine your mom trying to find math class? Can you picture your dad putting up with the bullying that goes on in the lunchroom, or keeping his mouth shut when Mrs. Taylor lectures in her squeaky voice?

God did enter our world and he does understand. God, Creator of the whole earth, became a human being and lived with all the stuff that we go through—the teasing, the schoolwork, the chores, the tension between brothers and sisters.

Not only that, his Spirit is with you every hour of the day, everywhere you go. He sees what your day is like. So when you pray, you're praying to someone who understands. He's been through it all, and he sees it all. He. Understands. You.

Dear God, you know what it's like to be me. You understand what it's like to live in my world, at school, at home, on the ball field, in my neighborhood. So I know I can pray and ask for help, and you understand. Thank you! Amen.

A LITTLE ODD

Suppose someone comes into your church meeting wearing nice clothes and a gold ring. At the same time a poor person comes in wearing old, dirty clothes. You show special attention to the one wearing nice clothes and say, "Please, sit here in this good seat." But you say to the poor person, "Stand over there," or, "Sit on the floor by my feet." What are you doing? You are making some people more important than others, and with evil thoughts you are deciding that one person is better.

JAMES 2:2-4 NCV

Ally looked up as the door to the church opened and a girl walked in. Her jeans were tattered and her coat had a hole in it. But it was the smell that made Ally want to turn away.

If this girl walked into your classroom, what would you think? How would you react if she walked into your church? Honestly.

Option #1: *I just thought of something I need to do. I'm out of here!*

Option #2: *So walking away would be rude, but there's no way I'm going up to her. What would I say? We obviously don't have anything in common.*

Option #3: *Okay, here goes. "Hi, I've never seen you here before. My name is...."*

What best describes you?

Dear God, it's so easy for me to walk away from people who make me uncomfortable. Help me treat them as important and special—because they are to you. Amen.

MOVE OVER, PLEASE!

"Love your neighbor as you love yourself." If you obey this law, you are doing right. But if you treat one person as being more important than another, you are sinning.

JAMES 2:8-9 NCV

Alessia and her friends looked up as a new girl walked into the lunchroom. She was beautiful. Stunning actually. Long, wavy black hair, olive skin, and a perfect figure—model perfect.

"That must be the new girl," whispered Alessia to her friend. "I heard Ms. Jackson say she does modeling in New York. And her parents are loaded."

Ms. Model walked over to Alessia's table. "Is anyone sitting here?' she asked with a smile.

Well, there was someone sitting here, Alessia thought, *but she's in the bathroom and can find somewhere else to sit.* "No, go ahead and sit down."

When we think of discrimination, we think about treating people badly. The opposite is true too. When we treat people like they're more important than others, we're saying, "You're better than so-and-so." Our over-the-top treatment says to others that we don't care about them as much as someone else.

When you're filled with God's love, you'll want to treat the poor and the rich and those who aren't popular and those who are just the same. Because you know inside that you're all equally loved just the same by God.

Dear God, I know I've given special treatment to some and then overlooked others. Help me to realize that you love all people. No one is better than anyone else. Amen.

THREE WAYS TO SAY THANK YOU

I thank my God every time I remember you.
PHILIPPIANS 1:3 NIV

Saying thank you can be fun! Whether someone gave you a birthday gift, did you a favor, or just came to mind because you think they're great, you have so many things to say thank you for. God puts people in your life who make you feel great. Telling them you appreciate them can make them feel great too.

Who are three people you're especially thankful for? List something specific they've done that you're thankful for.

Choose one of the creative ways below to thank each of them. Or, come up with your own creative thank you!

- Take a selfie of you smiling and text it to that person along with, "You put a smile on my face today. Thank you!"
- Take a video of yourself singing, "Thank-you, thank-you" to the tune of Happy Birthday. Email or text it to that person.
- Tell someone else what that person did for you. Good news travels quickly and you can be sure the person will hear about it.

Dear God, thank you for amazing people who fill my life with good things. I'm so happy they're in my life. Show me the best way to thank them for what they do. Amen.

153

KNOCK, KNOCK

"Everyone who asks will receive. The one who searches will find. And everyone who knocks will have the door opened."
LUKE 11:10 NCV

Knock, knock.
Who's there?
Cow says.
Cow says who?
No, silly, cow says moo!

A knock-knock joke wasn't exactly what Jesus had in mind when he told his disciples the verse above. (But hey, he probably would have liked it.) What Jesus was really saying is when you knock on a door, you expect the door to open. In the same way, when you pray you can expect God to answer.

First he says…
Ask: Come right out and ask God for what you need.
Seek: That just means be on the lookout for God's answer. Pay attention to anything he might be telling you.
Knock: Be persistent. Don't give up if the answer doesn't come right away

Be encouraged. God does answer prayer!

Dear God, you love to answer prayer! Thank you for that. Help me to keep hoping for the answer to my prayers and not give up. Amen.

LITTLE LAMBS

He gathers the lambs in his arms and carries them close to his heart; he gently leads those that have young.

ISAIAH 40:11 NLT

If you've ever seen a woolly little lamb or heard its tiny bleat, you can't help but think, *They're just so cute!*

They are cute. They nuzzle your head and shake their little tail. But they can also get into a lot of trouble. They wander off and get lost. They jump fences looking for a better patch of grass. They follow other sheep into dangerous situations. They're also stubborn and like to go their own way.

Sometimes we act the same way. We think we know best. We do what we want even though a parent or a friend might tell us, "That's not such a good idea."

That I-want-my-own-way heart is the reason Jesus died. He came to take away any hint of selfishness and make us clean. He scoops us up and holds us close to his heart.

Dear Jesus, thank you for dying on the cross to take away my selfishness. Thanks for your tender care for me. Amen.

REAL FRIENDS

*I pray that the God who gives hope will fill you
with much joy and peace while you trust in him.*
ROMANS 15:13 NCV

"I don't know, Mikayla," said Addie. "How am I supposed to go to a skating party if I can't skate? I don't want to sit around while the rest of you have fun."

"I'll teach you how to skate. Come on, it'll be fun!" said Mikayla. "If you need a break, there's a pizza place right next to the rink. Come on, Addie."

"Okay, I'll do it. Try at least."

Healthy friendships line up with the same things God brings: hope, joy, and peace. Unhealthy friendships do the opposite. They make you feel pressured, confused, discouraged, and stressed out.

A real friend builds up your confidence, encourages you, and reassures you. Listening to them fills you up with hope. Hanging around a real friend brings you joy. Being with a true friend doesn't make you confused and frustrated but brings you peace. There's no way a good friend would tear you down!

Dear God, help me choose friends that line up with who you are. Help me be that kind of friend too. Amen.

TOTALLY OFFENDED

Search me, God, and know my heart;
test me and know my anxious thoughts.
See if there is any offensive way in me,
and lead me in the way everlasting.
PSALM 139:23-24 NIV

I can't believe she did that?! That's just so...so wrong! She invited everyone in the class to her party—except me!

When someone does something wrong, it hurts. Big time. And it's easy to feel offended.

Sometimes we forget God has feelings too. "Do not bring sorrow to God's Holy Spirit by the way you live," says Ephesians 4:30. Doing what we know is wrong hurts God. That's because the laws he gives aren't just a bunch of random rules; they reflect who he is.

For example he says, "Do not lie" because he wants you to be honest. Why? Because he's a God of truth. If you do tell a lie it's like saying, "You're not right. I don't really like your rules. I don't really like you." And that makes God sad.

Take a minute to ask God if there's anything in your life that makes his heart sad. Then make it right.

Dear God, I know I'm supposed to do what's right just because I should, but I didn't realize that it hurt your feelings too. I'm sorry for thinking of me and not of you. See if there's anything in my life that makes you sad and guide me in what's right. Amen.

MUDDY LATTE WITH A SHOT OF EVERYTHING

Religion that God our Father accepts as pure and faultless is...
to keep oneself from being polluted by the world.
JAMES 1:27 NIV

What's your favorite thing to drink? Sweet tea? An icy Coke? What about a thick strawberry banana smoothie? Or perhaps you're more of a latte person.

Imagine you've got two glasses, one with latte and the other with muddy water. You pour a little latte into a third glass along with a little muddy water. (After all, they do kind of look the same, right?) Stir them together. How do you think it would taste? Probably like a whole lot of yuck.

When you follow God, you can't do what God wants most of the time and what you want a little of the time. You can't do a little of what he says and mix in a little of what the world says—like encourage your friend Melody, and then make fun of Krista. Or give money to a mission project, then refuse to give your little brother a piece of gum. Doing that is like polluting latte with muddy water.

God loves all of you. Love him with all your heart, all your mind, and everything you've got.

Dear God, I want all in. I want all of me to be yours, every area of my life—my studies, my relationship with others. Be the Lord of my life. Amen.

CREATIVELY YOU!

How many are your works, LORD!
In wisdom you made them all.
PSALM 104:24 NIV

God paints the sunset brilliant orange, pink, and purple. He flings a bright rainbow across the sky. He covers the salty ocean with rippling waves. He shapes each person with care and makes them special. Everything God makes bursts with creativity and imagination.

When you were born, God spilled a little of his imagination into you. You're God's creation, fearfully and wonderfully made (Psalm 139:14). People usually think of creativity as something artsy, like painting or doing crafts. Here are some more ways God can show his creativity through you:

- the way you think or solve a problem
- the way you make friends with others
- the way you come up with ideas on how to make things better or more beautiful
- the way you make people laugh

God made you creatively you!
How does God show his creativity through you?

Dear God, you made so many things. In wisdom you made them all and that includes—me! Take the creativity that you put in me and make it grow. Then use it for good. Amen.

GOOD, BETTER, BEST

Pay careful attention to your own work,
for then you will get the satisfaction of a job well done,
and you won't need to compare yourself to anyone else.
For we are each responsible for our own conduct.
GALATIANS 6:4-5 NLT

"Do your best!"

How many times have you heard that before?

Best is relative. It all depends who you're talking about. Michael Phelps' best is twenty-eight Olympic medals in swimming, twenty-three of them gold. Kelly Clarkson's best is over ten million dollars in album sales. Your kid brother's best might be nine out of ten correct words on a spelling test.

What's your best?

Unless you're an Olympian, someone somewhere will probably be better than you are—in track, in history, in tap dance, in Monopoly, or in whatever. So comparing yourself to others can make you feel like you're coming up short.

Focusing on *your* best and how hard you work and how far you've come, well, that brings satisfaction that can't be taken away.

Dear God, I want to do things really well—my best, not someone else's best. Help me focus on you and what I can do in and through you. If I'm starting to compare, let me know! Amen.

THAT'S THE BEAUTY

God is not a human being...and he does not change his mind.
NUMBERS 23:19 NCV

If you're what people call thin today and lived in the 1400s, you wouldn't be considered thin. You'd be called unhealthy and anemic. On the other hand if you were round and had large hips, the paparazzi would be following you around.

Depending on when a girl lived in history or even where she lives in the world today, the standards of beauty change. What's considered beautiful in Italy is different than in Kenya. What was considered beautiful in ancient civilization is different than what a girl wants to look like today. So unless you're born in a specific place at a specific time, you may or may not be considered beautiful.

The beauty of God's kingdom, though, is that even when other standards of beauty change, God's does not. "Your beauty," God says, "should be that of your inner self, the unfading beauty of a gentle and quiet spirit, which is of great worth in God's sight" (1 Peter 3:3-4).

With a standard that never changes, every girl can be beautiful!

You can develop your inner beauty by spending time with God each day, praying for others, reading God's Word, and learning from other Christians.

Dear God, thank you that your beauty standards never change. You'll always find me beautiful. Work in me true inner beauty. Amen.

JUNE

Be my rock of refuge,

to which I can always go;

give the command to save me,

for you are my rock and my fortress....

You have been my hope, Sovereign LORD,

my confidence since my youth.

PSALM 71:3, 5 NIV

BEING BOLD

Be on your guard; stand firm in the faith; be courageous;
be strong. Do everything in love.
1 CORINTHIANS 16:13-14 NIV

If you happened to be hiking in the western United States and came across an M-shaped paw print, you might get a chance to see a mountain lion. Admittedly, your chances of meeting a mountain lion in the wild are pretty slim. But if you did, what could you do?

- Be watchful.
- Stand your ground.
- Be bold. Don't turn around and run or "play dead."
- Be strong. If one approaches to attack, fight back. This can scare them away.

Unless you happen to live in a zoo, you probably won't face a lion any day soon. But what fears do you face each day? If you think about it, there are plenty of chances to take action.

- Be watchful. Be on guard for anything in your life that displeases the Lord.
- Stand your ground. Don't back down when friends try to get you to do something dumb, or worse something wrong.
- Be bold. Stand up for the weak. Stand up for what's right.
- Be strong in the Lord.

Dear Lord, I don't always feel bold, but teach me how to be bold and brave. Amen.

HOMEMADE ICE CREAM

There is a time for everything,
and a season for every activity under the heavens.
He has made everything beautiful in its time.
ECCLESIASTES 3:1, 11 NIV

Summers are made up of swimming, vacations, camps, sleepovers, sleeping in, and of course, ice cream. Double scoops of chocolate chip heaped high in a waffle cone or vanilla drizzled with chocolate and crushed Oreos. Yum!

All the deliciousness of ice cream comes when milk, cream, sugar and a bunch of other goodies are poured into an ice cream machine where it's churned and turned until it's frozen and creamy. Twenty minutes later, you can plunge your spoon into thick, icy creaminess. Take the mixture out any sooner, though, and all you'll have is a soupy mess. If you want ice cream, you've got to wait.

Some of the best things in life are worth waiting for. Like waiting for God to give you the close friend you've been praying for. Or waiting to start dating until your mom or dad thinks it's okay.

Waiting helps you appreciate it more when it does come. So instead of complaining, wait for God's timing. It's the best!

Dear God, your plans are perfect. Your timing is best. Help me to wait. Amen.

DEEP JOY

In Your presence is fullness of joy;
In Your right hand there are pleasures forever.
PSALM 16:11 NASB

"What's the matter, Alessandra? You don't seem like yourself," Dad asked.

Alessandra *was* feeling down. She wasn't sure why. She just felt restless, almost like something was missing.

When something like joy is missing, it isn't like looking for a missing sock. You won't find it under the sofa cushion, behind the dresser, or stuck to your sheets. Joy comes from Someone—Jesus. Being with Jesus fills you with joy.

That's not to say, of course, that two scoops of ice cream on a summer day don't make you happy, or that water skiing with friends or screaming down the side of a roller coaster won't make you smile.

But joy—deep down satisfaction—only comes from being with Jesus. It doesn't come from doing or having things, even though they might be fun. And it doesn't go away if something not-so-fun happens. The more time you read his Word and spend time with him, the more he'll fill you with joy!

Dear Jesus, you give me joy! You satisfy like nothing else can. Thank you. Amen.

SUNSHINE IN THE MIDDLE OF RAIN

I trust him with all my heart.
He helps me, and my heart is filled with joy.
PSALM 28:7 NLT

It was Cassie's first time flying. She walked down the aisle of the plane and looked around until she found her seat in 16A, next to her dad, and right next to a window. She buckled her seatbelt and looked out the small window as buckets of rain poured down. Not a very sunshiny day. She hoped it would be sunshiny where she was going on vacation—to the beach.

The plane engine rumbled and soon they moved down the runway until up they soared through the rain and into the clouds. After ten minutes, Cassie was enjoying a cold Coke. She looked out the window and was surprised—above the clouds the sun shone bright and clear!

The sun is never missing; it's just tucked behind the cloud. Sometimes it seems like God is missing or he's so far away—when a pet dies, when we get left out, when our parents argue. But tucked behind everything, his presence is strong. Because he's there you can have joy knowing he's got this. No matter what happens—whether things turn out like you want them to or not—God is still good. God still loves you. That will *never* change.

Dear God, I trust you—when things are going well, when things are going not-so-well, when I'm confused, and when I don't understand. You are always there, and you are always good. Amen.

WASHING MACHINE

Rest in God alone, my soul, for my hope comes from Him.
PSALM 62:5 HCSB

Back and forth, around and around, right side up and upside down.

That's what happens to the clothes you throw in the washing machine.

That's also what can happen to you, at least that's how life can feel. Too many commitments, too many decisions, too many to-do's, too many questions, and you just want to close your eyes and yell, "Stop!"

When that happens, here are a few things that will help you keep sane:

- Go for a walk. Sometimes looking at a great big sky makes problems seem smaller and gives you focus.
- Listen to some worship music. Music can powerfully impact your spirit, so listen to music that reflects how you want to feel not how you do feel.
- Go for a run. Exercise increases endorphins that trigger positive feelings and give you more energy.
- Turn your attention to someone else who might be having an upside-down day. Reaching out to others helps turn your focus away from your problems to someone else's.
- Go out for a latte and girl time with your mom or best friend.

Finally and most importantly, rest. Not the kind of rest that involves lying on the couch watching TV and eating a bag of potato chips. Rest in God. Go to him and pray about whatever is on your mind. Ask him to pull things together, give you wisdom, and do what's best.

Then, trust him!

Dear God, thanks for being my safe place, a place where I can rest. I can go to you when my life seems upside down. Amen.

THE HAND OFF

Commit to the LORD whatever you do,
and he will establish your plans.
PROVERBS 16:3 NIV

In the 2016 Summer Olympics, the United States' women's 4x100-meter relay track team dominated the sport and won the gold medal! In a relay race, four runners each take turns running as fast as they can. The first person carries the baton and sprints to the next runner on the team. Then she hands the baton off and the next runner takes it from there. Once she hands off the baton, it's not hers to worry about anymore.

Prayer works like that. Prayer is bringing our request to God and then handing it off. He takes it from there, so we don't need to worry about it. We commit things to the Lord. (That just means take things to him and trust him.)

That's our part. His part is "to establish our plans" or answer our prayers. The problem comes when we try to do both our part and his. Winning the race that way is impossible!

Why can it seem so hard to hand off our prayer requests to God?

Dear God, I realize that when I pray I don't always leave things in your hands. I take them back, like you can't be trusted. I'm sorry. Grow my faith. Amen.

GROWING!

We ought always to thank God for you, brothers and sisters,
and rightly so, because your faith is growing more and more,
and the love all of you have for one another is increasing.
2 THESSALONIANS 1:3 NIV

Spread out on the bed are magazines and books about horses. Posters of spotted Appaloosa horses, American Paints, and quarter horses cover the walls. Everywhere is horse heaven. This is the room of someone who loves horses.

If you're into horses (or dogs, ballet, soccer, or anything really) you'll read, collect, research, and enjoy. The more you do, the more you'll learn because you can't help it. It's fun!

Faith in God is like that. The more you read God's Word and really dig in, the more time you spend with him, the more you thank him for what he's done, the more your faith with grow. And, the more you'll realize how great his love is for you.

What are some ways to do that? Sing a worship song while you're in the shower. Learn a verse from the Bible and tape it to the bathroom mirror. Read it out loud every time you see it. Whisper a just-between-you-and-me prayer when you wake up in the morning. Before closing your eyes at night tell God you love him, and then just be still and listen.

Dear God, I want my faith to grow, not to be small and weak but strong and deep. Keep showing me creative ways to grow in you. Amen.

FAVORITE PERFUME

The LORD is far from the wicked,
but he hears the prayers of the righteous.
PROVERBS 15:29 NLT

When Angie and Alejandra went to the mall, their first stop was always the perfume counter.

"Here, smell this one," Angie said spraying her wrist. "Isn't it divine?"

"Too flowery for me," said Alejandra. "I love this one. If only it didn't cost eighty dollars."

A new fragrance can draw you in or make you wrinkle your nose and turn away, depending on what you like. God has definite likes too, not in perfumes but in prayers.

When someone who does what's right prays, God leans in to listen. When someone who is sincere prays, he hears and answers. But if someone who holds on to what's wrong prays, God steps away. If that person is insincere, God is far from them.

Sin might turn God away, but a right heart pulls him in. He loves to hear his children pray. Next time you spray on a little perfume or put on some fragrant lotion, whisper a prayer to the one who loves talking to you.

Dear Lord, it's hard for me to grasp that the creator of the whole world, you, loves it when I pray! I don't want to give up that privilege just because sin is in my heart. If I'm holding on to something wrong, please show me what it is. Thank you for listening when I pray! Amen.

HELLO, SUMMER!

You set the boundaries of the earth,
and you made both summer and winter.
PSALM 74:17 NLT

When you rolled out of bed this morning, slipped on your clothes, and walked into the kitchen for breakfast, did you notice that… it's summer?! Summer sun and summer sunflowers. Beach time and sandcastles. Bonfires and picnics. Warm weather and juicy watermelon. God outdid himself when he created summer.

Here are some ideas to start off your summer:

- Have a summer-kickoff party in your neighborhood.
- Go gaga for games and invite friends to bring over a favorite game and favorite snack. Have a game marathon day and a different snack between each game.
- With your friends, make crafts as gifts and take them to people at a local nursing home.
- Create be-my-friend bracelets. Make two bracelets, one for you and another for one of the kids at your church. Tell them you'll pray for them every week.

Dear God, I love summer! Thank you for a break from school and time with friends and my family. Thanks for sunny skies and long days filled with all things summer. Amen.

PARTY TIME!

*"Suppose a woman has ten silver coins and loses one...
when she finds it, she will call in her friends and neighbors
and say, 'Rejoice with me because I have found my lost coin.'
In the same way, there is joy in the presence of God's angels
when even one sinner repents."*

LUKE 15:8-10 NLT

If you could throw a party for your closest friends, what
kind of party would you have?
- ☐ arts and craft party
- ☐ pool party
- ☐ book exchange party
- ☐ make-your-own-pizza party

What kind of party you choose tells a lot about what you
like. What others choose can tell a lot about what they enjoy
too. A young boy probably wouldn't choose a spa-day party
and a twelve-year-old girl wouldn't choose to play in a sandbox.

God has a party preference too. He loves welcome-to-my-
family parties. Every time someone turns away from their sin
and asks God for new life, God and the angels celebrate. So
share the good news of Jesus. It just might result in giving
God a great reason to celebrate!

**Dear God, thank you for inviting me to be a part of your family.
Put on my heart the privilege of sharing that invitation with others
too. Then we can celebrate! Amen.**

LITERARY DEVICES

The Lord is my shepherd;
I have everything I need.
PSALM 23:1 NCV

"My brother was boiling mad," said Sondra.

"Well, talking to my sister was a breeze," said Cammie.

"I lucked out talking to my mom," piped in Zach. "She's a total rock!"

When you read the conversation above you know (of course!) that Sondra's brother hasn't reached a temperature of 212°F. Cammie's sister is a person, not a gust of wind, and Zach's mom is definitely not a large stone. The power of metaphor, though, helps make a point.

The shepherd and sheep combination is one of the Bible's favorite metaphors. Comparing Jesus to a shepherd tells us a little bit about what he's like and what he does.

- What does a shepherd do and how? (read verses Psalm 23:1-4 for some help)
- Why do sheep need a shepherd? What would happen if they didn't have one?
- So, how is Jesus like a shepherd?

The Lord is your shepherd. There's nothing you need that he won't provide. There's no place you need to go where he won't lead. He gives you strength; he gives you rest. He protects you; he disciplines you. Watching over you is his specialty.

Dear Lord, you are my shepherd. That means I have absolutely everything that I need. Amen.

NO SECRETS

*O Lord, you have examined my heart
and know everything about me.*
PSALM 139:1 NLT

Sometimes reading the Bible seems more about someone else than it does about us. Abraham and Sarah. Sampson and Delilah. *Their* stories are in the Bible and God's whole story *is* the Bible. But where do we fit in? What about what we're going through?

That's one reason Christians turn to the psalms. Psalms remind us that God is a personal God. Musicians have put the psalms to music, but the psalms are also great to use as prayers when we're not really sure what to pray.

Try this way of praying and personalizing Psalm 139:

Lord, you know everything about me. You know when I go to _____ (place) and when I do _____ (action verb).
You understand when I'm thinking about _____ (circumstance or person) even when I lay down.
Before I'm tempted to talk about _____ (person, topic), you know what I'm going to say.
When I think about your knowledge, it totally _____ (verb) me.

With you, Lord, there are no secrets!

Dear Lord, you know me better than I know myself. There's nothing you don't see and nothing you don't know. I'm amazed and humbled all at once. Amen.

MESSY ROOM

*Trust God all the time. Tell him all your problems,
because God is our protection.*
PSALM 62:8 NCV

"Shiloh, clear your homework off the counter."
"Hurry, pick up all those toys from off the floor."

When company comes over there's usually a scurry of cleaning the bathrooms, vacuuming the floor, washing dishes, and picking up. But there's usually one room, or maybe two, that doesn't get picked up or cleaned. Instead someone just closes the door.

That's the room that no one else is supposed to see. A bedroom piled high with dirty clothes, an unmade bed, and books, shoes, and stuffed animals spilling out of the closet.

Now imagine your life is like a house. When Jesus comes into your heart, he walks into the house of your life. There's nothing he doesn't see. There's no door you can close; he sees it all. He knows everything about you—what you're thinking, what you struggle with, the temptations you have, and any hurt that you try to tuck away out of sight.

Be honest with God. Just pour everything out and know that he'll listen. Tell an adult you can trust completely. Don't keep everything locked up inside.

Dear God, some things are hard to share. But I'm struggling and I need your help. Please help me. Show me what to do. Amen.

WHEN IT'S NOT OK FOR YOU

"For I hold you by your right hand— I, the Lord your God. And I say to you, 'Don't be afraid. I am here to help you.'"
ISAIAH 41:13 NLT

There are some things you can put up with. Like being teased by your dad, or having someone laugh when you trip on the stairs, or finding out your shirt is inside out and you've been wearing it all day long. Okay, it's not fun. But you can put up with it.

There are other things that you shouldn't put up with. Like being bullied on Twitter, or hearing that hurtful rumors are being spread about you, or being nicknamed a "beach whale" by neighborhood girls. Some things are just not okay.

It's important to stand up for those who are hurting and needy, and that includes you. Don't let anyone bully you. Stand up for yourself. Speak out—not in anger. That will only make things worse. If you need help, ask an adult you trust. You won't be sorry you did.

Pray and tell God how you're feeling. Then pray for the person or group of people who are being unkind to you. More likely than not, they're hurting too. Ask God for wisdom about what to do.

Dear God, sometimes it's hard to stand up for myself. I try but then I get afraid and back down. Give me strength, Lord, and give me people who can help me be strong. Amen.

WHEN IT'S NOT OK FOR OTHERS

Speak up for those who cannot speak for themselves; defend the rights of all those who have nothing. Speak up and judge fairly, and defend the rights of the poor and needy.

PROVERBS 31:8-9 NCV

There are some things you can put up with. Like wearing your red jersey because your blue one is dirty, or watching Clifford with your little sister instead of the show you want to watch, or not having red licorice for snack every day (although you probably don't have a choice on that!).

There are other things you shouldn't put up with. Like watching a girl cry because another girl made fun of her in the locker room, or seeing a boy your age shiver because his parents can't afford to buy him a coat, or letting someone sit alone in the lunchroom.

Some things are just not okay. You can be the one to stand up for those who are poor and needy.

What can you do? Pray for that person. Ask God what he wants you to do. Speak up in a sensitive way, by writing a letter or talking to an adult or raising money. Always pray and listen to what God says.

Dear God, I want to see those around me who need help. Show me what you want me to do and give me the strength to do it. Amen.

ALL OR NOTHING

You know the message God sent to the people of Israel, announcing the good news of peace through Jesus Christ, who is Lord of all.
ACTS 10:36 NIV

Just imagine… Inside the freezer is a peanut butter cookie dough ice cream cake topped with drizzles of caramel and chocolate. Yum! Your very best friend is having a surprise party and part of your surprise is giving her her favorite—an ice cream cake.

You wouldn't cut out a piece of the cake and eat it on the way there. Putting candles on a half-eaten cake would be totally awkward. You give it all or you give nothing.

That's what some people try to do when they give their lives to God. They keep part of their lives for themselves and then give the rest to God. Truth is, when you give your life to Jesus, he becomes *Lord of all*. He's the Lord of:

how you do your homework,

how you treat your mom,

that bad habit you don't want to give up, and

the money you earn.

Every part of your life.

Is there any part of your life where it's hard to let go?

Dear God, I want you to be Lord of all of my life, not just some of my life. If there's anything I'm holding back, please point it out to me. Amen.

WALKING THE DOGS

We take captive every thought to make it obedient to Christ.
2 CORINTHIANS 10:5 NIV

Every summer Nora took a job walking the four dogs in her neighborhood. At noon she went around to each house and soon four leashes attached to four dogs—Pulo, Joby, Chocolate, and Mocha—were wrapped around her wrist. The dogs would tug and race ahead and the leashes would get twisted up. Sometimes she felt like the dogs were walking her instead of the other way around.

"Mocha, stop that!" Nora would say, pulling him in. Or "Come on, Chocolate, be a good boy," and the dog would settle down.

Sometimes our thoughts need pulling in and settling down. Like a bunch of dogs on the loose they scurry and scatter in every direction. Creative thoughts. Funny thoughts. All those are fine. But when thoughts start drifting into not-so-good thoughts—*She's such a loser! Just you wait! I'll get you back*—then it's time to pull on the leash and bring them in. We keep all our thoughts under control and make them obedient to Jesus.

Instead of proud thoughts, get-revenge thoughts, sassy thoughts, and what's-the-matter-with-me thoughts, fill your mind with praise thoughts, thank-you thoughts, God-loves-me thoughts, and how-can-I-help them thoughts.

Dear God, I want you to be Lord of everything that swirls around in my head. Give me the strength and teach me the discipline to make all my thoughts obedient to you. Amen.

THE GREATEST THING!

"'Love the Lord your God with all your heart,
all your soul, and all your mind.'
This is the first and most important command."
MATTHEW 22:37-38 NCV

Who's the greatest chef in your family?
What's the greatest candy bar ever made?
Who's the greatest basketball player of all time?

The answers to those questions might depend on someone's opinion. The greatest commandment though is a for sure thing. God's *greatest* commandment (and forget about boring or complicated, it really is great!) is just to love God. That's it. If you wrapped up all the instructions in the Bible and put them all into one simple answer it would be loving God.

If you focus on loving God, you won't take what's not yours, tell a lie, or be envious of your friend's new designer jeans. If you focus on loving God, you will honor your parents, be kind, put God first, and find out what makes him happy.

Loving God takes care of everything else. As for loving him with all your heart, soul, and mind, that means loving him with everything you've got. Not kinda, sorta, I'll-think-about-it love but, "Wow! I love God so much I can hardly stand it." That kind of love!

Dear God, everything in me from the tips of my toes to the top of my head wants to love you. Amen.

BLOW POPS

Don't wear yourself out trying to get rich.
Wealth can vanish in the wink of an eye.
PROVERBS 23:4-5 NCV

What's the difference between a Blow Pop and a Dum Dum? If you lick a Dum Dum down to the stick, that's all you'll have left—a stick. But wrapped inside the candy shell of a Blow Pop is a bubblegum center that makes the lollipop treat last a little longer.

Money is like a Dum Dum. It really doesn't last and it can disappear—*poof!*—in an afternoon of shopping. What we buy with it doesn't last either. A new haircut, a pair of shoes, a new DVD, even a new bike. They're fun while they last but the problem is they don't. They grow out, wear out, or break down.

Jesus said instead of storing up wealth on earth, where moth and rust can destroy or thieves can break in a steal, store up treasure in heaven where it will last (Matthew 6:19).

Don't knock yourself out focusing on getting money. Put your energy and time into friendships, family, memories, and best of all a forever-life with God. Those are the things that last!

Dear God, help me focus on the things that last, especially the life I'll have with you some day. Amen.

EYEBALLS

The L{ord} took care of them and kept them safe.
He guarded them as he would guard his own eyes.

D{EUTERONOMY} 32:10 {NIRV}

If you've ever gotten a speck of dust in your eyes, you know it's more than just a minor inconvenience. You do everything you can to get it out. Until then, everything else gets sidelined.

We carefully protect our eyes. We squint in the bright sun. We buy sunglasses. Every night we rest our eyes. We're quick to close our eyes if dust is in the air. Quick to flush our eyes if a stray eyelash gets in.

After all, we've only got one set of eyes.

God watches over and guards us just like we protect our eyes. He's quick to respond and is never behind the ball on what's happening in our lives. He's got things covered, literally and figuratively; he guards us and drives away any danger. He knows we need rest; overworking just wears us out. He's definitely got our back (or maybe we should say our eyes).

What do you do to protect your eyes? How does that help you consider how God protects you?

Dear God, you watch over me as if I were the apple of your eye. I don't thank you enough, so… thank you! Amen.

SHOWDOWN

Summon your power, God;
show us your strength, our God,
as you have done before.
PSALM 68:28 NIV

It hadn't rained in over three years. The ground was hard and dusty. The rivers and lakes and wells were almost dry. People were running out of food.

But things were about to change.

During a showdown on top of Mt. Carmel, four hundred and fifty prophets prayed to their god Baal. From morning until afternoon they begged their god to answer. But nothing happened. No one answered.

Then Elijah stepped up to the top of the mountain. He prayed a single prayer. Fire swooped down from heaven and God answered. Shortly after, it began to rain. God had answered!

The same God that Elijah served and prayed to is the same God you pray to today. He is mighty to save! God can do anything! He is *powerful* to save.

Dear God, show me your power. Show me your strength.
Answer me and show me you are mighty to save. Amen.

DOUBLE BLESSING

Because we loved you so much,
we were delighted to share with you
not only the gospel of God but our lives as well.
1 THESSALONIANS 2:8 NIV

Pondtip (yep, that's her real name) grew up in a small town in Asia. Every morning Pondtip got up early to help her mom cook and then walked a mile and a half to the village school. The school in her village only went through sixth grade. To get more education, children needed to move to a big city. Since most parents didn't have money to do this, kids stop their education.

When Pondtip was in sixth grade, she learned that a family in a big city had a home where kids could go and live and get more education. The family invited Pondtip to the home, and her parents said yes.

Every morning at the home, the kids read the Bible and learned to worship God. It was there that Pondtip first heard about God. One day she realized God was real and he loved her very much. She decided, "I want to follow Jesus."

Because of that family, Pondtip not only got a great education but she came to know Jesus. She was blessed—twice!

You might not be able to travel all across the world to a place like Asia. But by sharing the good news of the gospel right where you are, you can give people the blessing of knowing God's love.

Dear God, please send people to share your love in different places around the world. Help me to be faithful sharing your good news right where I am. Amen.

PURPOSE

"This happened so the power of God could be seen in him."
JOHN 9:3 NLT

From the day he was born, the beggar couldn't see. He couldn't see the trees or the birds. He couldn't see his mom or dad. He couldn't see the clothes he put on or the food he was eating. Was he having rice or bread for dinner? He never knew unless he asked or put it in his mouth.

How he wished he could see! And he wished there was some kind of purpose for his life.

One day a man named Jesus came by and rocked his world! After that, he told everyone who would listen, "I used to be blind, but Jesus healed me. Now I can see!" He went from a man who had no purpose to someone filled with purpose—to give God glory.

That's the same purpose God gives you. Right now it may seem like the reason you exist is to go to school, do homework, do your chores, and take care of your little sister. Your real purpose, though, is to do whatever you do in a way that honors God. That gives God glory.

Ask God to show his power through you.

Dear God, show your power in my life. I pray that everything I do would give glory to you. Amen.

THE TOP THREE

What does the LORD require of you?
To act justly and to love mercy
and to walk humbly with your God.
MICAH 6:8 NIV

What are the top three girl names?
What are the top three music apps?
What are the top three selling snack crackers?

We all have our top three lists. Our top three favorite places to go on vacation. Our top three after-school snacks. Our top three excuses for avoiding homework. You get the picture.

God has a top three too. Here are the top three things he's looking for in our lives.

- Act justly: Always do what's right and fair and just. Don't try to manipulate people and get your own way. Don't treat some people more importantly than others.
- Love mercy: Give people a break when they've messed up. Treat them with kindness even when they don't deserve it.
- Walk humbly: Instead of acting like you know it all and are better than everyone else, think of yourself— and others—like God does. He loves everyone just as much as the other.

Which of God's top three comes easiest for you? What's harder to do?

Dear God, teach me to act with justice, to show people mercy, and to be humble. Amen.

A DOG NAMED ROSCOE

*As high as the heavens are above the earth,
so great is his love for those who fear him.*
PSALM 103:11 NIV

Once upon a time there was a girl named Lindsay who struggled to understand how God could love her. One day she prayed, "God, send me something that makes your love easier to understand."

Now Lindsay had a dog named Roscoe. When Lindsay went into the laundry, Roscoe went into the laundry. When Lindsay took out the trash, Roscoe went along with her. He never left her side.

Lindsay sometimes took Roscoe for granted. When school got crazy busy, Lindsay would go hours, even days, without paying Roscoe much attention. But that never seemed to lessen how much Roscoe liked her. He was still just as happy to see her.

One day Lindsay realized Roscoe was the answer to her prayer. Through Roscoe she realized that God is always with her. Though she often set God aside, he was always waiting, looking forward to connect. Even when she messed up, his love for her never changed.

God isn't like a dog of course. But the picture of Roscoe makes it easier to understand God's unconditional love. His faithful love never changes; it doesn't go up or down depending on the day. His love is forever strong.

Dear God, your love is unconditional. I pray that every day I'd understand a little bit more of your love. Amen.

BEACH SAND

God, your thoughts are precious to me.
They are so many! If I could count them,
they would be more than all the grains of sand.
PSALM 139:17-18 NCV

A day at the beach means a day of sun, water, and lots of sand. Sand sprinkled on your beach towel, sand squishing underneath your toes, sand clinging to your swimsuit, and sand sticking to your fingers when you're trying to eat your picnic lunch. Tiny grains of sand everywhere!

If you scooped up a handful of sand and tried to count the tiny grains, could you do it? Impossible! And it's just as impossible to count all the thoughts—the good thoughts—that God has about you. If you could count them, they would be more than all the grains of sand on the seashore.

Sometimes we have this picture of God with his arms crossed, tapping his foot, and impatiently frowning at us. We feel we've somehow disappointed him. But that smacks right into what the truth is—God loves us and his thoughts about us are precious.

How do you picture God? What do you picture him thinking and saying about you? How does it line up with this verse?

Dear God, whenever I start to question who I am and what you think of me, help me to stop, remember, and thank you that your thoughts are more than the sand on the seashore. Amen.

A SMALL JOB THAT WASN'T SO SMALL

*See how very much our Father loves us,
for he calls us his children, and that is what we are!*
1 JOHN 3:1 NLT

She was only a little girl and not particularly important. She was, after all, just a slave in the household of a very powerful master. But when she found out her master was sick, she thought, *I know God can heal him.* So she told her mistress and her mistress told her master and her master went to God's prophet and the master was healed (1 Kings 5).

Without the servant girl's small suggestion, something much bigger might have never happened.

You might think the tasks you have are pretty small or maybe even unimportant. But just because you're young and just because you might be small, doesn't mean God hesitates from using you. God loves you. He calls you his daughter, and he wants you to know he's working through you.

Dear God, I know I'm young but I'd sure like it if you used me to do something big. Remind me that no job you give me is too small. Amen.

BOYS

*"Just as you can identify a tree by its fruit,
so you can identify people by their actions."*
MATTHEW 7:20 NLT

Annoying. Cute. Friendly. Uninterested. Rude. Polite.

Boys are all that and a whole lot more. You like 'em and you can't stand 'em. How can they be so nice one minute and totally rude the next? Jesus said you'll know people by what they do and how they act. But sometimes figuring that out with boys seems impossible.

Growing from a boy to a man means being pulled in opposite directions. Boys try to fit in. Acting tough, cool, or funny puts them in that "in" category. But they kind of like girls too, and girls like warm and friendly. Somehow boys have to juggle friendly while keeping up a cool appearance. It's hard for them to know what to do.

So what do you do? Be understanding and pray for them. They're trying to figure life out just like you, and life can be tough. And how do you figure out what a guy is really like? Watch how he acts around his family. How does he treat his mom? How does he talk to his sister? Those are some clues into what's really inside.

Dear God, help me to be patient and understanding with the boys in my life. Help them to grow into the men you've created them to be. Amen.

GREAT WALL OF CHINA

A person without self-control is like a city
with broken-down walls.
PROVERBS 25:28 NLT

The Great Wall of China is a wall of stone, earth, and bricks. It was built as a fortress to protect the country of China. In some places today the wall is over thirty feet high and over 5,000 miles, although it used to be much longer. Years ago if enemies wanted to attack China, they looked for a gap in the wall. They searched for weak points and made that their entry point.

When we don't have self-control, we're like a country or city that has broken-down walls. Self-control protects us by keeping us from impatience, anger, and doing things we regret. Without it, we open ourselves up to trouble and a lot of heartache. If someone loses their temper and yells at a friend, for instance, those words can never be taken back.

When you have self-control, you don't let what other people do or say about you control you. You control yourself. You don't need your mom to tell you not to have six pieces of pizza, because you control yourself—you know you'd get a stomachache. You don't need the teacher to tell you not to argue with your classmates, because you control yourself.

Protect your heart and do yourself a favor—practice self-control!

Dear God, thank you for your Spirit who produces self-control in me. Help me to listen to your Spirit and say yes to self-control and no to anything else. Amen.

THE GOOD KIND OF FEAR

The fear of the LORD is the beginning of knowledge,
but fools despise wisdom and instruction.

PROVERBS 1:7 NIV

Morgan wasn't afraid to do anything—dirt biking, water skiing, surfing, skate boarding. She did it all. She wasn't afraid of spiders or snakes or mice (although she wasn't particularly fond of cockroaches.) She wasn't afraid of public speaking or being the center of attention. But there was one thing she feared—getting in trouble with her dad.

No, he wasn't mean. He didn't hit her or yell at her. He wasn't overly strict (if he was she wouldn't be surfing, skate boarding, and doing all the other things she loved). But he was firm. When he said something, he meant it. She didn't dare disobey because if she did she'd be grounded.

That kind of fear—the kind of fear that kept Morgan from doing wrong—is a good kind of fear. It's the fear that keeps you from cheating on a test or sneaking out at night. That built-in fear was put inside you by God to keep you listening to those who take care of you. That kind of fear protects. When you hear that voice of fear, listen up.

Dear God, I pray that my bad fears—being afraid of what people think and of things like the dark—would go away. But I pray that the good fear—the respect I should have for my parents and for you—would never go away. Amen.

JULY

Here is what we can be sure of when we come to God in prayer. If we ask anything in keeping with what he wants, he hears us. If we know that God hears what we ask for, we know that we have it.

1 JOHN 5:14–15 NIRV

WHAT TO DO WITH FEAR

"The LORD is with us. So don't be afraid of them."
NUMBERS 14:9 NCV

"I'm totally going to fall apart during dance tryouts," Natalie said. "My stomach is doing flip flops just thinking about it."

"You'll do great," her mom said, giving her a squeeze. "You might feel afraid but you always stick it out and do your best. That's one thing I admire about you."

"I just hope the coach thinks it's my best."

Everyone feels fear. That's normal. What you do with that fear is what matters. When you're faced with fear, you can take control and say, "Yeah, well I might be nervous but I'm going for it anyway." Or, you can let fear take control, telling you what you will or won't do. "There's no way I'm performing in the choir in front of all those people." Or, "I can't try out for the team; I'm too afraid of what'll happen."

Ultimately, God is in control and he promises to be with you. You don't have to face fears alone. When you feel afraid and remember God is with you, you're saying, "I believe you're big enough to protect me. I believe you will be with me."

When you're faced with something big, supposedly impossible, scary, or dangerous, what's your reaction? Can you believe that God is bigger than whatever that fear is and go for it anyway?

Dear God, I believe you're powerful enough and loving enough to take care of me. Please fill my heart with faith. Amen.

UNOPENED GIFT

Sing joyfully to the Lord. Sing to him a new song;
play skillfully, and shout for joy.

PSALM 33:1, 3 NIV

It was Christmas in July—for the kids at the orphanage in Guatemala, that is. Aria and the other mission team members watched as a little boy tore open his gift. He couldn't get the wrapping paper off fast enough. His eyes widened as he saw what was inside—a box of Legos, a plastic dinosaur, Play-Doh, and two new pairs of socks.

Each chapter in the Bible is like an unopened gift. God packs each one with tiny treasures and huge insights and waits to see if we'll discover what's inside. Maybe we'll discover a little more about him, a little more about ourselves, how to solve a problem, or make a friendship.

Check out the clues in this verse that tell us who God is:

Sing a NEW song: God is into creativity and originality. There's nothing wrong with doing what we've always done, but he likes new too.

What can you do or create that's unique?

Play SKILLFULLY: God is into things that are done really well. He admires things done with skill and the practice that it takes to do it that way.

What do you do really well? What are you working at so you can do it well?

SHOUT for joy: There's nothing timid about shouting. You shout when you're confident and bold.

Why do you think doing something with your whole heart makes God's heart sing?

Dear Heavenly Father, you're the creator of everything and you do everything well. Remind me to be bold and do things well, and teach me to be creative like you are. Amen.

BUT, WHY?

Do everything without complaining or arguing.
PHILIPPIANS 2:14 NCV

"But everyone has that brand of boots. Why can't I have them?"

"Church is the same every week, why do I have to go?"

"I hate creamy peanut butter. Why can't we ever buy chunky?"

Sound familiar? For forty years God heard similar things from the people of Israel. "Why did you have to bring us into the desert? We're so thirsty!" they complained. "Why can't we have bread?" they grumbled. "What's up with having no meat at all?" they muttered. Over and over God provided for all their needs but that didn't stop them from complaining.

We know we're not supposed to complain, but why not? What's the big deal? Psalm 78 says that complaining is basically telling someone, your parents for instance, "I don't trust you to take care of me. What you do for me isn't good enough" (verses 22-32). When you're thankful, you're saying, "Thanks for how you take care of me. I appreciate what you do."

That doesn't mean you can't ask for something. Just that when you ask, you don't dismiss the good your mom or dad has already done.

Dear God, help me appreciate all I have and the good my parent(s) do. Amen.

FOURTH OF JULY

When I look at the night sky and see the work of your fingers—the moon and the stars you set in place—what are mere mortals that you should think about them, human beings that you should care for them?

PSALM 8:3-4 NLT

What could be better than the Fourth of July? Lake time, pool time, picnics and barbecues, time with family and friends. But the best part of the day comes late at night when the sky lights up with a flash of fireworks. Stare up at the sky on the Fourth of July and see, hear, and feel an explosion of pink, red, blue, and white fireworks. People *ooh* and *ahh* and clap and cheer because it's all so beautiful.

Even the famous fireworks display in Washington D.C. can't compete with what we see every day. Brilliant sun, shimmering stars, and the soft glow of the moon are just a few of the amazing things that God made. He blankets the earth with blue seas and fills them with strange, weird, and wonderful creatures. The whole earth and heaven shout his power and beauty.

And still he pays attention to you. The world is so big and we are so small, but God still knows your name. He counts every hair on your head. He knows when you sit and when you stand. Best of all, he invites you to be part of his family.

What amazes you most about God's creation?

Dear God, you're the maker of heaven and earth, creator of the sun, moon, and stars, and still you think about me. You care about me. Who am I? I'm so thankful to be your child. Amen.

WHEN TOUGH THINGS HAPPEN

We know and rely on the love God has for us. God is love.
1 JOHN 4:16 NIV

Hayley went into her room and closed the door. She sat down on the bed. The worst thing she could think of had happened. The doctor said her mom had cancer. *Cancer.* She couldn't even say the word out loud. Why did her mom have to suffer? *Why?*

Some things are hard to understand—sickness, divorce, bankruptcy, or a parent's new job that means a move across the country. No matter how you look at it, it just doesn't make sense. You can't wrap your brain around it, and the more you try, the more frustrated you get. So what do you do?

It's not such much about what you can do as it is about what you can know—God is love. What's happening doesn't mean God doesn't love you or doesn't love the person who it's happening to. His love is something you can count on. It's the one fact in the middle of a confusing situation that you can rely on.

Dear God, when tough things happen remind me that your love hasn't changed. You still love me. You still care. And even though I can't figure it all out; you can. Amen.

I'M LISTENING

Be like-minded, be sympathetic,
love one another, be compassionate.

1 PETER 3:8 NIV

Joel walked in the door and dropped his backpack on the floor. *Thud.* Erica looked up from her algebra book. Her eyes tracked him as he stomped to the fridge and pulled it open.

"Why don't we ever have any chocolate milk?" Joel said and slammed the door shut.

Someone is having a bad day, Erica thought. At that point, she had a few options:

Option #1: Push Joel's buttons. He had no business making everyone else in the family feel as miserable as he did.

Option #2: Ignore him. Maybe if she kept her distance long enough, he'd get over whatever was bothering him.

Option #3: Find out what was going on.

One of the best ways to show compassion is just to listen. When you listen to someone, you can make them feel better. When you *really* listen to someone you:

- Look at them.
- Seem interested.
- Ask questions about what they said.
- Give them all of your attention, not just some of it.
- Try to understand their world.

Listening is more than just hearing. Listening is trying to understand someone's point of view and connecting with how they feel.

Dear God, thanks for the chance to step into someone's world and understand where they're coming from. Help me to listen with my heart. Amen.

199

TALL, DARK, AND HANDSOME

"I regret that I made Saul king, for he has turned away from following Me and has not carried out My instructions."
1 SAMUEL 15:11 NLT

He was tall. He was handsome. And he was rich. Saul seemed like the perfect pick for a king—and he was. Until he decided he didn't need to play by the rules and turned away from God.

So God sent the prophet Samuel to choose a different king. Samuel took a look at the first candidate and thought, "Well, he definitely has the look of a king."

God didn't agree. He said…

"Don't judge by his appearance or height, for I have rejected him. The LORD doesn't see things the way you see them. People judge by outward appearance, but the LORD looks at the heart" (1 Samuel 16:7).

There's nothing wrong with being good-looking. In fact, the king God did choose, David, was a handsome man. What David had that Saul didn't was a tender heart—a heart that loved and obeyed God.

Your outward appearance—your clothes, hair, makeup, and even how good you are at playing piano—isn't what God looks at. He sees your heart. Do you listen to what he says? Do you love him with all you've got? To God, that's what matters.

Dear God, help me see people the way you see them. Help me focus on the inside instead of the outside. Amen.

CANDYLAND

It was by faith that Noah built a large boat to save his family from the flood. He obeyed God, who warned him about things that had never happened before.
HEBREWS 11:7 NLT

Once upon a time in place called Candyland, the skies opened up and marshmallows floated down from the sky. Pink marshmallows. Blue marshmallows. Big marshmallows. Small marshmallows. Marshmallows covered the grass and reached the rooftops.

Right.

As much as you'd like to visit a real place called Candyland, you know it's just make-believe. If someone said Candyland existed, you'd never believe them.

When God said, "Noah, water will flood the earth," he might as well have told Noah he was going to Candyland. He warned Noah about something that had never happened before.

Noah could have brushed God aside and ignored what he said. But he believed God and built the biggest boat in history. God was so pleased, he saved Noah and his whole family.

You won't always understand what God says. But when you act in faith, God will be so pleased. Without faith, the Bible says, it's impossible to please God (Hebrews 11:6). If you want to please God, believe him. He can be trusted even when you don't understand.

Dear God, I like to understand things. I like to know what is going to happen and why. Help me believe even though I may not have everything figured out. Amen.

BEAUTY AND SENSE

*A beautiful woman who lacks discretion
is like a gold ring in a pig's snout.*
PROVERBS 11:2 NLT

Pigs are, as you well know, not known for their fine manners and polite eating habits. They aren't the kind of animal you'd take to the ice cream shop or have sit next to you at a restaurant table. A dog, maybe. A cat, maybe. But a pig? Definitely not. Pigs root around in the mud and roll around in the muck.

And putting a fine gold ring in a pig's snout? Well, that would just be wrong! The two don't belong together.

Beauty and indiscretion, or lack of good sense, don't go together any better. A girl who is indiscreet takes away from her beauty. A girl who's discreet adds to her beauty. And who doesn't want to be beautiful?

What can you do to be discreet?

- Think before you act.
- Think before you speak. Don't let your words get ahead of your brain.
- Be sensitive. Use words that won't embarrass or offend others.
- Be modest, both in what you say and in how you dress.
- Be smart. Look at the whole situation and make a decision that fits it best.

Increase your natural beauty by being discreet!

Dear God, would you give me a role model who can show me what being discreet looks like? Help me to be careful with what I do and say. Amen.

DRIVEN TO DO WHAT IS GOOD

"O Lord, please hear my prayer! Listen to the prayers of those of us who delight in honoring you. Please grant me success today by making the king favorable to me. Put it into his heart to be kind to me."

NEHEMIAH 1:11 NLT

If any knew what bad news was, it was Nehemiah. While he was a slave in a faraway land, he found out his home had been destroyed. The walls of his city had been torn down. The gates had been set on fire. His family and friends were in trouble. Things were a mess.

More than anything, he wanted to go back to his city of Jerusalem. But he had no money, no way of getting there, and no permission from the king to leave. Because his strong desire was God's desire too, God miraculously made a way for Nehemiah to rebuild his city.

Sometimes God puts a desire inside us to help someone or do something so big and so strong we can't think of anything else. It's his calling to us to do his important work in the world.

Has God put something on your heart like that? Pay attention to what it is. He'll give you his power and wisdom to do it. It might not be this week, this month, or even this year, but watch to see how God will use you to make a positive difference.

Dear God, use me to do your work in the world. If my deep desire is from you, make it grow and show me the best way to do It. Amen.

THUNDER LUNGS

*Your beauty should come from within you—
the beauty of a gentle and quiet spirit that will never
be destroyed and is very precious to God.*
1 PETER 3:4 NCV

"I'm doomed!" twelve-year-old Ellie said, shaking her head as she walked across the church parking lot.

"What do you mean you're doomed?" her older sister Vienna asked.

"My small group leader says that beauty means having a gentle and quiet spirit. Right. Like that's ever going to happen. Everyone calls me Thunder Lungs, remember?"

The verse above seems like it excludes anyone who is assertive, bold, outgoing, and loud from the beauty category. We read "gentle and quiet spirit" and it brings to mind someone who's timid, shy, and overly polite. Fortunately, that's just a stereotype. So what does it really mean?

What it doesn't mean:
You can't speak up or offer your opinion.
You're supposed to speak softly and sweetly.
You're not supposed to laugh out loud or joke around and have fun.

What it does mean:
You speak words that are kind, not hurtful.
You don't get all worked up on the inside.
Whether you give your opinion or choose to be quiet, you do it with respect not scorn.

How would you describe yourself on the genuine "gentle and quiet spirit" scale?

Dear God, I've had some mixed up ideas about what it means to have a gentle, quiet spirit. I'm so relieved! Teach me to speak kind, encouraging words. Instead of getting all agitated inside about things, teach me to trust you. Amen.

LIFE THAT IS SHARED

Be happy with those who are happy,
and weep with those who weep.
Live in harmony with each other.

ROMANS 12:15 NLT

Life is so much better when it's shared. (Unless you're talking about a big piece of chocolate cake with fudgy frosting. Then sharing might not be so appealing.)

Sharing life means…
Sharing good news: "We're going hiking in Colorado for spring break! I can't wait!"
Sharing something you just found out: "My new next-door neighbor has two bunnies. They're adorable."
Sharing jokes and laughing together: "How many bananas can you eat if your stomach is empty? Only one. After that it's not empty anymore."

And it means…
Sharing bad news, like your eleven-year-old dog Yolo just died.
Throwing an arm around someone's shoulders when they're feeling down.
Listening while your bestie tells you what is on her heart.

Sharing means togetherness. Sharing makes happy happier and sad a little more bearable.

Dear God, thank you for friends I can share with and friends who share life with me. Help me to be the kind of person people have fun sharing life with. Amen.

USE YOUR HEAD

*Trust in the L*ORD *with all your heart*
And do not lean on your own understanding.
PROVERBS 3:5 NASB

Swimming around in the icy Artic Ocean is an animal that's big, bulky, and weighs over 2,000 pounds. Beside its long tusks, which can grow up to 3 ft. long, one of the most unique things about it is its head. If ice starts to form on the top of the ocean, the walrus's tiny but powerful head can hammer a hole through the ice. Talk about using your head.

Using your head isn't such a bad idea, not to pound a hole of course, but to solve a problem. Sometimes the answer you're praying for is just a matter of good sense. What is it that makes the most sense?

While using common sense or your own understanding is a great idea, depending on that isn't. Check it out with a few others—your mom, your grandpa, someone you admire. Most importantly, go to God and ask him what he thinks.

When has your good common sense been an answer to prayer? Have you ever "leaned" on it and gotten into trouble?

Dear God, thanks for giving me common sense to make decisions every day. Help me to listen to that sense and not ignore it. But I don't ever want to depend on just that. Teach me to go to you first. Amen.

THE BIG PICTURE

We know that God causes all things to work together
for good to those who love God, to those
who are called according to His purpose.
ROMANS 8:28 NASB

Village women in northern Thailand weave beautiful patterns that start small and then grow into large stretches of cloth used for scarves, bags, and clothes. Their hand looms pull in different colored threads to create designs like blue and white stripes or purple with tiny white dots.

God uses everything that happens to weave a beautiful design: the ups and the downs and the days that are somewhere in between. He's taking everything, both good and bad, to create an amazing design. That design stretches beyond what happened Tuesday to everything in your life, your school, your country, and across the world. The pattern includes what's happened in history and what will happen in the future.

You just see a little piece of the design and it doesn't always make sense. When Jesus comes back and the pattern is finished, everything will make sense.

Has something ever happened to you that didn't make sense?

Dear God, thank you that you're taking everything and working it out for good. Even when I can't figure out what the pattern is, you have the big picture in mind. I trust you. Amen.

HORSE SENSE

*"I will guide you along the best pathway for your life.
I will advise you and watch over you. Do not be like
a senseless horse or mule that needs a bit and bridle
to keep it under control."*

PSALM 32:8-9 NLT

It was a perfect summer day for a horseback ride. AJ put her foot in the stirrup, swung a leg over the saddle and flipped the reins to nudge Silver forward. "Come on, boy," she urged. "We're going for a ride."

The path ran through the forest, over a stone arch bridge, to a large shimmering lake. *This is going to be great!* AJ thought.

Silver, though, had other ideas. He clip-clopped along as slowly as he could. When AJ tugged the reins to go left, he went left but circled around right. At this rate, they wouldn't ever reach the lake!

Sometimes we have our own ideas about what we should do, about what's right and wrong. And we question God's path because we don't feel like doing what he says, it doesn't make sense, or everyone else is doing something different.

But doing that means missing out on not just what's good, but what's great. "I will guide you on the *best* pathway for your life," he says. Don't settle for second best.

Dear God, I want what's best. Not just some of the time but always. You're so faithful to lead. I'll be faithful to follow. Amen.

WHAT'S FOR LUNCH?

Jesus asked, "How many loaves of bread do you have?"
They answered, "Seven, and a few small fish."
MATTHEW 15:33-34 NCV

For three days thousands of people had camped out on the mountain and listened to this man called Jesus. They watched him heal blind eyes and broken bones and heard people who had never said a word start to talk and sing. But after the excitement died down, the hunger set in. They'd eaten through all their ham & cheese sandwiches and PB&Js. There weren't any fast food restaurants in sight.

Jesus, though, wasn't interested in what they didn't have. He was more interested in what they did have—seven loaves of bread and a couple of fish filets. He prayed, passed out the food, and four thousand plus ate until they were stuffed.

God isn't limited by what we have or what we can do. He's far bigger than that. He can take what's not enough and make miracles happen including providing the money you need for your class trip, getting the medication your dad needs for his heart, and helping you with the pathetic-sounding (to you at least) speech you're trying to write.

God can do a lot with your little. Is there something big that God might want you to believe him for?

Dear God, teach me to think big, ask big, and believe big because you're a big God. Amen.

CHECK IT OUT: Read Matthew 15:29-38 to find out how much food was leftover.

A RACEHORSE

Let's not get tired of doing what is good.
At just the right time we will reap
a harvest of blessing if we don't give up.
GALATIANS 6:9 NLT

Dan Patch didn't have a patch and he wasn't a person—he was a horse. In 1896 a little colt with a little white star on his forehead was born. He was clumsy and had knobby knees and didn't look like he'd amount to anything. But someone gave him a chance and worked and trained him. Years later Dan Patch became a superstar racehorse and earned over a million dollars.

Some people will tell you, "You can do anything you want if you set your mind to it." That's not exactly true. But you can do what God created you to do—what is right. It takes work and practice and determination. Doing what's right is hard when you don't feel like it, or when no one else is doing it, or when everyone makes fun of you. The reward, though, is out of this world! It's everlasting life!

That's the best reason for never giving up!

Dear God, I don't always feel like keeping on but help me to remember the reward you promise when we don't give up. Amen.

THE SIZE OF A GIFT

*"All these people gave their gifts out of their wealth;
but she out of her poverty put in all she had to live on."*
LUKE 21:4 NIV

"Okay, girls," said Mrs. Monroe. "After Celia opens her last gift, it'll be time for cupcakes and ice cream."

"This gift is from Amanda," said Celia reading the tag. "I can't wait!" She unwrapped the gift, opened up the box, and saw a picture of a horse inside a small plastic picture frame. Normally Celia wouldn't have thought it was much of a gift, except she knew that Amanda's family didn't have much money.

"You like horses, right?" Amanda asked.

"I do! Thanks, Amanda," Celia said giving her a hug. "This really means a lot."

Jesus and his disciples watched one day as people dropped off gifts at the temple. Big gifts, fancy gifts, expensive gifts. Then a very poor woman walked in and gave two small coins. *One. Two.* It didn't seem like much but Jesus knew how much it had cost her.

"This poor widow has put in more than all the others," he said. The others had given what they could afford; she'd given all that she had.

If someone gives you a gift, its value doesn't depend on how big it is, how much it costs, how beautiful it is, or even how much you like it. You can determine the size of the gift from the heart of the one who gave it.

Dear God, teach me to see beyond the gift to the heart of the one who gave it. Help me to be grateful in every circumstance. Amen.

GOOD ENOUGH

*No one can ever be made right with God by doing
what the law commands. We are made right with God
by placing our faith in Jesus Christ.*
ROMANS 3:20, 22 NLT

"Ruby, I thought I asked you to pick up your room."

"Well, I made the bed," said Ruby, her eyes fixed on her video game.

"That's great. But how about picking up your clothes and vacuuming and dusting?"

Sometimes "not good enough" happens because we didn't put out our best effort. But sometimes we try and try and just never feel like we measure up. We feel like we need to work hard so God will love and accept us. But we can never meet his standards. We try to be good, but we mess up. We try to catch ourselves before making a sarcastic remark, but it flies out anyway.

If you are trying to meet God's perfect standards so he'll love and accept you, you'll end up feeling frustrated, ashamed, or like giving up. The great news is you don't have to earn God's perfect love. Jesus has done everything you need to have a right relationship with God. Accepting the gift of salvation is all that he asks.

Dear God, I'm going to stop trying to win your favor and just accept that you love me. I'm going to stop trying to earn my way into heaven and just accept your gift. Thank you. Amen.

CHANGED!

You were taught to be made new in your hearts, to become a new person. That new person is made to be like God—made to be truly good and holy.

EPHESIANS 4:23-24 NCV

When someone said the name "Saul," Christians scattered in every direction. Saul was brilliant, powerful—and cruel! He mocked Christians, threatened Christians, and even arrested them.

As he was traveling to the city of Damascus one day, Paul had a vision and God completely changed his life. From that day on, Saul used the name Paul. Paul spent the rest of his life powerfully reasoning with people and sharing his faith. He was a new person!

You may know kids in your neighborhood who are mean and rude. You may run into kids at school who bully you or act like total snobs. You might be hurt by what they say or feel like completely avoiding them.

But remember that God can do for them what he did for Paul. God can completely change their lives. So pray for them, be God's light to them, share his love for them, and remember that with God no one is a lost cause!

Dear God, is there anyone I've been treating as a lost cause? Remind me to pray for them and share your good news with them. Please completely change them, Lord. Amen.

DEAR DAD

Though good advice lies deep within the heart,
a person with understanding will draw it out.
PROVERBS 20:5 NLT

Dear Dad,

Camp is great! Horseback riding and swimming are my favorites. Late-night bonfires though are the best. I ate ten roasted marshmallow (burnt black like I love them) last night, but I made up for it by eating a lot of salad at lunch today.

Every morning we have chapel. It's mostly okay except I have to get up so early. Like 7 o'clock.

The speaker said that lots of kids have questions they wish they could ask their parents. But they just don't. He challenged us to ask one question. But I have two:

- What's the worst thing you ever did when you were my age?
- What's something I could do that would make you proud?

See you next week.

Aaliyah

Have you ever wanted to ask your dad or mom something but didn't know how? You're embarrassed or not sure what they'll say or afraid how they'll react. Conversations with parents can be awkward. But there are so many things parents want to share and sometimes you just have to ask.

Dear God, thanks for my parents. Remind me to take the time to really get to know them and tap into the advice they have. Give us some great conversations! Amen.

ACROSS THE WORLD

Ever since the world was created, people have seen the earth and sky. Through everything God made, they can clearly see his invisible qualities—his eternal power and divine nature. So they have no excuse for not knowing God.

ROMANS 1:20 NLT

In India a little girl giggles as she and her friends walk home from school for a lunch of *dahl*, or lentils, and rice. In Vietnam, a teenaged girl uses a sharp scythe to harvest rice and takes a break to wipe her forehead. In the USA, a sixth grade girl swings and hits a softball just beyond shortstop and dashes for first base.

Three very different countries. Three very different girls. But wherever they are in the world, they can look up and see the same big sky and the same brilliant sun or moon.

That sun and moon show God's power. They're proof that he is God. No one can say, "But I didn't get a chance to see what you've done!" Everyone, everywhere has the privilege of seeing that God is good. It's as if God says, "Look up and see all that I've made, and you'll know that I am God."

Dear God, you are great! The other gods of the nations are just idols. They can't speak or hear or answer. But you made the heavens! Thanks for showing everyone everywhere how powerful you are. Amen.

STAR LIGHT, STAR BRIGHT

The heavens were made by the word of the Lord,
and all the stars, by the breath of His mouth.
PSALM 33:6 HCSB

Look up at the sky on a clear summer night and you might see a white strip of very faint stars. That galaxy, called the Milky Way, has over 100 billion stars. The earth's bright fiery sun is just one of them.

Imagine a God so powerful that he made those billions of stars with a simple word. He spoke—and they came to be. He said, "Let there be light" and they appeared. He breathed and life was created. Imagine a God so powerful that he counts the stars in our galaxy and beyond. He keeps track of each one and calls them by name.

It's awesome and mind-blowing! That's the kind of God you serve. There's nothing he can't do: turn a tough situation upside down, change someone's heart, change your heart, provide what you need. He's an amazing God!

Dear God, you stretch out the heavens like a curtain. You sit above the circle of the whole earth. You are an amazing God! Thank you that there's nothing you can't do. Amen.

LOTSA LOVE

Your love, Lord, reaches to the heavens,
your faithfulness to the skies.
How priceless is your unfailing love, O God!

PSALM 36:5, 7 NIV

If you had to guess how far east is from west, what would you say? How about how far north is from south? And what about how far the sky stretches up into heaven. How far is that? If you can measure any of those things, you can measure how high and deep and wide God's love is.

God's love for you is extravagant, over-the-top, overflowing, persistent, infinite, gargantuan, mighty, astronomic, and towering.

We're talking mega-love here. There's no way to measure God's love; it's that big. His love for you, your family, the family who lives down the street, your classmates, your country and families around the world is colossal, staggering, and forever.

How could it change someone's world to hear about love like that?

Dear God, your love is amazing! It's more than I can take in.
What I most appreciate about your love is that it's for me.
I love you, Lord. Amen.

SPILLED LEMONADE

Trust in him at all times, you people;
pour out your hearts to him,
for God is our refuge.
PSALM 62:8 NIV

Aaah! That tastes so good!

Misty set her glass of lemonade on the counter and turned to put the pitcher away in the refrigerator. But it slipped from her hand and lemony goodness splashed onto the cupboards and poured out on the hardwood floor.

God encourages you to pour out your heart. Be real, be honest, and tell God what's on your heart. Let it all out. Even what's hard to express because you're not sure how to say it, because you're not sure you'd want anyone to know, because it sounds horrible, but that's really how you feel.

How you're excited that the popular girl in English class said hi.

How you're totally frustrated that your audition for the school play didn't go well.

How you're confused about what to do when your sister borrows your best sweater without asking.

What's on your heart today? Your Father in heaven would love to hear about it.

Dear God, thank you that you care about how I feel. I'm here to pour out my heart. Thank you for being a safe place for me. Amen.

BEYOND TALK

All hard work brings a profit,
but mere talk leads only to poverty.
PROVERBS 14:23 NIV

Jenna pulled out a pan of freshly baked cookies from the oven and set them on top of the stove.

"I wish I could bake," said Monica as she bit into a warm chocolate chip cookie and licked chocolatey goodness off her fingers.

"You could learn. I could teach you how to make my famous peanut butter and fudge cookies," Jenna said as she scooped cookie dough balls onto another cookie sheet.

"Well… I don't know. I'll think about."

You can wish or talk all you want or you can just do it. What have you always wanted to learn to do? Bake cupcakes, play piano, waterski, do a cartwheel, speak French? Go for it! Move past wishing and dreaming and make it happen.

- Write down your goal. What do you want to achieve?
- Write down the steps you'll need to take to make that goal happen.
- Assess your commitment. How badly do you really want to reach your goal?
- Ask someone to hold you accountable.

Write a plan and put it into action!

Dear God, I have so many "wants" swirling around in my head. Instead of sitting around talking and dreaming, give me the courage to take a chance and do! Amen.

POOL PARTY BUST

Be full of joy in the Lord always.
I have learned to be satisfied with the things I have
and with everything that happens.
PHILIPPIANS 4:4, 11 NCV

Ruined. Totally ruined. Jada watched rain pour down from the sky. Tears streaked down her face. She felt miserable. Her pool party birthday was a bust. All the cute beach decorations and party favors wouldn't work for anything else.

There's nothing so disappointing as making plans and then having them ruined. It's like everything you hoped for and worked for was for nothing! What are you going to do?

- Option 1: Throw yourself on the bed and cry.
- Option 2: Call up your friend and tell them how miserable you are.
- Option 3: Call a couple of friends and ask for help finding a creative solution. Take on the challenge: How fast can you come up with a Plan B that's better than Plan A?

Being full of joy isn't easy, much less being content with the way things turn out. But choosing to be thankful can turn a sour attitude into a positive one. Finding a creative alternative might just turn a flop into an unexpected surprise.

Have your plans ever flopped? What did you do?

Dear God, I have been disappointed. I really wanted one thing to happen, but something else did instead. Help me to be content no matter what. Amen.

THANKFUL FOR THAT?

Be thankful in all circumstances, for this is God's will for you who belong to Christ Jesus.
1 THESSALONIANS 5:18 NLT

Corrie and her sister lived in a prison camp during World War II. After a long day of hard work, they headed with the rest of the prisoners back to their bunks. One day everyone started to itch and itch and itch until someone discovered lice!

Why, God? Corrie asked. Wasn't being one of Hitler's prisoners bad enough? Why did they have to suffer with lice too? Corrie's sister reminded her that they had to thank God for the lice. God had said to be thankful in all circumstances and that meant with lice too.

All along, Corrie and her sister had been having Bible studies in their barracks. They were free to tell the women about God's love because the guards never went into their barracks. Later they found out why. Lice! Lice had kept the guards out.

You may not have lice at your house but is there anything you're having a hard time being thankful for? You can be thankful even when you don't understand why something is happening. Thankfulness is a choice and an action not a feeling. Could you ask God to change your heart and be thankful?

Dear God, help me to choose to be thankful whether I feel like it or not. Thank you for always caring for me. Amen.

CHECK IT OUT: Read Corrie ten Boom's true story, *The Hiding Place.*

GOT TO HAVE IT

*Buy truth, and do not sell it,
Get wisdom and instruction and understanding.*
PROVERBS 23:23 NASB

I've just got to have it, thought Kinsley.

For the last six months she'd saved every dollar of her allowance, babysitting money, birthday money, and Christmas gifts. She'd said no to the yogurt place. She'd said no to going out with friends. And tomorrow (finally!) she was going to walk into the store and buy herself an adorable purse. Because she had to have it.

"Buy the truth," says Proverbs, "and don't sell it." Why? Because it's *way* above the I've-got-to-have-that-purse category. More like I've-got-it-and-won't-ever-let-go category. Ever.

The whole, pure truth isn't watered down with just a little bit of lie. It isn't twisted a tiny bit or stretched out like a well-worn sock. The truth you've got to have is God's truth. Don't settle for anything less.

What would your life look like if you wanted truth that badly?

Dear God, I want to want truth that badly. More than a designer purse, more than anything. Building my life on truth is something I don't want to ever let go of. Amen.

POUND-A-PEG TOY

The LORD delights in those who fear him,
who put their hope in his unfailing love.
PSALM 147:11 NIV

Ever have one of those days? Your alarm doesn't go off so you oversleep and are late for school. You didn't have time to grab breakfast so your stomach makes strange noises in math class and everyone is giving you the look. You look down at your socks and realize you have one orange and another pink, and now Mrs. Jones is calling you out in social studies for an assignment you thought was due next week but evidently is due today. Go figure.

Some days you kind of feel like the peg in a pound-a-peg toy. Everything is pounding you down and you're sinking further and further into your started-out-bad-and-getting-worse day.

If that happens (and it will since that's just how life rolls), try to find a few seconds to yourself: in the bathroom, in the library, in your room, or just right at your desk. Close your eyes and whisper, "Jesus, I'm having a terrible, no good, very bad day. Could you help me? Could you push the refresh button and start things new from here on out?"

And he will.

Dear God, my hope isn't in the great day I'm having—because in case I haven't told you already, I'm not having one. My hope is in you. I believe you love me. I believe you're good even though this day seems pretty lousy. Amen.

HOW TO BREAK A HABIT

Some of you say, "I have the right to do anything."
But not everything is helpful.
1 CORINTHIANS 6:12 NIRV

Imagine two potted daisies are sitting next to each other on the sunny deck. For the next month you water one but not the other. What do you think will happen? The first one will grow. Unless it rains, the flowers on the one you didn't water will shrivel, petals will fall, leaves will turn brown, and that daisy will curl up and turn into a stick.

If you feed something it'll grow. If you don't feed something, it won't grow.

The same is true for a habit. Some things aren't wrong, they're just not helpful—like biting your nails. If you're trying to break a habit, the more do you it, the harder the habit becomes to break. The habit becomes stronger.

The less you do it, the easier it becomes to break. The habit shrivels up and becomes weaker.

Pray for God's grace; he'll definitely help. Just know you're in for hard work and a-day-at-a-time choices. The goal is to make the habit weaker one day at a time.

Dear Lord, I want to change. Give me strength. Give me grace. But also help me starve the habit even when feeding it might feel easier. Amen.

AUGUST

May he give you the power to
accomplish all the good things your
faith prompts you to do.

2 Thessalonians 1:11 nlt

TRASH TALK OR TRUTH TALK?

"When the Spirit of truth comes,
he will guide you into all truth.
He will not speak on his own
but will tell you what he has heard."
JOHN 16:13 NLT

We all know that telling the truth is important. But how about telling the truth to yourself? Picture this: You just found out you got a not-so-great grade on your science quiz. All of a sudden nasty thoughts start trickling into your head. *There must be something wrong with me. No matter what I do, I'll never succeed. I always mess up.*

When you've given your life to Jesus, God's Spirit comes inside of you. Because his Spirit speaks truth, you can know that none of those thoughts are from God. So put them out of your mind and replace them with God's truth. *I make mistakes but I can learn and do better next time. God made me special and created me in his own image. Are my goals realistic? Am I giving up too easily?*

When you're tired or something disappointing has happened, you're the most sensitive to untruth. Be on your guard. Take a break. Take a nap. Go for a walk or wait until after a good night's sleep. Things can look a lot different the next day.

Dear Lord, I sometimes find myself letting all kinds of lies dance around in my head. Give me discernment to spot the lie and wisdom to replace it with truth. Amen.

WHAT TO SAY WHEN YOU PRAY

God, be merciful to me because you are loving.
PSALM 51:1 NCV

Of all the kings of Israel, King David was the most famous. His career began as a shepherd boy who took down Goliath the giant with a sling and five stones. The king promoted David in his army, and David married the king's daughter. Later David became king.

King David had everything he needed—a palace, servants, money, a big family. But he wanted more. So he stole another man's wife and then had that man killed.

Psalm 51 is the prayer David wrote when he begged God for forgiveness. It shows us what was going on in David's heart and how he talked to God. The psalms can help us talk to God too. They give us words to say when we struggle to find words of our own.

If you did something wrong, for example, you could pray Psalm 51. God helps us even in our prayers!

Dear God, thank you for your Word. It gives me words to pray when my mind draws a blank or when I struggle with what to say. Amen.

TRUTH BONUS

LORD, try me and test me;
look closely into my heart and mind.
I see your love, and I live by your truth.
PSALM 26:2-3 NCV

Gina might be twelve years old, but she's a sales representative for a company. She hosts parties in her home for girls her age. She gets a percentage of everything she sells. If she gets to $500, she earns a special bonus. That bonus, more than anything else, drives Gina to do the best she can.

Bonuses aren't just for twelve-year-old entrepreneurs. God knew that we needed bonuses too, so he built them in to everything he asks us to do. Telling the truth, for instance, isn't just something we're supposed to do; it's something that comes with a bonus or two—for you.

Bonus #1: People will trust you because they know what you say is true.

Bonus #2: You'll have a clear conscience and won't be nagged by a guilty one.

Bonus #3: You won't have to stress out keeping track of which untruth you told to whom.

Being honest comes with definite bonuses. What other truth bonuses are the most meaningful to you?

Dear God, I want to live by your truth but I've always thought of truth as something I "have to" or "should" do. Help me to see the built-in bonuses you have for me too. Thank you for your goodness. Amen.

HAVING A MENTOR

*Remember your leaders who taught you the word of God.
Think of all the good that has come from their lives,
and follow the example of their faith.*

HEBREWS 13:7 NLT

When you need to talk about how you're feeling overwhelmed with homework, how your best friend isn't talking to you anymore, or how you think your teacher doesn't like you, who do you talk you? Your mom? Your friend? A youth group leader?

God knew we needed mentors in our lives: women to come alongside us and coach us in both practical and spiritual things. Women to admire and learn from. Women to tell us not just what to do but to give us a life we can imitate.

You can have mentors who help you learn a skill, mentors who help you explore a career interest, or even mentors who help you grow in your faith. God gave you a built-in mentor in your mom. But having others mentors is great too. You can have different mentors for different things, and all at the same time!

How do you find a mentor? Look for someone you can trust and someone who has qualities you admire. Ask if you can spend time with her, and tell her why. Ask her questions. Imitate what she does. Follow her example of faith.

Dear God, thank you for making me the girl I am. Give me a good role model, someone who can show me what it's like to be a godly woman. Amen.

DOWNLOAD

"I tell you the truth, anyone who believes in me will do the same works I have done, and even greater works, because I am going to be with the Father."
JOHN 14:12 NLT

"I feel so bad," said Clara. Mrs. J., Clara's favorite teacher, was out for the rest of the school year. She was going through chemotherapy. "We've got to do something to cheer her up. What can we do?" asked Clara.

"I'm thinking, thinking…" Lizzie said tapping the side of her head.

Whenever Lizzie did that she was downloading one of the great big ideas God gave her. "Got it!" Lizzie said, her face breaking into a smile. "We'll ask for donations from everyone and buy a month of meals and put together a basket of her favorite things. It'll be fun! It'll be great!"

God's plan all along was for you to do great things. He is a great God after all. You can be a part of someone else's great big thing, helping to make it a reality. Or he can give you a great big thing to do, an idea that swells up inside you until you're about to burst. You can create a new design, feed a village, help someone in need, land a jump, or run a race.

What great thing does God want to do in you?

Dear God, you are so great! Show me the great things you want me to be a part of. Do your great things in and through me. Amen.

230

WHY PRAYER IS POWERFUL

The prayer of a righteous person is powerful and effective.
JAMES 5:16 NIV

Shelby was just placing the final ingredients for her smoothie into the blender. She had started with yogurt and a touch of milk then added strawberries and a banana. Now she drizzled honey over a few ice cubes. After placing the lid on top, the next step would be to press "pulse" until completely mixed, and voila: the best smoothie ever!

By themselves, the ingredients to that smoothie tasted great. But the power of the blender changed them into something completely different.

When you pray, things happen. Prayer changes situations. Prayer changes people. Prayer is powerful and effective. Not because we say the right words, we repeat them often enough, we pray hard enough, or we're good enough.

When we pray, things happen because the one we pray to is powerful! Yes, we believe and pray persistently. Yes, we make sure we're living in a way that's right. But everything else is up to God. He makes things happen, not us. Prayer is powerful because God is powerful!

If someone asked you why prayer is powerful, how would you explain it to them?

Dear God, you are mighty! Your power covers the whole earth. You give power and strength to your people. Help me to pray knowing that you'll answer because you are powerful. Amen.

ABIGAIL'S INFLUENCE

"May the Lord bless you for what you have done.
You have shown a lot of good sense."
1 SAMUEL 25:33 NIRV

A beautiful woman name Abigail was married to a man named Nabal. He was a brute, a mean fool. One day Abigail was running errands when messengers came to the house. Nabal insulted them so badly, they left to report to their leader. Their leader was so furious he threatened to destroy Nabal, Abigail, everyone!

Now Abigail wasn't just drop-dead gorgeous, she was extremely smart. When she found out what had happened, she quickly put together many gifts and offered them to the leader. She spoke calmly and wisely to him. Because of her quick thinking and influence, the entire situation changed. (You can read what happened in 1 Samuel 25.)

When you act with good sense and wisdom, you can influence situations and people for good. Freaking out only makes a difficult situation worse. Being calm settles a situation and makes other people calm down too.

Be quick to think and unafraid to act and use your influence for good.

Dear God, give me wisdom to do what is right and help me be an influence for what is good. Amen.

DOUBLE CHECK

Plans go wrong for lack of advice;
many advisers bring success.
PROVERBS 15:22 NLT

"Are you sure?" Mrs. Alvarez said into the phone. "I'm swamped at work. Having everyone pitch in would be great!"

Every year Renata's mom insisted on making all the food for their neighborhood block party. She was a caterer and her Mexican food was to die for. This year instead of taking everything on herself, everyone in the neighborhood was bringing something to eat.

The next day neighbors showed up to the block party with grilled chicken, pasta, corn on the cob, chips, and enough brownies and cookies to cover a whole table. Thanks to everyone's contribution, Mrs. Alvarez didn't have to pull it off herself.

When it comes to making decisions, the same thing is true. Instead of feeling like you need to know it all, instead of feeling the pressure to make a decision yourself, tap into the experience others have to offer. Parents, teachers, and others you respect have more life experience than you. They might have a different perspective and can help you think through something you hadn't thought of before.

Even when the answer seems obvious, ask God what he thinks. He knows things that you don't. If you want plans that succeed, double check with him first!

Dear God, thanks for friends and family who love me. Remind me to take advantage of their good advice. Amen.

CAUSE AND EFFECT

Just as stirring milk makes butter, and twisting noses makes them bleed, so stirring up anger causes trouble.
PROVERBS 30:33 NCV

If you want to make butter, put heavy cream into a mixer and start to whip it. After a while, the color will turn from fluffy white to pale yellow. Turn off the mixer, drain off the little bit of water in the bottom of the bowl, and add a sprinkle of salt. Spread it on a muffin or piece of toast. Congratulations! You've just made homemade butter.

Everything you do has a cause and an effect. If you whip cream it will turn into butter. If you walk outside in the rain, you'll get wet. If you pour milk on your cereal and forget to eat it, it will get soggy. If you punch someone in the nose (don't really do it, please), they'll get a bloody nose and you'll get a sore fist. Actions have consequences.

When you stir up anger, that is, if you're rude and offensive, don't be surprised if an argument breaks out.

The good news is that you can change the result by changing your actions. Get a different result by doing something different. Instead of being rude, you can be kind. Instead of talking back, you can listen. You have a huge impact on what goes down.

Is there someone you find yourself arguing with a lot? How could you change what you say to get a different result?

Dear God, help me do my part in making situations and conversations healthy, safe, and free from anger. Amen.

POOR, POOR HANNAH

Her rival, however, would provoke her bitterly to irritate her….
It happened year after year…she would provoke her;
so she wept and would not eat.

1 SAMUEL 1:6-7 NASB

If anyone knew what it was like to be teased it was Hannah. Every day Penninah (how's that for an interesting name?) made fun of Hannah because she had children and Hannah didn't. Back in the day when having children was the most important job a woman had, this was a really big deal. Hannah would get so frustrated she'd sob and completely lose her appetite. Who wanted to eat with all that bullying? This went on for years.

One day she prayed and wept. "Lord," she said, "if you will give me a son I will give him back to you." God gave Hannah a baby boy and she named him Samuel, because she asked and the Lord heard.

If you've ever gone through endless teasing or know someone who has, God hears. He gets the tears, frustration, and even anger that can result. Tell him how you feel. Then go to a parent or a teacher you trust to help you make sense of what's happening and find a solution. But make God your go-to person; he always understands.

Dear God-who-hears, please be near me. I need to know what to do. Help me, Lord. Amen.

ADVENTURE!

You will fill me with joy in your presence.
PSALM 16:11 NIV

One bright Texas morning, Macie took her horse Samson out for a gallop. They dodged mesquite bushes scattered across her ranch and then cut across the path that led to her aunt and uncle's ranch.

This is the best! Macie thought as she leaned forward in the saddle. She lightened up on the reins and Samson surged forward. A rush of air whipped through her hair and she felt on top of the world.

You're on an adventure every day, an adventure called life. God's packed it with freedom, exhilaration, and pure joy! Don't let all your to-dos quiet the excitement of discovering what's new every day. Explore and enjoy everything God has for you.

Dear God, I'm looking forward to my life adventure with you! Fill me with your joy. Help me find and embrace the new opportunities you bring my way. Amen.

A GIRL NAMED KAY

The God of all grace, who called you to his eternal glory in Christ, after you have suffered a little while, will himself restore you and make you strong, firm and steadfast.

1 PETER 5:10 NIV

Kay had a lot of things going against her. She was poor. She lived in the projects. Her dad drank a lot of alcohol. Her mom couldn't support her so she moved in with her aunt and uncle.

But Kay had a lot of things going for her too. Her dad loved her even though he didn't show it sometimes. Her mom loved her and taught her about Jesus. Her aunt and uncle took good care of her. Kay learned to work and study hard.

When Kay grew up she worked for the president of the United States. She started the Gloucester Institute that helps train African American young leaders for the future.

It's easy to make a list of the things we don't have going for us. Kay had a long list. Part of the reason she succeeded was because she didn't forget the good things in her life. Trouble doesn't have to stop you from becoming everything God created you to be.

What do you have going for you? What are the good things God has put into your life?

Dear God, thank you that no matter what happens, I can walk through it when I lean on you. Make me strong, firm, and steadfast. Amen.

MIXED UP

*Love never gives up, never loses faith, is always hopeful,
and endures through every circumstance.*
1 CORINTHIANS 13:7 NLT

Hope knew her grandpa loved her. He called her "princess" and gave her pretty gifts and always teased her. "Do you have any clue how much I love you?" he'd ask. Hope would guess a billion or a trillion, and he'd laugh and say that it was way more than that.

But Hope's grandpa also drank a lot, and when he did he wasn't nice to her or her mom or dad. He was still her grandpa, though, and she still loved him.

Sometimes the people we love do bad things. But we still love them because that's what real love does. That doesn't mean we let them do bad things to us. That doesn't mean we can't find someone who can help us be safe. Love doesn't give up. It keeps praying and encouraging. Love never loses faith. It keeps hoping that God who is big can change a heart and hear a prayer. It perseveres even though things are sometimes hard.

That's what real love is.

Dear God, I want to love everyone even though people do things that aren't nice. Please show your love to those who are the most difficult for me to love and change their hearts. Amen.

KEEP IT SUPER SIMPLE

The soothing tongue is a tree of life.
PROVERBS 15:4 NIV

"What's the matter, Aurora?" asked Charlotte. "You seem kind of sad."

"It's my mom and dad," said Aurora. "They're getting a divorce." Her eyes started to fill with tears.

"I'm so sorry!" said Charlotte who gave her a big hug.

One of the greatest gifts you can give a friend is two words—I'm sorry. That's it. Not...

"It could be a lot worse. Did you hear about so-and-so?"

"I've been through the same thing. It was awful."

"Well, if you want to make things better you should..."

Do say you're sorry. Give them a hug. Write them a card or send them an IM. Don't try to fix things. Don't say anything more than "I'm sorry." Don't compare what they're going through with what someone else went through.

The bigger the hurt, the fewer words you'll want to say. Just it keep simple.

Remember a time someone comforted you? What wasn't helpful? What was helpful?

Dear God, I want to support those who are hurting. Remind me to keep my words few and kind. Show your love through me. Amen.

239

TRUE LOVE

God shows his great love for us in this way:
Christ died for us while we were still sinners.
ROMANS 5:8 NCV

"Tuck your shirt in, Lucas," his mom said. "Here, let me fix your hair. It's sticking up all over."

"Mom, I already did!" complained Lucas.

"Well, not good enough. Hold still. Luciana, go get Lucas's nice shoes, will you. They're in the downstairs closet."

"Sure, Mom," Luciana said. Boy, was she glad piano recitals came just twice a year.

Going to a special event usually means getting ready with your best. Best clothes. Best shoes. Best appearance. Nothing dirty. Nothing messy. Good enough and presentable enough to pass inspection and hopefully make an impression.

You don't need to make yourself presentable before you put your faith in Jesus. You don't need to try to be better before asking for forgiveness. You don't need to get your act together before asking him for help. Jesus died for us while we were sinners, not after we cleaned up our act. We can come to God just like we are. We don't have to make an impression to secure his love. We already have it.

Do you feel like you need to do something so God will like you better? God says, "Come to me just the way you are. I love you."

Dear God, I'm coming to you just the way I am. I'm not pretending to be someone I'm not. Take away my sin and change me, the way only you know how. Amen.

THAT KID

You created my inmost being;
you knit me together in my mother's womb.
PSALM 139:13 NIV

Hi, my name is Emma and my little brother has Down Syndrome. People call him "that kid," but he has a name. His name is Riley. Riley is super creative and likes doing art projects. He's really organized and likes being on a schedule. Riley is really friendly too. At school he loves to greet people. "Hello, how are you today?" he'll say to people who walk by.

One day our family went to Riley's open house at school. A kid walked in and saw Riley. "Oh," he said sounding disappointed. "He's going to be in my class." When people say things like that, it makes me sad. God made Riley special, and I love him a lot.

When people look, sound, or act differently than we do, we aren't always sure what to do or how to act. Here's some of Emma's advice:

- Be friendly to them. They have feelings too.
- Don't talk down to them. They're really smart.
- Treat everyone fairly. God created everyone; no one is better than anyone else.
- Don't stare, but don't avoid them either. Say hello.
- Love and treat people like you would want to be treated.

Dear God, you created me in a wonderful way. Give me eyes to see them just the way you do. Amen.

TAKE MY ADVICE

The wisdom that comes from God is first of all pure, then peaceful, gentle, and easy to please. This wisdom is always ready to help those who are troubled and to do good for others. It is always fair and honest.

JAMES 3:17 NCV

"What am I going to do?!" Allison asked her best friend Claire. "Alyssa's telling everyone that *I'm* the one who pulled a prank on Mrs. Jarret. But that's totally not true!"

"Well," said Claire, "I think you should…"

Imagine that the situation above is yours, and your best friend is about to give you her advice. You're listening because she is your best friend after all. She knows you better than anyone else (except maybe your mom). How do you know if the advice she gives you is good?

In the Bible, God gave us a type of checklist to use to see if the advice we get is wise or not.

☐ Does the advice line up with what's pure?
☐ Does the advice provide a gentle way of solving the problem?
☐ Is the advice fair and honest?
☐ If you took the advice would it lead to peace or make waves?
☐ If you took the advice would it help others?

If you can check what's on the list, go for it. Take the advice. If not, maybe the advice isn't as wise as you thought. Real wisdom will have good results.

Dear God, thank you for showing me how to decide if the advice I get is good or bad. Remind me to compare the advice I get with what your guidelines say. Amen.

BEING THE BOSS

Remind the people to be subject to rulers and authorities, to be obedient, to be ready to do whatever is good, to slander no one, to be peaceable and considerate, and always to be gentle toward everyone.

Titus 3:1-2 NIV

Sara squealed. She'd just landed her first babysitting job. She loved playing with the four-year-old Anderson twins but this time—she was going to get paid. *Hello, brand new jeans!*

Everything started out fine until Bella started drowning her Goldfish in apple juice at lunch. Then, Brian turned rest time into jumping-on-the-bed-waving-his-light-saber time. Bella threatened, "I'm telling Mom!" and Brian teased her back. Bella started to cry and pushed Brian and his light saber off the bed. Sara tried to referee but they just wouldn't listen. Ack!

Being in charge sounds awfully fun. But when people don't want to do what you tell them to do, when they don't agree with what you've said, when they argue that your rules don't make sense and fight you on everything, it's exhausting!

You can support someone who's the boss—whether that's a teacher, parent, principal, or even a president—by influencing others to do what's good. Even when you're not in charge you can lead by being an example of working together and being kind. Be the kind of follower you would like to have if you were the leader.

Dear Lord, help me lead others in keeping peace and being considerate. That's what I want to be known for. Remind me that I'm reflecting you wherever I go and whatever I do. Amen.

COURAGE

Wait for the LORD:
Be strong and let your heart take courage;
Yes, wait for the LORD.
PSALM 27:14 NASB

Esther was beautiful and rich and she was queen. While that may sound like a fairy-tale life, the truth was Esther would rather have been at home. She missed eating homemade food and walking to the market with friends. She missed her family and hearing her cousin Mordecai laugh. She missed worshipping God together.

But circumstances were out of Esther's control. She could have cried. She could have pouted. Instead she took courage and made the best of her strange, new surroundings.

Courage isn't how you feel; it's what you do. You might not feel courageous about moving to a new school, making new friends, or taking a hard test. But courage is realizing God is with you. It's what you do in spite of how you might feel.

Dear Lord, when I'm in circumstances that are tough to face, help me to go to you. Give me courage to be strong and courageous, knowing you're always with me. Amen.

DID YOU KNOW? In ancient times when a king wanted a young woman, he could force her to come to the palace. Once she was part of his household, she wasn't allowed to see her family again.

244

STANDING UP

Who will stand up for me against those who do evil?
PSALM 94:16 HCSB

Have you ever faced a dilemma that kept you up at night and turned your stomach into knots? That's exactly how Queen Esther felt. She was staring a problem in the face. Not just a little, it'll-go-away-in-a-few days problem; but a huge problem. Her people and her family were in danger. She had to ask the king for help.

If she *didn't* ask for help, her people were in trouble. If she *did* ask for help, *she* could be in trouble. No one, absolutely no one, went into the king's throne room without being called. Not even the queen. The punishment? Well, let's not go there.

Three days later Queen Esther walked into the throne room, not knowing what would happen. She just knew that she had to stand up.

God gave Queen Esther courage to do what she did. God gives you courage to stand up for what's right too. Courage to love someone who doesn't particularly like you. Courage to stand up for someone who can't speak up for herself. Courage to speak the truth even when it's not popular.

What is God asking you to be courageous about?

Dear God, I'm not normally a courageous person. Please take away my fear. Help me to stand up for what's right. Amen.

WHAT HAPPENED? Read Esther 5–8 to find out.

245

SUMMER SPLASHES OF JOY

The whole earth is filled with awe at your wonders;
where morning dawns, where evening fades,
you call forth songs of joy.

PSALM 65:8 NIV

Paisley stared outside her bedroom window at the rain. Rain had been coming down in buckets all day. The sun was nowhere to be seen and the skies were a dingy gray. Leaves and branches were drooping from the weight of constant rain. The small pond outside had been churned to a murky brown. *Not exactly the kind of day for a campout,* Paisley thought.

Ever had one of those days? A day when everything looks gloomy and nothing seems to turn out. You might be tempted to complain but what about going outside and catching raindrops with your tongue, or pulling on boots and jumping in a puddle (who says little kids get to have all the fun?), or cozying up inside with a book, or camping inside with blankets and pillows.

A day is what you make it. You can't always control what happens, but you can find the gift inside each day. Embrace your day!

Dear God, thank you for this day. I choose to wrap my arms around it and enjoy it as a gift. Help me discover new joys along the way. Amen.

WHEN GOD IS FAMILY

God is in his holy Temple. He is a father to orphans, and he defends the widows. God gives the lonely a home.

PSALM 68:5-6 NCV

"How was your day?"
"Did you finish your homework?"
"Are you wearing your retainer?"
"Don't forget to say thank you."

You've probably heard those phrases so many times you don't realize what they mean—you have someone to take care of you, like a dad, a mom, or even a grandparent. For some kids, that's not the case. Maybe their dad is in jail. Maybe their mom has passed away. Or maybe, just maybe, they don't have either a mom or dad.

God says he's a father to the fatherless. He's an advocate for those who are orphans. He steps in when someone doesn't have a mother. When someone is lonely, he puts that person in a family.

If you know someone who's missing a dad, mom, or even both, let them know that God is looking out for them; they aren't forgotten. And if that someone is you, just know that God sees and cares.

Dear God, thank you for the family I have. Thanks for watching over me. Amen.

PURE RELIGION

Pure and genuine religion in the sight of God the Father means caring for orphans and widows in their distress and refusing to let the world corrupt you.
JAMES 1:27 NLT

God loves simple, so following him isn't complicated. If anything, people are the ones who make it confusing. He takes religion, something we think of as hard to understand, and strips it out down to the bare basics:

1. Take care of orphans who need help
2. Take care of widows who need help
3. Keep yourself free from being polluted by what's wrong

Real religion expresses itself in helping those who are helpless and refusing to ignore them. Genuine religion shows itself by staying far away from anything that's questionable or wrong.

What are some ideas you could do to express true religion? What could you do to help someone who doesn't have a mom or dad? What could you do to encourage a woman whose husband has died? What would encourage you to say no to what's wrong and yes to what's right?

Pray and ask God to give you ideas.

Dear God, thanks for making things simple and helping me focus on what's important. Please show me how I can hold true to what you have in mind. Amen.

HOLES

The believers studied what the apostles taught. They shared their lives together. They ate and prayed together.
ACTS 2:42 NIRV

Unless you're talking about bagels or doughnut holes—think sugar, cinnamon, dipped in chocolate doughnut holes (yum!)—we don't care much for holes, like…

holes in your socks

holes in your shoes

holes in your backpack

or a big rusty hole in the side of your car.

When you see a hole, it can mean something is missing and needs to be fixed or filled. You want to put something in the hole, like putting a puzzle piece into place or inserting a key into a keyhole.

God gives us each other—friends, family, teachers, pastors, and other believers in Jesus—to share life together. Without each other our lives would be full of holes. Praying together, sharing a pizza together, worshipping God together, and laughing together fills us up.

Dear God, thanks for friends, family, and especially those at church who give me good advice, who I can laugh with and hang out with. Most of all, thank you for being my God and friend. You fill me up. Amen.

PATIENCE POWER

With patience you can convince a ruler,
and a gentle word can get through to the hard-headed.
PROVERBS 25:15 NCV

That noise is driving me crazy!

For the last fifteen minutes, a woodpecker had been drilling into the side of the house outside Kennedy's window. Obviously it hadn't found what it was looking for, because it kept on pecking. Kennedy pulled the pillows around her ears to try and muffle the sound.

I just wish it would stop!

A woodpecker will drill constantly—up to twenty times per second—to get at tiny insects buried in wood. In order to get that lunch it pecks over and over again, drilling deeper and deeper every time. Even though it takes time, the bird keeps at it. That's patience!

Patience is what you need when you're in the middle of a math problem that's long and hard, or you're doing a complicated dance routine, or you're trying to wash the dog and it keeps shaking its fur. More importantly, patience is what you need when dealing with someone who won't listen, someone you might be trying to help, someone who's about to make a mistake. Arguing won't convince them. Getting frustrated won't persuade them. Patience paired with gentleness usually wins.

When someone is trying to persuade you, what usually works?

Dear God, teach me to be patient and persistent in small things and big things. Help me keep the final reward in my mind so I don't give up. Amen.

HELP IS ON THE WAY

My help comes from the LORD,
who made heaven and earth!
PSALM 121:1-2 NLT

The minute someone dials 9-1-1, they know help is on the way. Within minutes, a police car, an ambulance, and possibly a fire truck will be in the driveway. They can call 9-1-1 with complete confidence.

Psalm 121 is called a psalm of confidence. The author basically says, "I'm confident that God is our help. He is our protector." What do you think he meant when he wrote…

The LORD himself watches over you! Why is it a big deal that God himself watches over you and not someone else?

The LORD stands beside you as your protective shade. How does the shade protect you?

The LORD keeps you from all harm and watches over your life. What are some ways God keeps you and your family and your church from harm?

The LORD keeps watch over you as you come and go, both now and forever. How long is forever?

Dear God, you're the one I go to for help. When I call, you answer. Thank you for watching over me and my family. I trust you completely. Amen.

BACK-TO-SCHOOL MERCY

I have hope when I think of this:
The LORD's love never ends; his mercies never stop.
They are new every morning;
LAMENTATIONS 3:21-23 NCV

It's the beginning of a new school year and everywhere around us we see "new"!

- New school clothes without stains or holes
- New notebooks free of eraser marks or writing
- New shoes with bright white shoelaces
- New pencils with extra pointy tips

God talks about a different kind of new—new mercy. New mercy means God isn't remembering what we should have done yesterday, and didn't. His new mercy isn't worn thin by the things we did wrong in the past—making fun of a teacher, ignoring a little brother's request for help, procrastinating on an assignment and turning it in late—again.

Every morning God hands us a fresh notebook of mercy with blank lines that have no record of our mistakes. His faithfulness is so great! That undeserved love means every day begins with hope that today is going to be different.

What if we showed mercy like that? What if the sting of the sarcastic remark flung our way yesterday, or the fact that our best friend forgot our birthday, or the misunderstanding and tension with our mom or dad wasn't carried over to today because we're doing what God does and handing them new mercy every morning. What would life be like then?

Dear God, your faithfulness is so great! Your love never ends. Every day you give me new mercy. I want to do the same! Amen.

JUST BELIEVE

Sarah had faith....Sarah believed that the God who made the promise was faithful.
HEBREWS 11:11 NIRV

Two people come up to you and they both promise the same thing: by the end of the day, they'll get you tickets to the summer's blockbuster movie premiere. You know one person and you don't know the other. Who are you more likely to believe?

A promise is only as good as the one who makes it. "Just believe" won't get you far because *who* you believe in matters. You can count on the promise if you can count on the one who made it.

God promised Sarah she'd have a son and she believed him—not because what he promised seemed to make sense— it didn't. She was too old to have kids. She believed God because she knew he was someone who kept his promises.

If you get to know God, you'll discover he's a promise-giver who is also a promise-keeper. He's faithful and honest and totally trustworthy.

If you're having trouble trusting God, spend a little time getting to know him and that will probably change. Read his Word and talk to him—then believing and trusting will come easier and easier.

Dear God, thank you that I can believe in you. You are faithful to keep your promises. I want to know you more, so my faith will grow stronger. Amen.

A SMILE ON HIS FACE

Without faith it is impossible to please God, because anyone who comes to him must believe that he exists and that he rewards those who earnestly seek him.
HEBREWS 11:6 NIV

What Morgan liked best about Mrs. Peters was that she looked Morgan in the eye and really listened to her. To Mrs. Peters, Morgan wasn't just another student; she was a real person. Her next-door neighbor Jack, on the other hand, acted like she didn't exist. He looked right through her. When she was around, he talked like she wasn't even there.

There's nothing you can do to please God more than believing he exists, talking to him like a real person, and listening to what he says. Having faith like that puts a smile on God's face.

Believing God will give you courage for the first day of middle school makes God happy. Believing God will show you how to love the girl in science class who keeps kicking your chair makes God happy. Pouring out your heart to God on a bad day makes him happy. Why? Because it shows that you believe he is who he says he is—loving, kind, and caring enough to answer.

Dear God, I believe! I believe you are who you say you are—a powerful, mighty, loving Father. Help me keep reading, praying, learning, and growing in faith. Amen.

SURPRISE!

My child, listen and accept what I say. Then you will have a long life. I am guiding you in the way of wisdom, and I am leading you on the right path.

PROVERBS 4:10-12 NCV

Avery remembered the day like it was yesterday. Her dad had walked in the kitchen, sat down at the table, and said, "Avery, I want you to pack a bag tonight. You and I are going on a short trip tomorrow." She should have been excited but she really didn't want to miss hanging out with her friends that weekend.

"Where are we going? What are we going to do?" she asked.

All her dad said was, "You're going to need a swimsuit."

The next morning they drove north to a summer cabin. For the whole weekend, they swam and went tubing and skiing. Best of all, Avery got to be with her dad for three whole days. She closed her eyes and smiled. She loved remembering that day.

One day God told Abraham and his wife Sarah to leave their home and head to a new place. They had no idea where they were going. They left anyhow, knowing God would show them what was next. God surprised them not with just a home but with a promise for a whole country that would be their own.

You won't always know what God has in mind when he tells you what to do. Sometimes he asks you to take the first step even if you don't understand, even if it doesn't make sense, even if you'd rather do something else.

What you can be sure of is this: God will lead you on the right path and it'll be good.

Dear God, I like to plan ahead and know what's coming next. Thank you for being a God of surprises. I trust you to do what's best. Amen.

S'MORE, PLEASE

*"If two or three people come together in my name,
I am there with them."*
MATTHEW 18:20 NIV

Mia thought summer church camp was the best time of the year. She loved sitting around a crackling bonfire on a warm summer night, singing worship songs, hearing the stories of how God had changed people's lives, laughing together, and wrapping up the night by passing around a bag of marshmallows to make her favorite treat—s'mores. Ooey-gooey marshmallows squeezed between two layers of graham crackers with chocolate. Yum!

Nights like that just made her want s'more. Not just more s'mores but more campfire-singing-talking-worshipping-hanging out time. Being together was so much fun.

When two or more people who believe in Jesus come together, God's Spirit is with them. Whether it's worshipping together at church, canoeing together at a youth retreat, biking together down a forest trail, or praying around a campfire under a summer sky, God's Spirit is there.

How does God's Spirit bring us all together in ways that nothing else can?

Dear God, thank you that I can pray, worship, and hang out with other people who love you. We love you and want to praise you in whatever we do. Amen.

SEPTEMBER

Be on guard. Stand firm in the faith.

Be courageous. Be strong.

And do everything with love.

1 CORINTHIANS 16:13–14 NLT

BOLD AND BEAUTIFUL

*The wicked flee when no one is pursuing them,
but the righteous are as bold as a lion.*
PROVERBS 28:1 HCSB

Have you ever been so afraid your heart started racing, your palms started sweating, and your knees felt wobbly? That describes the people of Jericho when they heard that God's people were just across the river from their city. They'd heard of God's power, and they were afraid.

Rahab should have been afraid, but she wasn't. When Joshua, the leader of Israel, sent spies into the city, she welcomed them. She took action and hid them. She stood up to the king who was trying to hunt them down—all because she believed that their God was the true God. Because of her bold faith, God saw Rahab as beautiful and included her with his people.

God still values faith and boldness. When you're filled with faith, when you defend what's right no matter what everyone thinks, when you're confident and not afraid of hard situations, God sees you as beautiful too.

Speaking up, standing up, and being unwilling to let things slide can be tough. But it's when you're bold that things begin to change.

Dear Lord, I want to be bold. Teach me to be confident doing what's good and right. Use me to be a strong voice for you. Amen.

CHECK IT OUT: Read the whole story of Rahab's boldness in Joshua 2 and 6:1-17.

CORN MAZE

Oh, how great are God's riches and wisdom and knowledge!
How impossible it is for us to understand his decisions
and his ways!
ROMANS 11:33 NLT

Every September and October when leaves turn golden brown, brilliant orange, and earthy brown, family farms all around Iowa put on fall festivals with pumpkins, apples, hayrides—and life-size corn mazes. People come from miles around to wind their way through ten-foot high cornstalks from one end to the other. It's complicated—but fun!

Sometimes life is like a maze. You don't know which way to turn or where you're going to come out. Things happen that are totally out of control. It's complicated—and not always fun.

Even though you can't see above your circumstances and figure things out, God is a master at mazes. He sees confusing situations from above, even when you can't. When you're in the middle of a life maze, you don't have to know how to make sense of it all. You just need to know that God is big and trust in that.

Dear God, you are great and I can't even grasp how wise you are. That's what I'll trust in—your bigness, your greatness, and your wisdom. Amen.

STRESSED OUT AT SCHOOL

"I will be with you as I was with Moses. I will not fail you or abandon you. Be strong and courageous."
JOSHUA 1:5-6 NLT

Ack! This is just stressing me out! thought Kayla. Just thinking about going to middle school was enough to make her want to crawl back into bed. Sure it sounded a little exciting, but how would it all turn out?

Joshua in the Bible faced something similar. For the first time in his life, he was being asked to step up and take on more responsibilities. Joshua had always been the follower; Moses, the one God had used to part the Red Sea, had been the leader. After Moses died, it was up to Joshua to lead and decide. He was feeling a little shaky inside, unsure of how everything would work out. So God said, "Joshua, just like I was with Moses, I'll be with you. Be brave."

God says the same thing to you. When you were a kid, your parents made the decisions. Now you're owning more decisions and responsibilities—keeping track of when basketball practice is, turning in your assignments on time, getting to the right class on time. It can be confusing!

God says he'll be with you. Just like he helped your parents when they were growing up, he'll help you. So be brave!

Dear God, sometimes I feel like my life is crazy busy. I have a lot to keep track of and school especially can be stressful. Please give me wisdom to set priorities, trim back my schedule to what's really important, and be brave. Amen.

CHANGES

There is a time for everything,
and everything on earth has its special season.
ECCLESIASTES 3:1 NCV

Every fall, oak, maple, dogwood, and birch trees, turn from deep green to bright orange, ruby red, and golden yellow. The change in season means a splash of brilliant new colors that will eventually lead to winter. That change is normal and good.

Life is full of change that's normal and good. Two of the biggest changes we experience are the outside and inside changes from a girl to a woman. On the outside, your body is changing. You're getting taller. Your body has more shape to it. You're getting hungrier because your body needs more energy for all the changes. It's busy changing, changing, changing!

On the inside changes are happening too. You might feel full of confidence some days and extra sensitive on others. Happy and energetic on one hand, and more serious and introverted on the other hand. You might question things you always took for granted because even your thinking is changing, changing, changing!

All these changes are normal; all these changes are good. They can feel awkward (adjusting to something new always is!) but God has watched over these types of changes many times before and all with a wonderful result—a beautiful woman. Exactly the way God planned you to be.

Dear God, thank you that you're directing all the changes that are going on, both outside and inside of me. Nothing is out of control. Nothing catches you by surprise. Help me to trust in you. Amen.

A REAL BULLY

*What should we say then? Since God is on our side,
who can be against us?*
ROMANS 8:31 NCV

What would it feel like to stand up to a nine-foot tall bully?

Every day a bully that tall named Goliath strutted out and bullied the people of Israel. He made fun of them. He teased them. But no one dared take him on; everyone, even the king, had chickened out.

Until David came along. David realized what everyone else seemed to have forgotten—God stands up for his people. To mess with God's people was messing with God. And Goliath was messing with God's people. So with a sling and five strategically placed stones, David brought Goliath down.

God stands behind his people. He is for us, not against us. Nothing escapes his notice. Nobody messes with God's people without him noticing.

Dear God, you are for us! Remind me of that when I feel like everything is going against me. You don't ignore. You don't overlook. You see what's happening and you'll do something about it. Amen.

THE FUNNY SIDE OF THINGS

Splendor and majesty are before him;
strength and joy are in his dwelling place.
1 CHRONICLES 16:27 NIV

What do you think: Does God have a sense of humor or not?

The word "joy" pops up all through the Bible. Joy is in God's presence. God's Spirit gives joy. God's joy is our strength (Psalm 16:11; Galatians 5:22; Nehemiah 8:10). Joy is everywhere God is. With that joy comes laughter and a good dose of humor.

He made an elephant with a six-foot nose and family-pizza-size ears.

He made a giraffe with a neck as long as its legs.

He made tickle spots and funny bones and giggles and laughter.

Does God have a sense of humor?

Absolutely.

What's something that strikes you as funny?

Dear God, help me spot the creative, goofy, funny things you've created and learn how to laugh. Amen.

263

JUST IMAGINE

"In everything, do to others what you would have them do to you, for this sums up the Law and the Prophets."
MATTHEW 7:12 NIV

"Come on, Elena. It's time to go. We can come back to the park another day."

"I can't, Maya. I'm talking to Gio."

Maya smiled. Gio was her little cousin Elena's imaginary friend. Elena lived in her imagination. She imagined the clouds were giant balls of cotton candy. She imagined the trees blowing in the wind were waving at her so she always waved back. She imagined she was a famous chef and served up Playdough cookies and pancakes.

What if you imagined you were a mom for a day? What would you like your daughter to say about you? Imagine you were a teacher for a day. What would you want your class to do for you? Imagine you were a little kid for a day. How would you want your big sister to talk to you?

Imagining can help you figure out what others like. Doing to others what you'd have them do to you gives you a chance to show them love in practical, down-to-earth ways.

Dear God, remind me to think of others—how they feel and what they need—before I act. Amen.

PRAYER LAUNDRY

*Give your burdens to the L*ORD*,*
and he will take care of you.
PSALM 55:22 NLT

Imagine you came home from school and said to your mom, "Mom, someone bumped in to me in the cafeteria today and spaghetti got on my jersey. Can you wash it before the game tomorrow?" What would your mom do?

It your mom is like most moms she'd say, "Sure. I'll take care of it." (After, of course telling you to take it off and soak it in cold water.) Then you'd hand her the jersey and go do your homework or walk the dog or whatever it is you do after school. Simple enough, right?

That's what prayer is. Prayer is taking things to God and handing them over. Prayer is letting him handle whatever you've talked to him about. Prayer isn't making things happen on your own (that would be like washing your own jersey). Prayer isn't asking God for something and then worrying about it. (That would be like asking your mom to wash your blouse and then grabbing it back from her.) Prayer is leaving things with God.

Do you have any prayer laundry that needs handing over to God?

Dear God, I've really got a lot on my mind these days. It's bothering me. Please show me what to do. In the meantime, I'm handing it off to you. Thank you that I can trust in you. Amen.

NOTHING TOO SMALL

*Dear friends, if God loved us in this way,
we also must love one another.*
1 JOHN 4:11 HCSB

Thirteen-year-old Briana was sitting on her bed when her brother walked in. "Hey, Briana, look at my new Lego man," said five-year-old Brandon. "He's Luke Skywalker and he just landed from a different galaxy."

"Uh yeah. That's nice, Brandon," said Briana without looking up.

"Look, Bri. He's got a cape. See," her brother said, sticking Luke in front of her phone.

"Stop it, Brandon. I'm busy. Can't you see?"

God loves you and cares about each detail of your life. That's true for you and for those around you—your little brother or sister or little cousin or the neighbor boy who is *always* ringing the doorbell and asking to play. God cares about them; shouldn't you?

Little kids need to be shown love in a certain way. Love to a little kid means listening, even if you've heard the same thing a million times; looking, even if you see something else more interesting; being interested, even if you don't feel like it; or spending time with them, even if you'd rather be doing something else.

That's how Jesus loves. When you're with younger kids, what do you do to let them know they matter?

Dear Lord, thanks for giving me an example of what loving little kids looks like. Show me creative ways to show them they matter. Amen.

SECRETS

Would not God find this out?
For He knows the secrets of the heart.
PSALM 44:21 NASB

Do you know how to keep a secret?

You know that Michael, your next-door neighbor, likes your cousin Stacey. But it's a secret. You know that your mom hides a bag of chocolates behind the peanut butter in the cupboard. But it's a secret. (And you aren't supposed to know.) You know there's a surprise birthday party for your grandma. But it's a secret. Those secrets are easy to keep. But is there any secret you shouldn't keep?

You know that Lacey cheated on her English test. But it's a secret. You know that Susan told her mom she's going to the library but she's really going to a friend's. But it's a secret. So what do you do? After all, you don't want to be a snitch.

One thing you can do is talk to that person and encourage them to share their secret. If keeping a secret means someone might get hurt in any way, find an adult you can trust and let them know. Doing that might keep that person from getting hurt. If keeping a secret means helping someone do something wrong, then keeping that secret is hurting, not helping, them.

Be wise with your secrets!

Dear God, I want to be a loyal friend who my friends can trust. But I don't want to help them do what's wrong. Help me be wise with my secrets. Amen.

HE GETS IT

How can you say the LORD does not see your troubles?
The LORD is the everlasting God, the Creator of all the earth.
He never grows weak or weary. No one can measure the
depths of his understanding.
ISAIAH 40:27-28 NLT

I just wish someone would understand! Olivia thought. *I'm trying my best but this homework is just too hard!*

Frustrated. Helpless. Discouraged. Feelings like these can tumble around inside you when someone doesn't understand how you feel. When people step out of their world to understand something from our point of view, we feel affirmed. They're taking us seriously. Instead of dismissing our feelings, they're saying, "I get it. What you're feeling is real."

God says, "I get it. I see where you're coming from. What you're feeling is real." The Bible says no one can even measure God's understanding. It is limitless!

At the same time, God turns you around to look, not at that pile of homework sitting on your desk, but at him. It's like he says, "What you're going through is tough. But look at me. Ask me for help. I'm God, and look"—he gestures to the big world around him—"at what I can do!"

God created the whole world. If anyone understands, he does. If anyone can help, he can.

Dear God, you understand me even when I can't express myself. There's no limit to your understanding! Please help me. Help me realize how big and awesome you are. Amen.

KNITTING

I am certain that God, who began the good work within you,
will continue his work until it is finally finished on the day
when Christ Jesus returns.

PHILIPPIANS 1:6 NLT

Click. Click.

"Hey, Ella. Whatcha doing?"

"Knitting a scarf for my fundraiser."

"A scarf?" said Harper looking at the small blue knit circle. "That doesn't look like a scarf. It looks more like a, well, like a coaster."

"Well, I'm not done yet. It'll be a scarf when I'm finished."

God isn't making a knit scarf, but he is making those who believe in Jesus into something beautiful. God has started a good work in you. You're not finished, but you're on the way. He's doesn't constantly compare you to perfection or point out your failures, and neither should you. He's still working to make you more and more like him.

What's true for you is true for others—God's not done with them yet. They're a work in progress. So while you may be tempted to complain or compare or criticize, don't. Encourage, believe in them, and pray for them instead. God is doing a good work—in them and in you!

Dear God, thank you for loving me the way I am and at the same time working to make me like you. Fill me with hope that you're doing a good work in me and others. Amen.

LOOKING BEHIND

I know your deeds, your love and faith,
your service and perseverance,
and that you are now doing more than you did at first.
REVELATION 2:19 NIV

"Paddle harder, Madison!" her dad called above the wind and rain. Madison plunged her paddle into the water and pulled back hard. In the canoe next to her, Madison saw her brothers do the same. *Plunge, pull, and out.* Repeat. *Plunge, pull, and out.*

Their campsite was all the way across the mile-long lake. Even though they'd been paddling for half an hour, the opposite shore seemed far away. That was when Madison looked back and saw how far they'd actually come. All this hard paddling *was* paying off.

Working toward a goal is great. But when that goal is still a long ways off, looking back can be encouraging. It shows you how far you've come. Maybe you're science grade isn't up to an A, but you got an A on the last quiz. Maybe you can't do a cartwheel on the beam, but remember when you struggled to learn the split jump? Maybe you can't reach high E on your horn, but remember when you didn't know a quarter note from a half note? Look how far you've come!

On your way to moving forward, take a break and look back. See how far you've come!

Dear God, thanks for progress. On my way toward my goals, remind me to look back and appreciate how far I've come. Amen.

NO LIMITATIONS

With God's power working in us, God can do much,
much more than anything we can ask or imagine.
EPHESIANS 3:21 NCV

Josiah looks like any other boy. He's got a big smile, curly brown hair, and wears glasses. But Josiah can't talk and can't play like other children. That's because Josiah has severe autism.

God saw Josiah's limitations. But since he is God, he decided those limitations weren't an obstacle. They wouldn't stand in the way of God using Josiah to tell others about him. So God talks to Josiah, and Josiah listens. Then Josiah uses his iPad to communicate to other people and tell them what's on God's heart.

Sometimes we think that what we can't do limits God. But it doesn't. He's God. With a willing and quick-to-listen heart, God can use anyone, anywhere, anytime to do anything. And that includes you.

Have you ever asked God how he wants to use you?

Dear God, there's nothing you can't do! You aren't limited by anything. Stretch my imagination to see what your power can do in and through me. Amen.

CHECK IT OUT: You can read Josiah's amazing true story in the book, *Josiah's Fire.*

PRAISE!

I will praise the LORD at all times;
his praise is always on my lips.
My whole being praises the LORD.
PSALM 34:1-2 NCV

"Can I have everyone's attention please?" Mrs. Dahlen said. "After this last assignment, I came across the perfect essay. Giovanna, you gave us an example of strong writing," she said glancing at Giovanna in the second row. "Your introduction and colorful choice of words immediately catches the reader's attention. Your…"

With every word the teacher spoke, Giovanna's heart soared. Her smile got wider and her heart swelled with pride.

Is there anyone who doesn't like it when people say good things about them? God isn't any different. He's strong, he's perfect, he shows mercy, and he's loving! (Just to name a few things.)

When we praise God—with our words, with our singing, with our gifts, with our offering—we lift him up. No matter how much we praise him it never comes close to lifting him high enough—but he sure likes it when we try.

Dear God, I appreciate so many things about you. With everything that I am, I praise you! Amen.

KNOW FOR YOURSELF

*It was your own eyes that saw all these great things
the Lord has done.*

DEUTERONOMY 11:7 NIV

The event was just a few weeks away and Anna still didn't have a dress. Not that she didn't want a new dress; her family just couldn't afford one.

"Dear Lord," Anna prayed. "I'd really like a new dress. And please make it blue."

A week later Anna's aunt called. "My neighbor has a daughter your age. She's had a dress sitting in her closet for several months and decided she doesn't want it. It's new; the tags are still on it. Would you like to come over and take a look?"

When Anna walked into her aunt's kitchen that afternoon, she saw a pale blue dress draped over the table. Anna knew without even trying it on that the dress would fit. *Thank you, God,* she whispered.

We read in the Bible about the miracles God did. People like Moses and Esther and Hannah prayed, and God answered their prayers in amazing ways. Sometimes you want to know for yourself that God is great. Experiencing things up close and seeing with your own eyes can encourage and make your faith strong. Be honest with the Lord and ask him to show you that he is God.

Dear God, you're the same God that many of the Bible heroes prayed to long ago. Thank you that you still hear, you still answer prayer, and you still do miracles too. Amen.

STYLE WITH A SMILE

Happiness makes a person smile.
PROVERBS 15:13 NCV

"Grace!" Grace's mom called from down the stairs. "Are you dressed yet? We're leaving for the wedding in ten minutes."

Grace looked at herself in the mirror. Party dress. *Check.* Matching shoes. *Check.* Matching purse. *Check.* Hair styled. *Check.*

"Coming, Mom!" Grace spun around, looked again in the mirror and put on the finishing touch—a big smile.

Whether you're in a swimsuit at the beach or suited up in your hockey gear, a smile is the finishing touch on whatever you put on. A smile makes you look good and feel good. It makes those around you feel good too. Wouldn't you rather hang out with someone smiling than someone who's always frowning?

A smile starts when you choose joy. That doesn't mean nothing bad ever happens or that you never feel sad. You look for the good things God gives. When you do, it'll show on your face!

Dear God, thank you for your joy that bubbles up inside me. Just thinking about all you do puts a smile on my face. Amen.

A WORLD OF POSSIBILITIES

Then he told them, "Go into all the world and preach the Good News to everyone."
MARK 16:15 NLT

Carol grew up with her nose in a book. She read books about people and places and ideas. She read poems and novels and biographies. She even read the Bible from cover and cover. When she grew up, Carol decided she wanted to tell people about God—through books! She studied hard and worked harder to write interesting stories that would tell kids about God.

When we think of sharing the good news about the life that God gives, we usually think of pastors or preachers or people who travel overseas. In reality, there are as many different ways to do that as there are different people, including becoming a teacher or an author or a businessman or a singer or a coach. We can tell people about God in a conversation, through a letter or song, or on a website. The possibilities are limitless!

Here are some ideas for sharing the good news about Jesus:

- Become a pen pal with someone from a different country (write).
- Pack an Operation Christmas Child box for a child overseas and tuck a verse inside (give).
- Volunteer at a local soup kitchen and pray for those you serve (serve).
- Start a blog and post creative stories about how God is using real kids today (create).

Dear God, I want to share the good news of Jesus and what he's done in my life. Show me what I can do best. Amen.

CHOOSING JOY

I will give you hidden treasures,
riches stored in secret places,
so that you may know that I am the LORD,
the God of Israel, who summons you by name.

ISAIAH 45:3 NIV

Elsa's grandmother was folding clothes in her laundry one day. When she finished, she bent down to pick up the full basket of folded laundry. When she stood up, her head jammed into the corner of a cupboard. It hurt a lot. Then it hurt even more.

Ten years later Elsa's grandma's head still hurts. Every day. All night. No one has ever been able to figure out how to make it better. But Elsa's grandma chooses joy! She knows that Jesus is her friend and that he loves her a lot.

When bad things happen you can say, "Well, this stinks. This is awful. This doesn't make me happy." Or you can let God uncover sweet treasures of joy in the middle of hard times.

Even in dark times, God walks beside you. You can choose joy and no one can steal it away.

Dear God, I want to choose joy. I know you see me and I know you call me by my name. I am yours; I am loved. Amen.

SOUR MILK

Do everything without complaining and arguing, so that no one can criticize you. Live clean, innocent lives as children of God, shining like bright lights.
PHILIPPIANS 2:14-15 NLT

Brooklyn threw open the doors of the fridge. Where was the milk? There! She grabbed the gallon of milk and splashed it on her bowl of cereal. *Crunch, munch—yuk!* Brooklyn ran for the sink and spit out a mouthful of sour milk.

Rotten. Sour. Bad. Whatever you want to call it, that's what complaining is. Nasty stuff that you might just want to spit out of your mouth. It doesn't change anything. It doesn't make you feel better. And it's not particularly fun to hear.

Complaining doesn't belong in your mouth because you're a child of God, shining like a bright light for all to see. He takes care of you. He loves you. He gives you many good things. Give people an earful of thanks-filled, kindness-filled, honest-filled words.

Dear God, you are so good and I don't want to complain like you're not and make you look bad. You do take care of me. Thanks for all I have and get to do. Amen.

BAND PRACTICE

*How good and pleasant it is
when God's people live together in unity!*
PSALM 133:1 NIV

"Attention! Let's run through the song one more time. Percussion, pick up the tempo. Woodwinds and brass, when you come in on the fourth measure be sure you come in strong."

Five other schools were coming for the marching band competition the next day. Even though she wouldn't admit it to her friends who thought she should have joined the dance team instead, Rosa was pumped. When she played the trumpet, it sounded pretty good (at least that's what Mr. Reetz, the band director, said.) When you added the other brass instruments, the percussion, and woodwinds, everything sounded amazing. Rosa loved being a part of something big.

Each person who belongs to the family of God is part of something bigger than just themselves. We can do together what we never could do alone.

- We can influence a classroom.
- We can impact a community.
- We can pray for a country.
- We can change the world!

Dear God, thanks for the great big family I belong to—your family. I pray we'd love each other and work together. Protect us from the things that divide. Amen.

WHAT IT WILL BE LIKE

Before me was a great multitude that no one could count, from every nation, tribe, people and language, standing before the throne and before the Lamb....And they cried out in a loud voice: "Salvation belongs to our God."

REVELATION 7:9-10 NIV

If you saw Delaney and Janella together, you'd never think they were sisters. Delaney has wavy brown hair and skin the color of white chocolate. Janella has a smile as bright as a full moon and skin the color of a midnight sky. Delaney was born in America. Janella was born in Uganda. Because of adoption though they are sisters in every way possible.

Delaney and Janella's family looks a lot like the big family we'll see in heaven. Because of Jesus, God has adopted people from every country, tribe, and language. Heaven's streets will be filled with different people who are all part of the same family—God's family!

People who love and follow God live all over the world. They don't look like you. They might not speak the same language you do or have the same traditions. But you're family. What makes you family is who you belong to—God. And God's family sticks together.

Dear God, remind me to pray for the brothers and sisters in my great big God family. I pray that we'd stick up for each other, love each other, and pray for each other. Amen.

COUNT ME IN!

She is clothed with strength and dignity.
PROVERBS 31:25 NLT

On their way home from school, Cayla and Skylar spotted a new, designer handbag left alone on the public bus bench.

"Look! Someone must have forgotten their purse!" Cayla exclaimed. "It's beautiful."

Skylar said, "It must have cost a fortune! What are we going to do?"

Sometimes it's hard to have the courage or confidence to do the right thing.

One woman in the Bible wasn't short on courage or confidence. Deborah was called the mother of Israel. She led the nation and wasn't afraid to stand up to those who were doing wrong. When she succeeded, she turned to everyone else and said, "Why did you sit around wondering what to do? Why did you take so much time trying to decide whether to help me or not?" (See Judges 5.)

What's your reaction when someone asks for help standing up against what's wrong?

- I'm not sure.
- Let me think about it.
- Sorry, that's not my thing.
- Count me in!

Dear God, I don't want to be ashamed, timid, or unsure of what to do. Fill me with confidence, strength, and the boldness that comes from you. Amen.

THE GOAL OF GOLD

The lazy will not get what they want,
but those who work hard will.

PROVERBS 13:4 NCV

Allyson's nickname was Chicken Legs. She had long skinny legs that never seemed to end. In her freshman year, Allyson decided she wanted to try out for track. She worked hard and when she was eighteen years old, Allyson competed in her first Olympics. She won a silver medal. She worked even harder and eight years later won her first Olympic gold medal.

We all have dreams. Many times what we want comes as gift. Most of the time though, those dreams don't just happen. They're paired with a lot of hard work. Many times the difference between those who succeed and those who don't is just hard work.

Some people want to be good at Spanish but don't feel like doing the homework. Some want to make the track team but don't bother exercising. Others want to write a book when they grow up but don't want to excel in English.

Instead of dreading the work, think of how sweet it'll be to reach your goal. The reward will be worth all the work!

Dear God, instead of feeling discouraged or lazy, help me to focus on my goal. Teach me to work hard, stick with it, and remember the reward. Amen.

A GOOD KIND OF STUBBORN

Where you go, I will go. Where you live, I will live.
Your people will be my people,
and your God will be my God.
RUTH 1:16 NCV

If anyone had a reason to give up it was Ruth. She got married and her husband died. Then her brother-in-law died. Her mother-in-law, who she lived with, was always complaining. Talk about depressing. You can understand why Ruth would just want to give up and leave.

But Ruth was stubbornly strong. When Naomi said, "I'm leaving town," Ruth went along with her. Ruth said, "I'll go where you go and live where you live." What drove her to do that was a fierce belief in God. God gave her an incredible reward later on.

Have you ever felt like you want to throw up your hands, walk out the door, and forget about whatever is staring you in the face? Like, why bother?

Don't give up. Have faith in God that things will turn around, and be stubbornly strong!

Dear Lord, you are my God and nothing is going to change that. You are my help. Please help me. Put a deep determination inside me to face this problem that seems giant-tall. Amen.

EYES WIDE OPEN

Praise the LORD, everything he has created,
everything in all his kingdom.
Let all that I am praise the LORD.
PSALM 103:22 NLT

Sheila hopped on her bike and headed down the gravel road away from her house. She was in a hurry to meet up with Bailey at the park just a mile away. But then she started to notice…

A long skinny cloud that looked like it was lined with purple cotton.

A squirrel bouncing across an oak branch, his bushy tail waving behind him.

Ducks bottoming up in the pond.

The way the sun's rays glittered on the pond.

The huge grasshopper that jumped out of the way of her bike.

Little things she'd never noticed before.

Sometimes it's the little things that make us smile. We can miss them if we're in a hurry to do "important" things. We can skip over them if we're too wrapped up in the school-sports-church-home again routine.

What are the little things that you might be missing? Look around you and ask God to open your eyes to his wonder.

God, open my eyes to the little but amazing things you do all around me—the creatures you make and the little miracles of life, like just waking up every day. Amen.

ONE-OF-A-KIND DESIGN

*We were chosen so that we would
bring praise to God's glory.*
EPHESIANS 1:12 NCV

"I just can't sleep!" Brittany sat up in her sleeping bag. "Of course it probably has something to do with this," she said, and held up a book she'd been using as a pillow.

Brittany and her family were camping in Colorado, and she'd forgotten her travel size pillow at home. Her solution? In the last hour she'd tried a sweatshirt, a book, and another sleeping bag. But they were too bumpy or big or hard. None of them were meant to be pillows.

You're a one-of-a-kind design who was meant to give God glory. You were made to live for him. When you glorify God in what you do, what you think, and what you say, you're at your best. Anything else will seem slightly off.

Dear God, when I do things your way it's for your glory, but it also works out for my good. Instead of fighting you and resisting what you say, teach me to listen and walk with you every day. Amen.

284

BREAKDOWN OR BUILDUP?

An honest answer is like a kiss of friendship.
PROVERBS 24:26 NLT

On the Outer Banks of North Carolina stands a beautiful black-and-white candy cane stripe lighthouse that's over 120 years old. In the 1990s, people thought storms might make the lighthouse collapse. The ocean surf had pounded against the beach for many years and worn away the sand around the lighthouse. In order to save the lighthouse from the eroding beach, a team of people moved the lighthouse 3,000 feet inland to keep it safe.

The lighthouse is a little like the relationships you have with friends and family. Truth makes those relationships stand strong. Dishonesty erodes trust and breaks it down; truth builds it up.

When someone doesn't tell the truth—even once—how can you tell if they won't be dishonest again? If someone always tells the truth, you count on them. If someone gives you their word and keeps it, your confidence in them grows.

That's the kind of person you can trust to keep a secret, follow through on a promise, and do what's fair. When truth grows, trust grows. When trust grows, friendship does too.

Are you the kind of person other people can trust? If not, what would build that trust back up?

Dear God, help me build friendships on honesty and trust. I want relationships that are strong! Amen.

HIDDEN LOVE

*Better is open rebuke
than hidden love.*
PROVERBS 27:5 NIV

There aren't many things more important than friendship. Good friends are loyal, kind, trustworthy, and fun to be with. They accept you like you are. They like you on your good days and on your bad days.

Friends laugh together and hang out together. They help each other when the other is down. But true friends, ones who trust each other, can also be honest with each other.

Loving somebody isn't always about telling them what they want to hear. And loving somebody means listening to what a friend has to say, even if hearing it isn't easy.

Real friends build each other up by being open and honest.

Dear God, please give me friends that I can be open and honest with. Help me be the kind of person others can be open and honest with too. Amen.

MEMBERSHIP PRIVILEGES

Don't let anyone look down on you because you are young,
but set an example for the believers in…purity.
1 TIMOTHY 4:12 NIV

Membership has its privileges. If your family belongs to a fitness club, you've got access to a basketball court, a workout gym, a swimming pool, tennis courts, fitness classes, and maybe even a restaurant or a hair salon.

Being a Christian has its privileges too. God gives us many amazing privileges and gifts to enjoy at the right time. But we have to be patient and trust that waiting for God's timing is best.

Don't let anyone make you feel like you're not as important as they are just because you don't do everything they do. You're being smart by setting an example of purity! Being obedient to God and waiting for his timing is something you won't ever regret.

Dear God, I want to set an example in purity. Please help me be patient while I wait for your timing. Amen.

OCTOBER

May the favor of the Lord
our God rest on us;
establish the work of our hands for us—
yes, establish the work of our hands.

PSALM 90:17 NIV

PRETTY PACKAGES

Dear brothers and sisters, when troubles of any kind come your way, consider it an opportunity for great joy. For you know that when your faith is tested, your endurance has a chance to grow.

JAMES 1:2-3 NLT

Most gifts come packed in tissue, wrapped up in brightly colored paper, and topped with a bow or ribbon wrapped around the box.

When it comes to opportunities, though, that's not always the case. Sometimes the best gifts come wrapped up in trouble. Seriously.

- That toilet you're supposed to clean Saturday morning? It's a chance to serve.
- That science homework assignment you've been putting off? It's a chance to learn something new.
- The new church your family started going to? It's a chance to make new friends.
- The money you need to raise for the youth retreat? It's a chance to trust God.

Thinking "possibility" instead of "problem" transforms trouble into opportunity—and a chance for joy.

Is it easy or hard for you to see opportunity in every day things?

Dear God, help me to see the possibility inside what looks like a problem. And give me your joy. Amen.

A GOOD NIGHT'S SLEEP

In peace I will lie down and sleep,
for you alone, LORD, make me dwell in safety.
PSALM 4:8 NIV

It's been a looong day! Up early for breakfast, off to school for six to seven hours of class, a piano lesson, and a quick dinner followed by cheerleading Picture Day. After that it's a shower and homework, and well, it's really been a long day! *Stre-e-e-e-tch.*

After you pull on your PJs and slip under the covers and before you close your eyes and drift off to sleep, take a minute to remember that the Lord watches over you and your family.

When you close your eyes, you can sleep in peace. Even when you sleep, God stays awake. He never gets sleepy; he's never distracted. He's always watching over you.

Dear God, thanks for my day. Thank you that wherever I am and wherever I go, you're always watching over me. Even when I'm sleeping, you're awake and alert. Amen.

THE DEEP, DEEP BLUE

Once again you will have compassion on us.
You will trample our sins under your feet
and throw them into the depths of the ocean!
MICAH 7:19 NLT

If you poured out all the water from Lake Superior, it would cover North and South America. It's the largest fresh water lake in surface area in the world and has more water in it than all the other Great Lakes combined. At roughly 1400 feet, it's deeper than the Empire State building is high. We're talking deep!

Hundreds of shipwrecks have happened on Lake Superior, but because the lake is so deep, those wrecks will stay buried under the icy cold waves forever.

When you do something that makes God sad—slam the door, disrespect your dad, cheat on a test—and confess it and forsake it, God forgives you. Then it's like he throws your sins into the ocean. They sink down, down, down into the blue never to be seen again. No one is going to haul them up. They're gone. Out of his sight. Out of his mind. Big ocean, big God, and really big forgiveness. Isn't God amazing?!

Dear God, the deep, deep sea of your forgiveness is bigger than the ocean. Thanks for forgiving me. Amen.

PLEASING GOD

Live as children of light...
and find out what pleases the Lord.
EPHESIANS 5:8-10 NIV

Of all the teachers you've had, who was your favorite and why? That's the kind of teacher you'll do anything for, the kind of teacher you want to please, love to help, and want to work hard for.

When you like someone, making that person happy doesn't feel like work—it comes naturally. It's like searching for the perfect gift for a friend or helping your dad rake the lawn because you like hanging out with him. It's not a have-to; it's a get-to.

When you love someone, you also want to make that person proud. The same is true with God. "Find out what pleases the Lord"—because you get to. Because you love God and want to make him proud. Instead of thinking about what he asks as a list of to dos, you're looking to make God smile. There's a world of difference!

Dear God, I want what I do to come from a get-to not a have-to heart. Show me what pleases you, Lord, so I can make you smile. Amen.

RESET

Do not be fooled: "Bad friends will ruin good habits."
1 CORINTHIANS 15:33 NCV

The three friends were sitting around the lunch table talking about Mrs. French, who happened to be the Spanish teacher.

"Don't you think her eyes look a little close together?" asked Taisha.

"Kind of," said Amanda as she took a bite of chicken pasta. "The one who really has weird eyes is Tory. They're crossed or something. I can never tell which one to look at."

"Well, I don't think it's very nice to talk about someone's eyes like that. Even if they are crossed," Jailee piped in.

"Lighten up, Jailee," said Taisha. "It's not like she heard us or anything."

Still, Jailee felt uncomfortable. Her friends were always pointing out everyone's defects.

The people we hang out with have a huge influence on us. The more we're with them, the more like them we become—whether we plan for that to happen or not. If what friends are doing makes us feel uncomfortable, it may be time to hit reset and slowly pull away.

When you choose close friends, choose those who will encourage your values and your relationship with God.

Dear God, thank you for my friends. If any of them are starting to be a negative influence on me, give me wisdom to know what to do. Amen.

BUILDING EACH OTHER UP

Encourage one another and build each other up.
1 THESSALONIANS 5:11 NIV

What do you do if you've got a friend who is always putting herself down? You like her (she is your friend, after all), and you wish she'd realize how much she's got going for her—or at least realize how awesome you think she is.

Let's say she's always pointing out how uncoordinated she is. "I'm such a clutz!" she says. How do you encourage her?

Don't bother contradicting her. Instead, be honest and remind her of the truth. Tell her what she is instead of what she isn't. You can say, "Maybe you're not an athlete. So what? You're kind and funny, and I like you."

What you say can take her one step closer to feeling encouraged and built up. And isn't that what friendships are for?

Dear God, show me ways that I can build my friends up when they're feeling discouraged or down. Amen.

DEAR DIARY

I remember what the LORD did;
I remember the miracles you did long ago.
I think about all the things you did
and consider your deeds.
PSALM 77:11-12 NCV

Dear Diary,

The most amazing thing happened to me today! I sat behind Josh in school. He dropped his pencil and reached down to get it. When he sat back up, he looked at me—and smiled! He looked so cute in his black sweatshirt. I almost died! (*gasp*) Then my friend Mia stopped me in the hall after class. She was all bubbly and happy and I couldn't figure out why. Guess what? She wants to follow Jesus! I could burst. I've prayed for her every day for, well, forever. And now this. Two awesome things in one day.

Having a happy day,
Alexa

Journaling helps us express our feelings, whether they're happy or sad. The cool thing about journaling is it can help us remember. When a week goes by and Alexa's feeling discouraged, she can flip back to this diary entry and remember the good thing that God did.

When you're feeling down, sometimes what helps is to remember. Remember who God is. Remember what God has done. And journaling goes a long way toward doing that.

Dear God, remind me of all the times you've answered my prayers. You are so good. I can't help but think of your amazing power. Amen.

PRICKLY PEOPLE

"Love your enemies. Pray for those who hurt you.
Then you will be children of your Father who is in heaven."
MATTHEW 5:44-45 NIRV

Thistles are tall prickly weeds topped with a bright purple flower. Just touching them or stepping on them hurts.

People can be like thistles—prickly, crabby, and mean. Their bad mood spreads gloom all around. They're hard to get close to, and being around them can hurt.

Underneath that prickly surface is a person that God genuinely loves. He understands why they seem crabby and say what they do. He's not intimidated by how they come across and you don't need to be intimidated either. Remember, he cares for them just like he cares for you!

Do you know someone who seems prickly? What would happen if you prayed for them for a month and then took the chance of reaching out?

Dear God, instead of avoiding or reacting in anger to the prickly people around me, remind me to love and pray for them. Amen.

APPLE PICKING

Do you have the gift of prophecy? Then use it according to the faith you have. If your gift is serving, then serve. If it is teaching, then teach. Is it encouraging others? Then encourage them. Is it giving to others? Then give freely. Is it being a leader? Then work hard at it. Is it showing mercy? Then do it cheerfully.

ROMANS 12:6-8 NIRV

Every fall Adeline, her friends, and their families went apple picking. Adeline's favorite apple was a Fireside apple. They made the absolute *best* after-school snack. Her friend, Jocelyn, liked picking sweet Honeygold apples and dipping the slices in caramel sauce. Jacinda and her family picked McIntosh apples. Her mom was always making homemade apple crisp. Each different apple was used for different things.

God gave each person different gifts. One gift isn't better than the other; they're just used for different things. A giver helps people in need. A leader gives people direction. An encourager gives those who are down a boost.

Not any one person has every gift. We need each other. Together we build each other up. Whatever your gift is, use it and excel at it!

Dear God, show me what gift you've given me and how to use it well. Remind me that it's not for me but to help others. Amen.

DIY PROJECT

I want to do the things that are good,
but I do not do them. I do not do the good things
I want to do, but I do the bad things I do not want to do.
ROMANS 7:18-19 NCV

DIY picture frames, hair ribbons, bracelets, crafts, and even room décor. They're fun to do, you can do them with friends, and they save a lot of money! Plus, they let you be creative and invent something that's uniquely you.

When it comes to our own lives, though, "Do it yourself" projects just don't work. We can't make ourselves a DIY project.

You want to be patient but say something nasty to your brother. You want to keep from losing your temper, but that last taunt makes you pummel your ex-friend instead. You know you shouldn't gossip but the story about how Jason dumped Cassidy is just too good not to talk about.

It's like this tug-of-war going on inside. You want to do what's right but end up doing what's wrong! You can't *Do It Yourself.*

Romans 8:1-2 offers an answer. The little individual sins aren't the full problem; it's the big sin—selfishness—that has to go. And there's only one person who can change you—Jesus!

Dear Jesus, I want a complete change. Please take away my selfishness and make me new. Amen.

NEVER ASHAMED

Never be ashamed to tell others about our Lord.
2 TIMOTHY 1:8 NLT

Having amazing news and keeping it to yourself is like trying to put out fireworks. You can't be quiet or it will explode! Then when you share your great news, you want everyone to be excited and think it's great too, right? To jump up and down and say, "That's awesome! I'm so happy for you!"

Unfortunately, that's not what happened when Jesus healed a blind man. The former blind man was so excited he started to tell friends, neighbors, and strangers on the street who'd seen him begging every day.

Some believed Jesus had healed him, but many did not. Others were jealous Jesus was getting so much credit. But the former blind man didn't back down. He kept telling them that the one who had healed him was from God.

When you share the good news about the life that Jesus gives, people might listen. But they might not. They might believe what you say. Or they might make fun of you or ignore you. Be like the man Jesus healed and don't back down. The truth you're telling them is real.

Dear God, help me not to back down, give up, or even get discouraged when people don't listen to me when I tell them about you. Give me the courage to tell the truth. Amen.

CHECK IT OUT: Read the whole story in John 9:7-38.

BARREL RACING

I will hurry, without delay, to obey your commands.
PSALM 119:60 NLT

Marta sat on top of her quarter horse and zeroed in on the three barrels in the middle of the arena. *Okay, Diamond. We can do this.* She clucked her tongue and Diamond flew into the arena, heading for the first barrel. With a gentle pressing of the reins, Diamond rounded the barrel tightly and accelerated to the next challenge. Marta's prompts combined with Diamond's quick responses got them around all three barrels in record time.

In barrel racing as in life with God, precision is important. Following his instructions without delay will make your life powerful and effective.

If God gently reminds you to apologize for a sarcastic remark you made, do it right away. If God encourages you to help at church, talk to someone about it. Don't put it off. Train yourself to listen to God's prompts and respond right away. The result? Success and a whole lot of joy.

Have you ever felt prompted to do something? Did you follow through? What happened?

Dear Lord, I know I drag my feet sometimes. Teach me, and remind me, to be quick to listen and obey. Amen.

A UNIQUE WHISTLE

"They follow him because they know his voice. But they will never follow a stranger. They will run away from him because they don't know his voice."

JOHN 10:4-5 NCV

Who am I?
I'm excellent at solving problems.
I'm known for my acrobatics
I like to hang out in a pod.
I'm the smallest member of the whale family.

If you guessed a dolphin, you're right. Dolphins talk through clicks, whistles, and squeals. Grown dolphins have a unique whistle. A mother dolphin begins using that whistle more and more when a baby calf is born. By learning to recognize the mother's whistle, the baby calf can find its way back if it's been separated from the pod.

From the time you were born, you learned to recognize your parents' voices. Learning to recognize God's voice is just as important. You've got to know the difference between what's true and what's not.

Practice listening. Run from voices that don't belong to God. Follow the voice that is really his.

Dear Lord, I know it takes practice and a lot of listening to really learn to hear your voice. Teach me to hear your voice. Amen.

THE NO GOOD, VERY BAD DAY

*When Job's three friends...heard about all the troubles
that had come upon him, they set out from their homes....
Then they sat on the ground with him for seven days and
seven nights. No one said a word to him, because they
saw how great his suffering was.*

JOB 2:11, 13 NIV

If there was anyone who could say they had a terrible,
horrible, no good, very bad day it was Job. In a single day,
Job lost everything—his cattle, sheep, donkey, camels, and
servants.

A servant who had survived delivered the final blow late
in the day. "A windstorm blew through the desert. The house
where your family was staying collapsed. All your children have
died."

What can you possibly say to someone in so much grief?
Job's friends started out by getting it right. Read the verse
above. What did they say to him?

Absolutely nothing. Sometimes the best thing to say is
nothing. Just being there for your friend is enough. Anyone
can rattle off a bunch of meaningless words. Instead, be strong
by coming alongside them and being silent.

**Dear God, sometimes I think words will make things better, and I
stress out about what to say. Remind me that it's okay just to be
there and to be quiet. Amen.**

SHOW OFF

Don't brag about tomorrow,
since you don't know what the day will bring.
PROVERBS 27:1 NLT

"What is your family doing for summer vacation? "Rosa asked.

"We're going to the beach! We get to go snorkeling and swimming," gushed Fatima. "It'll be the best vacation ever!"

"Well, we will be going to the beach and swimming with the dolphins," bragged Maria. "And we'll go out to eat every night because we can, you know, since my dad is such a VIP. That means very important person."

Rosa rolled her eyes and Fatima just looked hurt.

When people are excited, talking comes naturally. They just want to share with everyone. Looking forward to something is exciting! Bragging, though, is different. When people brag, they aren't taking others into consideration. People might feel left out or hurt by the competition that bragging creates.

You may feel frustrated if you've been around someone who brags. Whether that person intends it or not, they can come across like they're better than you are. Even though what they're doing isn't right, look beyond their bragging and choose to be happy, without feeling competitive or jealous.

Dear God, it's hard for me to be around people who brag. I pray that they'd know you love them and they don't have to show off to be important. They're special because you created them that way. Amen.

STARTING SMALL

Do not despise these small beginnings,
for the LORD rejoices to see the work begin.
ZECHARIAH 4:10 NLT

Regan really wanted to teach Sunday school to the preschoolers. All Mrs. Martin seemed to think Regan was good for was handing out glue sticks, wiping noses, and tying shoes. Regan never got to read the story or show the kids how to make the craft: the things she was really excited to do. She felt discouraged and tempted to give up.

By the middle of the year, though, Mrs. Martin seemed to give more important jobs to Regan. By end of the year, Regan was helping with craft ideas and greeting the kids when they arrived. Regan was having fun and feeling useful. She was so glad she had stuck with it.

We all want to start out doing big things, important things. But big things start with little things. When you do the small things well, you earn the respect of others. They won't always give you more responsibility, but when someone comes along who does, you'll be ready. Pour yourself into what you've been given and give it your best!

Have you ever been in a situation where you felt you couldn't do as much as you were capable of?

Dear God, sometimes small things seem—well, kind of small and unimportant. Help me to remember to do my best at it all. Amen.

PAINTING PUMPKINS?

By faith Abraham, when called to go to a place he would later receive as his inheritance, obeyed and went, even though he did not know where he was going.

HEBREWS 11:8 NIV

"You want to *paint* pumpkins?" Alisha asked her brother. "But we always *carve* funny faces in our pumpkins."

"Yeah, I know, but I saw this picture of a painted pumpkin frog," said Micah. "It was funny! I thought maybe we could try something different this year."

Alisha wasn't convinced, but she decided she'd give it a try. Their dad took them shopping for paint and brushes. When they got home, the painting began. Alisha turned her pumpkin into a painted pink pig with Styrofoam ears. Micah made a Frankenstein pumpkin face with green and black paint and shiny screws for its neck.

"Great idea," said Alisha. "This was different, but fun!"

Different doesn't have to be bad. In fact, different can be good. Moses was a prince who grew up in a palace; yet, God chose him to live as a pioneer. Abraham had lived the city his whole life; yet, God sent him out on an adventure to find a new home.

The different things you face might not be as big as moving to a different home. Maybe it's a smaller adventure—like trying a new food or doing something you've never done before, like riding a horse. Whatever your different is, don't let it intimidate you. Think of it as a chance to discover something that will become a new favorite. Give it a try!

Dear God, I usually like what's familiar and comfortable, but give me the courage to try what's different. Thank you for being with me on big and small adventures. Amen.

WHEN EVERYTHING SEEMS TO FALL APART

*Each day the Lord pours his unfailing love upon me,
and through each night I sing his songs, praying to God
who gives me life.*
PSALM 42:8 NLT

Tricia had come home from school so excited. That weekend she was going to a pep rally, a homecoming football game, and then to a friend's. The weekend was going to be awesome! And it had been—until she found out her mom was leaving her dad.

Tricia was frustrated. She was angry. She was confused. *How could God let this happen?* she thought. *Doesn't he even care?*

When something difficult happens, it doesn't mean God doesn't care. Even if families separate, nothing can separate any of them from God's love. God isn't thrown off by the situation. He still has a plan and purpose for each person in that family. Absolutely nothing can change that.

If you know someone whose family is going through a tough time (or if *your* family is going through a hard time), encourage them to be open and honest with their mom or dad and ask them the questions on their mind. Encourage them to be honest with God about how they feel. He understands.

Dear God, thank you for caring for everyone in my family. Help me trust that your love never changes even when things seem to be falling apart. Amen.

WHAT YOU SEE

Lord, may these words of my mouth please you.
And may these thoughts of my heart please you also.
PSALM 19:14 NIRV

Have you ever torn the wrapping paper off a gift, seen the logo on the box inside, and felt your heart leap? You're so excited! You open the box and—*oh no!*—something completely different is inside. And your heart sinks.

Some people say all the right things. If you unwrapped their words, though, you'd find something completely different inside. They might say, "You look so cute!" while thinking, *Who taught her how to dress?*

Psalms says that your words should please God and your thoughts too. What's inside should line up with what's outside. Easier said than done, right?

Thinking I'm-so-thankful, how-can-I-help-her thoughts instead of Why-do-I-have-to-do-this, I-wish-she'd-get-lost thoughts takes practice. You have to constantly wrap your thoughts around God's Word.

What's a verse you could bring to mind when a not-so-good thought pops up?

Dear God, please help me line up my thoughts on the inside with who I am on the outside. I pray that they'd both line up with what pleases you. Amen.

GET UP AND DANCE

*Let them praise his name with dancing
and make music to him with timbrel and harp.*
PSALM 149:3 NIV

Trees that clap and mountains that sing and fields that burst out in joy. That's how the psalmist describes celebrating and praising the Lord.

He says…

sing,

praise,

worship,

make music with the harp (but a piano or guitar will do),

be happy,

dance.

Let that inside joy burst into an outward expression of praise! Why? Because the Lord is great and he's coming back. He'll make wrongs right, punish those who do wrong, and give those who love him special care.

So just get up and dance.

Dear God, I'd like to get up and dance. You are great! You are good! One generation after another praises you. I want to praise you too. Amen.

BEHIND THE BRAGGING

I always remember you in my prayers, asking the God of our Lord Jesus Christ, the glorious Father, to give you a spirit of wisdom and revelation so that you will know him better.
EPHESIANS 1:16-17 NCV

"What do you mean, 'Do I know what the answer to the math equation is?'" said Violet. "Of course I know. I'm the smartest girl in the class, aren't I?"

Emery didn't answer. Sure, Violet was the smartest in the class. But did she have to point out that Emery wasn't and make her feel like she'd asked a dumb question?

When people brag about what they know or what they get to do, they can make the rest of us feel pretty small. Like we're not as smart or lucky as they are. Feeling hurt can come easily when that happens.

Try to look behind the bragging. People do brag when they feel proud. But they also brag when they don't feel good about themselves. If they talk others down, they feel they can boost themselves up. If they knew God and understood that he and others really, truly loved them, maybe they wouldn't try to prove themselves or draw attention to themselves.

If you come across a person who's always bragging, pray for them. Pray that God would show them how much he loves them—through you!

Dear God, even if others try to make me feel small, remind me of your love. Then help me to see them through your eyes and love them too. Amen.

FACE FORWARD

The righteous keep moving forward,
and those with clean hands become stronger and stronger.
JOB 17:9 NLT

It would be hard to go through a day without facing forward. Walking to the bus stop. Stepping onto the bus. Practicing for volleyball. Pushing a shopping cart. Now, that would be interesting.

We were made to face forward (that's one reason why your nose, ears, mouth, and eyes are not on the back of your head)—and not just when it comes to texting a friend or sitting at the lunch table. But when it comes to life. You can't go back but you can decide to move forward.

- You wish you had taken piano lessons—but you didn't. That's okay; you can start now.
- You wish you had studied harder for the science test—but you didn't. That's okay; get a jump on studying for the next test.
- You wish you had signed up for volleyball—but you didn't. That's okay; you can choose to do something else.

You can't control what's behind. But you can embrace and step into new opportunities, make new friends, and try something else. The world's an endless place of possibilities!

Dear God, I don't want to live looking backwards at what I wish I would have done. Help me forget what's behind and face forward toward the possibilities you have ahead. Amen.

DREAMING BIG

*To him who is able to do immeasurably more than all we ask
or imagine, according to his power that is at work within us,
to him be glory...for ever and ever!*
EPHESIANS 3:20-21 NIV

If you could imagine a day filled with your favorite things,
people, and places, what would be on your list? Go ahead
dream, and dream big!

No matter how big your big is, God can top it. He can
dream bigger. He can dream better. Trying to describe or
measure his big will blow your mind. You can't squeeze it into
your brain.

God showed how big he thinks when he chose Abraham
who was married to Sarah. That couple became a family. That
family grew to a whole nation. But God still wanted bigger;
he still wanted better. He wanted the whole world—every
language, people, culture, country, tribe—to belong to him.
So he had a plan that would make that possible.

Through faith in Jesus *everyone*—people who speak
French and people who speak Thai, people from Kenya and
people from Iran, Native Americans and second generation
Americans—can be part of God's big family.

If you could imagine God doing amazing things in and
through you, what would you dream? Go ahead imagine, then
ask, and do it big!

**Dear God, when I think I'm dreaming big, I've just scratched the
surface of your imagination. Stretch my idea of big. Instead of
believing you for little things, help me know you more so I can
believe in your kind of big. Amen.**

311

SALAD BAR

Accept one another, then, just as Christ accepted you,
in order to bring praise to God.
ROMANS 15:7 NIV

Half the fun of going through a salad bar is getting to choose what you want. Lettuce? Yes. Spinach? Maybe. Black olives and garlicky croutons? Definitely.

Being a part of a family is a little different than eating at a salad bar. You can't decide who you do and don't want in it. And can you can't push aside the qualities or quirks that you don't like.

You love how your mom dresses to kill and always welcomes your friends. You don't like how she's such a neat freak. You love how your dad believes you can do anything. You wish he wouldn't brag about you in front of your friends. You love how generous your sister is. You wish she wouldn't be so generous with her advice!

With family, the hard parts, the easy parts, and the parts we don't understand all come together. You can't separate one from the other.

Make a list of the things you appreciate most about those in your family. Then thank God for those things.

Dear God, thanks for accepting me the way I am. Thanks for my family—just the way they are. Help me focus on what I appreciate about them. Amen.

THE WAY WE THINK AND LEARN

There are different kinds of gifts, but they are all from the same Spirit....And there are different ways that God works through people but the same God.

1 CORINTHIANS 12:4, 6 NCV

"We have to talk about our cookie sale on Saturday," Judy said. "We have to research the best cookies to bake and how much we'll charge."

"Forget research," said Joanna. "I say we get to baking."

"I have a great idea! Why don't we make cookie pops? Or ginormous cookies people could bid on!" said Ariel growing more and more excited.

When God pours his Spirit inside us, he gives us each gifts. The verses above are talking about gifts like teaching, preaching, and hospitality. But the way we learn and look at a situation can be a gift too.

- Some people show curiosity. They want to know why.
- Some people analyze. They like to think and plan.
- Some people are practical and want to get right down to it.
- Some people love to come up with ideas.

Of course no one way is right; they're just different ways of looking at a situation. How would you describe yourself? How about those in your family?

Dear God, I'm so glad you made us all different. Help me appreciate the way you pour different types of creativity inside each of us. Amen.

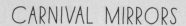

CARNIVAL MIRRORS

God created human beings in his image.
In the image of God he created them.
He created them male and female.

GENESIS 1:27 NCV

Ben looked at himself in the mirror. "Hey look! My arms shrunk down to little hands"

"And look at my nose! It's *huuuge*! And there are two of me." Sarah said.

Standing in front of the carnival mirrors made the real Ben and Sarah look weird, wacky, tiny, monstrous, and bizarre. In a funny sort of way.

When God created people he created them to look like him—not with their eyes or ears or noses—but by who they are inside—kind, loving, bold, and confident. But of course when sin came into the world, all that changed.

The faults you see in other people, and even in yourself, are a distortion of God's image. Through sin, our enemy, Satan, twists what God planned for good. He twists confidence into bragging or generosity into wastefulness.

Instead of complaining about people's weaknesses, pray that they'll reflect God's real image.

Dear God, I want to reflect who you really are. Amen.

ITTY BITTY KITTY

Gentle words are a tree of life.
PROVERBS 15:4 NLT

"I'm going to die; she's just so cute!" Adriah cupped her kitten, a birthday present from her mom, in her hand and stroked its tiny nose. "I'm going to call her Penny," she said.

"Can I have a turn?" asked her brother Charlie.

"Sure, but you have to be gentle. Careful or you'll hurt her."

When we're careful to speak gentle words, we show people we care about them. Speaking kind words to them says, "You matter to me." If we're not gentle with our words, we can hurt people.

If something you said came out harsher than you meant, or if something you said hurt someone's feelings (even if you didn't mean to), go to them and speak gentle words. Make sure that everything is all right.

Kind words bring a smile! Gentle words bring life!

Think back to a situation where someone didn't use gentle words. How would things have been different if they had?

Dear God, help me to be gentle with my words. Show me how to use my words to build people up and make them feel good. Amen.

IMAGINATION

God's voice thunders in marvelous ways;
he does great things beyond our understanding.
JOB 37:5 NIV

If you walk into any theatre and wait until the lights go down (after you've bought that supersize bag of popcorn, of course), you'll soon be lost in a world of imagination. The soundtrack and special effects, the script and characters, all come together to tell a story that stretches your imagination.

God uses words to stretch our imagination, to help us visualize what he's like. He's a master at painting pictures with words. So he said about himself...

He wraps himself up in light like a cloak and stretches out the heavens like a tent.

The clouds are his chariots, and he rides on the wings of the wind. His voice is in the thunder. He splashes lightning across the sky, and when he breathes icicles form (Psalm 104:2-3; Job 37).

What word pictures could you use to describe how amazing God is? Give it a try!

Dear God, thank you for your Word and your world around me. They help me understand a little of what you're like. No words can describe how amazing you are. You're beyond imagination! Amen.

HANDS AND FEET

When God's people are in need, be ready to help them.
ROMANS 12:13 NLT

One day Gail's dad came home from work. He said to Gail's mom, "I don't want to be a part of this family anymore." After a while, he left. Gail's mom's heart started to break (and of course Gail's heart hurt too). Sometimes it felt like the weight piled up on her heart would make it break.

But Gail's mom had a lot of friends. They gave her hugs. They brought her favorite meal over for dinner—chicken soup. They went on walks together and they encouraged her with verses (Psalm 23:1 was her favorite!) One pastor friend prayed with her every week. Every day someone called or came over to her house.

"Every day God wrapped me up in his arms using real people that I knew," said Gail's mom. "God used my friends to show me he loved me and that he was near."

God doesn't have arms and hands and feet, but you do. So he uses you to help other people when they are in need, someone they can see, hear, and touch. Prayer is good; prayer is great! But pairing up prayer with something practical is even better.

Dear God, open my eyes to see people who need help. Give me ideas to show them how much you care and how much I do too. Amen.

AN UNOPENED GIFT

Be very careful how you live.
Do not live like those who are not wise,
but live wisely.

EPHESIANS 5:15 NCV

On the dining room table sat a gift beautifully wrapped with purple and shimmering gold. It was topped with one of those curly cue ribbons that bounce and wiggle. Some people would walk by and give the gift a shake, trying to discover what was inside. But it sat there unopened until the day the person the gift was meant for appeared.

You are like that gift. Every inch of your skin, every lock of your hair, every curve of your body is a gift that God made. When you dress in a way that shows too much, you're showing people part of the gift that you want to keep for the right person to open.

Be wise and keep the gift pure and beautiful. Save your gift for the one that God gives you.

Dear God, your plans are perfect, wise, and best. Thanks for thinking of me as a beautiful gift. Help me keep that gift wrapped up and saved for the special someone you have for me. Amen.

EVERYBODY'S DOING IT

I envied the proud when I saw them prosper despite their wickedness....Did I keep my heart pure for nothing? Did I keep myself innocent for no reason?

PSALM 73:3, 13 NLT

Everybody's doing it. They're swearing, watching R-rated movies, texting at night without mom and dad's permission. They're saying they're going to a friend's when they're really headed to the mall. "Everybody's doing it," you say. "So why can't I?"

That's exactly how the author of Psalm 73 felt. In the worst way, he wanted to say, "Why do I bother? Am I doing what's right just for nothing? Everyone else has it so easy. They're out having fun while I'm trying to be 'good.'"

Maybe that's how you feel. The more people you see getting away with what you thought was wrong or were taught was wrong, the more you start to wonder, *Is it really such a big deal?*

Knowing the whole picture might help you keep your focus strong. Things won't end well for them; a reward is in your future though. God will show himself to be good, and he'll gently lead you and care for you. So hang in there and stay strong! It'll pay off in the end.

Dear Lord, sometimes I'm tempted to go ahead and just do something because everyone else is. Help me remember the reward you have for those who do what's right and the end for those who don't. Amen.

NOVEMBER

Take delight in the LORD, and
he will give you your heart's desires.
Commit everything you do to the LORD.
Trust him, and he will help you.

PSALM 37:5 NLT

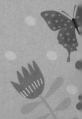

BITTER TO BLESSED

We who are strong ought to bear with the failings of the weak and not to please ourselves.

ROMANS 15:1 NIV

Naomi was just plain old cranky and she knew it. "Just call me bitter," she said. Her life read like a series of unfortunate events. She'd left her home. She'd lost her husband. She'd lost both her sons and now she was about to lose her land. She was convinced God had forgotten her and let everyone know it.

Naomi had a friend and daughter-in-law, though, named Ruth. Ruth stuck with Naomi—even though she was bitter, even though she complained, even though she wasn't always fun to be around. Ruth was a kind and loyal friend. Soon Naomi's heart changed and God used Ruth to do it.

Maybe you know someone like Naomi, someone who is always down, always complaining, and convinced the world is against them. God can change that person's heart and maybe if you're willing he can use you to do it. It all starts with one smile, one kind gesture, or one patient word.

These might make a world of difference. And praying for someone will for sure.

Dear God, when I'm around someone cranky, I sometimes just want to leave. Remind me how much you love them, and help me to reach out even if it's in a small way. Amen.

VOICES

"Whether you turn to the right or to the left, your ears will hear a voice behind you, saying, 'This is the way; walk in it.'"
ISAIAH 30:21 NIV

Once you've heard Adele's voice, you won't forget it. Her deep, distinct, powerful voice has sold millions of albums. If you heard your teacher's voice, you'd recognize that too. You've heard it over and over through the school year. If you heard a random person's voice in the grocery store, though, you wouldn't give it a second thought.

You pay attention to voices you know. If you believe in Jesus, God promises to speak to you and guide you. You'll hear a voice behind you, says the prophet Isaiah. "This is the way; walk in it." The key is recognizing that voice. If you know his voice, you'll know to listen.

How do you learn to know God's voice?

- Believe in Jesus. Those who belong to him are the ones who will hear his voice.
- Learn how God's voice is distinct. What he says and how he says it are all consistent with his Word. By knowing his Word, reading it, and thinking on it you'll be well on your way to knowing his voice.
- Practice. The more you read his Word and the more you're still and actually listen, the more you'll learn to recognize it.

God loves to speak, and he loves it when you listen. Has God ever spoken to you? What did he say?

Dear God, thanks for showing me who you are through your Word. Amen.

PERFECTLY GOOD PERFUME

*Happy is the person whom the LORD does not consider guilty
and in whom there is nothing false.*

PSALM 32:2 NCV

"I found some perfume on my desk earlier this morning,"
said Mr. Cox to his sixth grade class. "If it's yours, you can pick
it up at break."

After break, Carla noticed no one had claimed the
perfume. *Well, if no one is going to claim it, I will. No use
wasting perfectly good perfume.*

Carla told Mr. Cox it was hers and took it home. She felt
so guilty, she couldn't use it. She knew it wasn't hers. Perfectly
good perfume was only perfect, she decided, if you got it
honestly. In the end, she brought the perfume back and told
Mr. Cox she was sorry. She was so happy she did.

God blesses those who are honest with a happiness that a
guilty heart doesn't have. People might never know if you're
dishonest. But you'll know, and it'll eat away at the joy that
God always meant to give.

Honesty means your homework is your own and no one
else's. Honesty means taking credit for something you really
did. Honesty means calling in sick when you're actually sick.
Honesty means taking what belongs to you, not what belongs
to someone else. Honesty means telling the truth even if you'd
rather avoid the consequences.

A natural result of honesty? A happy, guilt-free heart.

**Dear God, honesty matters to me, not just because I want to be
happy, but because I want to be like you. Help me to be honest all
the time. Amen.**

INSIDE BEAUTY

Your beauty should not consist of outward things....
Instead, it should consist of what is inside the heart.
1 PETER 3:3-4 HCSB

"Hey, girls. I'm heading to the thrift store to look for some photo shoot props," said Becca's mom. "Want to come along?"

Thirty minutes later Becca and Lydia were having a blast trying on some super cool old-fashioned dresses and posing for selfies. One caramel-colored dress had puffy lace sleeves.

"Oh, that one looks so cute on you!" said Becca.

Another had bold black flowers splashed on a white background.

"You look like Grandma in her picture album," said Lydia.

Depending on what they tried on, they looked silly, pretty, or just plain weird.

How we look matters. Nobody wants to be known for really bad style choices, after all.

But how you look doesn't matter as much as who you are on the inside. Are you honest? Are you kind? Do you think of others over yourself? It's not that pretty clothes and cute hats and totally awesome shoes are bad—they're not—but they don't need to be the focus.

You might think, "Of course how I look on the inside is more important!" Just to be sure, you might want to ask a friend. Ask them if they think you're focusing more on outside stuff or inside stuff.

Dear God, I want to be noticed not for the way I look on the outside but for how I reflect you from the inside. I want my true beauty to come from within. Amen.

HIDEAWAY

You are my hiding place;
you protect me from trouble.
You surround me with songs of victory.
PSALM 32:7 NLT

If you traveled to the Arctic, one of the animals you'd find is a ringed seal. A mother ringed seal takes unusual steps to hide her young pups from danger. She dives into the freezing water, under a layer of ice, and finds a place where snowdrifts have covered a hole in the ice. In this small cave, or lair, she gives birth to her young pups. Hiding them inside the small cave protects them from polar bears.

That's just a small example of how the Lord God protects his children. Psalm 121 says that he is our help. He watches over us. He's a hiding place: a place where we can go when there's trouble.

Is there somewhere you go when you feel like hiding? A place where you feel safe, cozy, and warm? Take a few minutes and head to your hideaway. Journal a prayer, play or sing your favorite worship song, or draw a picture that reminds you God is your protection. He is your hiding place!

Dear God, you protect me from trouble. Thanks for being a hiding place—somewhere I can go to feel safe, understood, and loved. Amen.

A SOFT SPOT

When the Lord saw her,
his heart overflowed with compassion.
"Don't cry!" he said.
LUKE 7:13 NLT

"Pleeease, Auntie Beth. Please can I have another cookie? Just one," begged Makayla's little sister, Mila, her blue eyes wide and curls bouncing.

"How can I resist a cutie like that?" said Auntie Beth. She handed Mila a cookie then turned to Makayla. "I'm afraid I've got a soft spot for little kids."

Some people have a soft spot for little kids or elderly people. Jesus had a soft spot for the poor and the "nobodies" in society. In Jesus' time, the nobodies included widows. So when Jesus saw a widow whose only son had died, he had compassion. Jesus brought the son back to life.

If you're a follower of Jesus, you can show his compassion to those who others might overlook or even ignore. Who are some people that often get overlooked? What are some ways you could show them compassion?

- Be a friend to a widow or widower. When you live alone, life can get lonely.
- Talk to your mom or dad about sending a care package to someone in prison.
- Write a thank-you note to the mail carrier. They'll appreciate it!
- Volunteer to help a student from a younger grade with their homework.

Dear God, give me ideas for showing compassion to those who might get overlooked. Amen.

BUT IT'S WRONG!

*Be still in the presence of the L*ORD*,*
and wait patiently for him to act.
Don't worry about evil people who prosper
or fret about their wicked schemes.

PSALM 37:7 NIV

"But it's wrong, Dad! That farm belongs to Jada's family. Why is someone going to force them to sell their house? They don't want to go. It's theirs!"

A lot of injustice happens these days. Bad people seem to do so well while good people can't catch a break. We wonder, "If God is so powerful, why doesn't he do something!" So we try to do something, like start a petition, or call a representative, or hand out flyers. Which can be good unless we get all worked up and stressed out. "Those people aren't going to get away with shoving people aside and ignoring how they feel!"

Doing something about injustice is a good thing. But sometimes the best action is stop and pray. Just be still, and know that God is on the way. Even if you're tempted to freak out, don't. Be still and wait.

Dear God, I see so many things that are wrong and I want to make them right. I try, but some problems are too big for me. Please come and rescue those who are suffering injustice. Amen.

GETTING ALONG

Every time I think of you, I give thanks to my God.
PHILIPPIANS 1:3 NLT

"I call the front seat," said Taylor as they walked toward the van.

"But you had it last time," said his older sister Elizabeth.

"Actually, you had it last time, Elizabeth," interrupted her mom.

"But I never get a turn. He always gets a turn. And why," Elizabeth said turning to Taylor, "did you eat the last cupcake today when you knew it was mine?"

Their mom sighed, "Why can't you two just get along?"

Inside you know that if anything happened to your brother, you'd feel terrible. If anyone tried to pick on your sister, you'd be the first to step up. But sometimes, just sometimes, the house (or the car) doesn't seem to be big enough for you all. You'd like a little space.

You're precious to God. He made you; he loves you. The same is true for your siblings. They're precious to him. When you get into it with them over chores, over who owns what, and whose space is whose, you're getting into it with someone God loves. They are a divine creation too, fearfully made, wonderfully made. Don't treat them like a bother; remember they're a gift.

How does thinking about your brother or sister as a gift change your perspective?

Dear God, I appreciate my family. I don't always think of them as a gift but I know they are. Help me be quick to see the good things in them and point those out. Amen.

PRIORITIES

*We set our eyes not on what we see but on what we cannot
see. What we see will last only a short time, but what we
cannot see will last forever.*

2 CORINTHIANS 4:18 NCV

If you could take three things with you on a camping
vacation, what would they be?

If you were stranded on a desert island, what four things
couldn't you live without?

If you were headed to a party, what five things would have
to go in your purse?

Questions like these force you to decide what's priority?
What *are* the things that matter most? Having a boy you
like, like you back? Knowing when to start shaving your legs
or when to ask your mom if you can start wearing make-up?
Avoiding an embarrassing situation?

Sure, they're important. The question is, What's *more*
important? They're the things that last. And while you make
think you'll *never* get over an embarrassing situation, that's not
exactly what God was talking about when he said, "We set our
eyes not on what we see but on what we cannot see."

When you follow God, you remember that what you
don't see—heaven and a forever life with him and all that it
includes—is what matters. All your other decisions are made
with that in mind. So remember what really matters. Know who
really matters.

**Dear God, help me to remember what matters most—living for
you. Remind me who matters most—my family and you. Help me
make them a priority. Amen.**

CHEERLEADING

We are surrounded by a great cloud of people whose lives tell us what faith means. So let us run the race that is before us and never give up.

HEBREWS 12:1 NCV

"Nice job, girls. Get in your cheer lines, and let's try it one more time," Madeline's coach (who just happened to be her mom) said. "And remember, it's picture day tomorrow."

Poms up, Madeline started, "Give me a G! G! Give me an O! O! Gooooo Lakers!"

Madelyn loved cheerleading. She liked hanging out with her friends, and she liked cheering for the football team. When she cheered, the crowd cheered. When she clapped, the crowd clapped. It felt good to be supporting her team.

God describes a huge cheerleading squad in heaven (Hebrews 11 &12). Great men and women of faith like Queen Esther and King David and Moses and Noah are cheering us on as we walk with God every day. They know what it's like to love God. They know what it's like to be discouraged and face problems and overcome!

Imagine them saying "Don't give up!" "You're doing great!" "It's going to be worth it." "Keep looking at Jesus." "Remember what matters." Not only are they cheering you on, but Jesus himself is praying for you (Hebrews 7:25).

You've got a cheerleading squad behind you. How does that make you feel?

Dear God, thanks for men and women who believed in you and showed me what faith looks like. When I get distracted or discouraged, remind me to follow their example and remember you're cheering me on! Amen.

INFLUENCE

*Don't let anyone look down on you because you are young,
but set an example for the believers in speech, in conduct,
in love, in faith and in purity.*
1 TIMOTHY 4:12 NIV

"Come on, Dad. You should do it."

Martina's hockey coach needed an assistant coach and Martina had the perfect person in mind—her dad.

"I'm not sure, Martina. I've got a lot going on already, and I haven't coached hockey for a long time.

"It'll come back to you, Dad. Promise. It'll be fun! Besides, you'll get to spend more time with me, right?" Martina flashed him her best smile.

Just because you're young doesn't mean you can't influence others. You do it all the time, right? You influence your mom to buy you a new pair of jeans. You persuade your brother to swap chores so you can leave early for a friend's. You "strongly encourage" your coach that you are the best person to play goalie.

You can also influence people to believe what's true about God and live in a way that's right. Use the power you have to encourage others to do good. Know that because of you things can change!

Dear God, I love you with all my heart and I want to do whatever I can to show, tell, encourage, and set an example for truth and faith. Amen.

A LITTLE RESPECT

Show proper respect to everyone,
love the family of believers, fear God, honor the emperor.
1 PETER 2:17 NIV

Peanut butter and jelly, monkeys and bananas, pen and paper, macaroni and cheese, shoes and socks. Some things seem inseparable. To say one is to think of the other. They come in pairs.

The same is true for respect. One of the coolest things God has called us to do is to show people respect. It doesn't sound like much, but if you've ever been on the other side of disrespect, you know it's huge. Certain things pair really well with respect. To think of one is to think of the other.

What are some of the things that pair well with respect? Listening, trying to understand, assuming the best, using common courtesy and words like "please" and "thank you."

Things that don't belong with respect? Ignoring, interrupting, name-calling, sarcasm, back talk, or talking bad about others.

One thing that's not on either list is agreeing or disagreeing. You can respect someone without agreeing. You can disagree and still show respect. Common courtesy unites; unkindness divides.

Dear God, I want to give you a good name. How I treat people is important to me because people are important to you. Help me to hit "pause" if I'm getting out of line. Amen.

DOUBLE THE FRIENDS

All things work together for the good of those who love God:
those who are called according to His purpose.
ROMANS 8:28 HCSB

One night during dinner, Susie's dad said, "My company is transferring me to a different city. We get to move to Denver."

At first Susie was excited, but after a while she realized how much she'd miss her friends.

When they first moved to Denver, Susie hated it. Her mom told her that God had a purpose for them in Denver. Susie was still upset.

"I felt really scared because I only knew one person from her old neighborhood: Luke."

That friend Luke was a gift. He stood up for Susie. He invited Susie to his Super Bowl party. He introduced her to his friends.

"Luke made me feel really happy," said Susie. "Now, I know everybody and I have twice as many friends as I did before."

You can make a difference in the life of someone going through a change. Just reaching out in one small way to include them can help them find God's purpose. Encouraging and showing them support can bless them—maybe even with double the friends.

Dear God, thank you for being with me when things change. You aren't intimidated by new jobs, new schools, and needing to make new friends. Help me to be strong and trust you. Amen.

A HEAVEN HOME

"I am going there to prepare a place for you. After I go and prepare a place for you, I will come back and take you to be with me so that you may be where I am."

JOHN 14:2-3 NCV

"Okay, now close your eyes and don't peek. I want it to be a surprise," said Mrs. Chang. "Here, give me your hand, Stella."

Mrs. Chang led Stella down the hallway, past the master bedroom to Stella's own room.

"Surprise!" she said.

Stella opened her eyes and gasped. "Mom, it's…it's… beautiful! I love it!"

Stella was staring at a total bedroom makeover complete with freshly painted pale yellow walls and a brand new loft bed with a desk underneath. A cute paisley comforter and flower pillows decorated the bed. Stella hugged herself and squealed. It seemed too good to be true.

Before Jesus rose up into heaven, he said he'd be preparing a place for us. It'll be far better than the most amazing room makeover. Everything will be brand new! A new earth and a new heaven, gates made of pearls, walls made of jewels, streets made of gold, a tree of life whose leaves heal, and complete peace (read Revelation 21 and 22).

If you belong to Jesus, that's what you have to look forward to! What excites you most when you think about the new home God is preparing?

Dear God, I'm excited to see the home you're preparing for us. I don't know exactly what'll be like, but I know it will be amazing. Most of all, though, I'm excited to see you and be with you. Amen.

THEY CALL IT KARMA

"I—yes, I alone—will blot out your sins for my own sake and will never think of them again."
ISAIAH 43:25 NLT

They call it *karma*. What you do is what you get. What you put in is what you get out. Who you are in this life is what you'll be in another life. So they say.

In karma, everything you've ever said or done is strapped like a heavy bag to your chest. It never comes off; it's never undone. The only way to lighten the load is by what you do and don't do from here on out. Talk about pressure.

In God's kingdom, he offers something else—grace—because he *is* someone else. He's love. Because of that love, he gives free and undeserved grace.

So strike that word karma out of your conversations because thankfully that's not how things roll. The truth is that if you believe in Jesus, you're free. He doesn't hold your sins against you. He doesn't force you to earn something better. He gives grace to you because he loves you. You're free!

Dear Jesus, you came to set me free from what I really deserve and give me grace. You give me love. Neither of which I deserve. Thank you for loving me. Thank you for your grace. Amen.

COMPLIMENTS

Let someone else praise you, and not your own mouth;
an outsider, and not your own lips.
PROVERBS 27:2 NIV

"Hey, Brianna. I like your flower braid," said Miranda as she checked her hair in her locker mirror.

"It's okay," said Brianna. "I mean, I did it myself and it didn't turn out so good. My sister does a way better job than I do."

"Well, I think it looks nice," Miranda said.

How to handle compliments can be tricky. It can feel like someone has passed you a sign that says, "Hi, I'm really great." In which case, you might be embarrassed with all the attention and want to hand the sign back.

Honor, like a compliment, is a gift. It isn't something you take; it's something given. So treat it like the gift it is. Don't compliment yourself. You wouldn't buy yourself a gift, so don't hand yourself a compliment. Don't hand the compliment back. Rejecting a compliment is telling the person who said it that they're not telling the truth.

The best way to handle a compliment is saying two words—Thank you. How do you usually respond to compliments?

Dear God, thank you for compliments. They're a nice gift to get. Remind me to treat them as the gifts they are and just say a sincere "thank you." Help me to give that kind of gift out freely to others. Amen.

LUNCHROOM DILEMMA

My dear brothers and sisters, as believers in our
glorious Lord Jesus Christ, never think some people
are more important than others.

JAMES 2:1 NCV

It was a week into sixth grade, and Erin and Anna were already friends. As they huddled over turkey wraps and chips in the cafeteria one day, one of the popular girls from another table walked right over to them.

"Hi, Erin," she said without looking at Anna. "You want to come sit with us?"

"Sure," Erin said, "You mind if Anna comes too?"

"I'm asking *you*," she said crossing her arms. "Guess you'll have to decide. It's us or her."

Part of Erin wanted to be included with their group. The girls were fun, pretty, athletic, and had a ton of friends. The other part was angry and sad. How dare they force her to pick sides?

The friendships God designed don't leave any room for treating one person more important than the other. If it's a real friendship, you won't be excluded and you won't be asked to do the same. Real friends don't make you pick one person over the other.

If you were in a dilemma like Erin's, what would you do?

Dear God, help me to be a true friend even if others aren't. When I'm faced with a tough choice that might cost me a lot, give me the courage to do what's right. Amen.

OPEN ARMS

"While he was still a long way off, his father saw him and was coming. Filled with love and compassion, he ran to his son, embraced him, and kissed him."

LUKE 15:20 NLT

Once upon a time a man had two sons. One son did everything right. He worked hard, obeyed all the rules, respected his dad, and never gave him a reason to complain.

If the first son did everything right, the second son did everything wrong. He ran away from home, ditched all his responsibilities, totally disrespected his dad, took his money and left.

After his money was all gone, he thought, *What am I doing? I'll tell my father I was wrong and beg him to take me back.* As he headed toward home he wondered, *What will Father's reaction be? Crossed arms? Clenched fists? Disapproving face?*

Instead he found his father waiting—with open arms.

That father is a picture of how God welcomes those who have done wrong. Maybe you know someone who feels like they've done so much wrong that God will never forgive them. Or they've made a huge mistake that cost big time. Goofed up. Totally messed up. It's never big enough to turn God away. When someone comes to God with a sincere "I'm sorry," he's quick to forgive.

Dear God, show me how much you love me. Use me to show others that you don't hold what they've done wrong against them. You welcome us with open arms. Amen.

GRACE

We wait in hope for the LORD;
he is our help and our shield.
PSALM 33:20 NIV

When Grace was little, she found out she had asthma. Sometimes she had trouble breathing; it was kind of scary. Grace could have been discouraged, and sometimes she was, but she loved God and listened to God and decided she could have hope. Even though she often felt sick, she didn't let it keep her from doing what she could. She played hockey; she played lacrosse. She volunteered with the children at her church.

Wherever God is, there's hope. If God lives inside you, you can have hope too. Hope when things go great. Hope when things go all wrong. Hope when you're sick; hope when you're healthy and strong. Hope when you have lots of friends, and hope when you don't. God is always there, so there is always hope. How is it possible to have hope when what you're hoping for doesn't turn out?

Dear God, I'm waiting in hope for you. Even if things don't turn out the way I want, my hope doesn't ever need to go away because I've got you. Amen.

WHAT DO YOU MEAN, I'M WRONG?

Anyone who loves learning accepts correction.
PROVERBS 12:1 NCV

How do you handle it when someone tells you you're wrong? Do you thank them, or do you wish they'd bother someone else?

Most people don't enjoy being told "You're wrong" or "That's not the way to do it." But like brushing your teeth or eating your vegetables, you don't have to like it to accept it. Accepting correction shows that you love to learn and have a humble heart.

Of course what is said or how it's said can sometimes make you want to cringe. In that case:

- Take a deep breath.
- Listen. Resist the temptation to argue back.
- Later on ask yourself and ask God, "Is there anything about what that person said that's true?" (Even a little bit of it.)
- Use what they've said to make yourself a better and stronger person.

What does accepting correction say about you?

Dear God, telling other people they're right sometimes means admitting I'm wrong. Teach me to listen and use what's said for good. Thanks for putting people in my life who care. Amen.

HIGH TICKET ITEM

You are not your own; you were bought at a price.
Therefore honor God with your bodies.
1 CORINTHIANS 6:19-20 NIV

If your parents paid everything they owned to buy something, how valuable would that item be? Very!

Jesus gave up everything so that you could have life. He died on the cross to give you life and poured his Holy Spirit inside you. That's how valuable you are to him!

Not just your heart but everything about you belongs to God. So honor him. What you wear, how you talk, how you act, everything should honor God because you are his and he thinks you're precious!

What does the price Jesus paid say about your value?

Dear Jesus, the price you paid for me shows me how much value I have. I'm precious in your eyes. Thank you for loving me that way! Show me how I can honor you best. Amen.

RIPPLE EFFECTS

The words of thoughtless people cut like swords.
But the tongue of wise people brings healing.
PROVERBS 12:18 NIRV

"Here, Casey, go like this." Casey's older brother Chris picked up a flat rock from the shore. "Throw it low with a little spin so it hits the water flat. It'll skip like this." He threw the stone and it skipped once, twice, three, then four times before sinking into the water.

Casey took a deep breath and launched her stone across the water and then—down, down, down it plunged, creating rings of ripples all around.

"It's okay," said Chris. "You just have to practice, that's all."

The words we say can create ripple effects. They can influence those around us. Our words can hurt or our words can heal. Thoughtless, cutting, accusing, angry words can stay with someone for a lifetime. "What did you do that for?" "Well, that was dumb."

Kind words that compliment, encourage, and affirm can soothe, bring hope, and stay with someone for a lifetime too. "You can do it." "I believe in you." "I'm praying for you." "I'm sorry."

Dear God, I've never realized the power my words have. Help me to be the kind of person who brings healing instead of hurt. If I do make a mistake, let me know so I can make it right. Amen.

LAUGH A LITTLE

A joyful heart makes a face cheerful.
PROVERBS 15:13 HCSB

In the middle of the fifth inning, the Cosmos best hitter got up to bat. Sofia was on first base and her twin sister, Sadie, was on second. A base hit landed in the infield where the shortstop whipped it to Sofia. Overthrown. As the runner rounded first and headed to second base, Sofia finally scooped up the ball and threw it to second.

Sadie jumped high to make the catch then reached down to tag the base. "We got her! Out!" she yelled. But when she looked down, her glove was empty. She turned and saw the ball on the ground behind her.

Talk about embarrassing. For a long time after that, Sofia would tease Sadie. "We got her, huh?" And they'd both laugh.

We all do dumb stuff. When that happens, sometimes the best thing you can do is laugh at yourself. Most people don't mean any harm when they tease you. Even if you're dealing with a bully, the best way to disarm them is to laugh right along with them. If you react and look bothered, it's an invitation to get teased again.

So lighten up and laugh a little.

Dear God, sometimes I do really dumb things. Help me to keep my head up and see the humor in the situation. Amen.

WHEN NO ONE NOTICES

*"Your Father sees what is done in secret,
and he will reward you."*

MATTHEW 6:18 NCV

How would you feel if you did something impressive or difficult or creative and no one noticed? You cleaned up your room without asking and no one noticed. You came up with a cool idea for the school fundraiser, and someone took your idea and you never got credit.

It's nice to be noticed. No one has to throw you a party or make a big deal. Just a simple "That was great!" or "I can tell you're trying" can go a long way toward making you feel good. But people don't always notice. And even when they do, they sometimes don't say a thing.

God does notice—always. He pays attention to what you do, the good things others might overlook. Even more importantly, he says something about it. "Your Father sees what is done in secret, and he will reward you." He will reward what others may not notice. Maybe not right away. Maybe not in a way you expect. But he will keep his promise.

Dear God, thank you for noticing. When I feel discouraged because others don't notice, remind me that you appreciate my efforts. You see what I do. Amen.

STUFFED

From the fruit of their mouth a person's stomach is filled;
with the harvest of their lips they are satisfied.

PROVERBS 18:20 NIV

"I'm stuffed," Hailey said leaning back in her chair and rubbing her stomach. After a Thanksgiving dinner of turkey, cheesy potatoes, and her grandma's famous oatmeal bread (yum!), Hailey wasn't sure if she'd have room for chocolate cream pie.

Well, maybe a little room, she thought. *After all, there's always room for chocolate.*

If your words were food, would you want to eat them? How would they taste? "When you talk," says God's Word, "do not say harmful things, but say what people need—words that will help others become stronger. Then what you say will do good to those who listen to you" (Ephesians 4:29).

Saying the right words at the right time and saying things that build up and encourage satisfy like a Thanksgiving meal—only better.

What kind of meal describes your conversations?

Dear God, teach me to think of my words like food I'm serving up to those around me. I want my words to be like the best ever Thanksgiving feast. Amen.

GOING TO BE GREAT

*"Whoever wants to become great
among you must be your servant."*
MARK 10:43 NIV

When Juliette was ten, she developed a website idea that's now worth millions. When Nadia was fourteen, she won three Olympic gold medals.

By most standards, these girls are great! Look at where they started and look where they ended up. Hard work, creative thinking, and perseverance brought them success and fame. In our society that's what great is.

In God's kingdom, great is defined by how well a person serves others. Jesus said being great in his kingdom is learning to serve and put others first.

That doesn't mean you can't aim for great grades or do great things. It means that others come first.

- Clear your dishes, empty the dishwasher, take out the trash and recycling—without being asked.
- Let your little sister get ready for school before you, without complaining.
- Hold the door open for the person behind you.
- Get on the volunteer schedule at church or school.

Doing "great" things doesn't make you great, serving others does.

Dear God, teach me to be great in your kingdom. Amen.

FAMILY NIGHT

Children are a gift from the LORD;
they are a reward from him.
PSALM 127:3 NLT

For as long as Natalia could remember, Friday night was family night. In the spring, Natalia, her two brothers, and her mom and dad would go biking. In the summer they'd go swimming or play mini golf. In the fall they'd go apple picking or roast marshmallows around a bonfire. In the winter, they'd eat popcorn, play board games, and watch movies.

For the most part Natalia liked family night, but sometimes she wished she could go to the mall or cheer on the football team or stay home and do nothing (and sometimes they did that, but it was always together).

Family is special. Not everyone has a family. Have you ever realized you are one of the most precious gifts your parents have ever been given? Nothing compares to the amazing privilege of having a child and having a family. So if they want to spend time with you and have family dinners or have devotions together, it's because they like you and because family is important to them.

Dear God, thank you for my family. We're not perfect but we're family and we stick together. Amen.

A LETTER IN THE ATTIC

*My child, listen to your father's teaching
and do not forget your mother's advice.*
PROVERBS 1:8 NCV

When she was helping her grandpa pack up his house and move into a new townhouse, Meghan found a box of old letters in his attic. She snuck a peek at one worn letter her great-grandma had written to her grandpa when he was younger.

Dear David,
Have I ever told you how much I love you? You don't like all that touchy-feely stuff, I know, but sometimes even a twelve-year-old boy needs to know he's loved.

Your dad and I waited two years to be able to have you. Then we waited nine months to be able to see you. I remember the day you were born. Holding you was one of the greatest joys I've ever had. I kept thinking, "This is my son!" Saying those words seemed like a dream come true.

If I ask you things like "Where are you going?" or "Who are you going out with?" I'm only caring for a precious gift God gave me—you. When I give you advice, I only want your best. I made many mistakes growing up and don't you to want to make the same ones. I love you so much.

Mom

When your mom or dad asks you to check in or sit you down for some one-on-one advice, they do it because they love you. You are their DNA, and they care. Listening to them will give you an advantage in life that you'll never regret.

Dear God, thanks for the advice that my mom/dad give me. Help me value their advice and really learn from them. Amen.

WINTER COATS AND WARM WEATHER

Our homeland is in heaven, and we are waiting for our Savior,
the Lord Jesus Christ, to come from heaven.
PHILIPPIANS 3:20-21 NCV

Hannah's first stop when she got off the plane in Colorado was to buy a down winter coat. She was a west Texas girl and used to stretches of flat land and blazing hot temperatures. She'd never seen snow before and definitely had never needed a winter coat. But if she was going skiing with the rest of her cousins, she'd have to have one.

Once she went home, she'd hang the coat in the closet; it wouldn't do her any good in warm weather. That coat was just for now.

If you've put your faith in Jesus, your forever home will be in heaven. All the stuff you have now—your phone, your books, your stuffed animal collection, your shoes and clothes, even your home—you won't need any more. They're just for now. Everything you have now is a gift. But eventually it will fade away and what will matter most is what lasts—ultimately that's your forever home with God. So invest your time in what will matter then.

When you think that heaven is your forever home, is there anything you'd change about how you live now?

Dear God, I appreciate everything you've given me. Thank you! Please teach me not to get so caught up in now that I forget about then—the day I'll live with you. Amen.

DISNEY WORLD

*Their trust should be in God,
who richly gives us all we need for our enjoyment.*
1 TIMOTHY 6:17 NLT

Friday morning before school Mr. and Mrs. Jensen called their three girls into the living room for a family meeting. Maddie thought she was in trouble. Kyra and Kenzie didn't think anything; they just didn't want to miss breakfast.

"Your mom and I have something to tell you," Mr. Jensen said. "We're going on a trip—to Disney World. Tomorrow."

Maddie looked at Kyra. Kyra looked at Kenzie and suddenly the three girls were dancing around in their pajamas, jumping on the couch, and giggling on the floor.

Mrs. Jensen looked at her husband. "Don't you just love seeing them so happy?" *Sigh.*

The only thing better than enjoying something yourself is giving someone a gift and seeing *them* enjoy it. God loves to give you what you need (and sometimes what you just want). Watching you enjoy it puts a smile on his face.

When you pray, don't ask like he's bothered. Ask with confidence. Then turn around and give the same way God does—freely, generously, and with joy.

Whose day could you brighten up by giving them a gift?

Dear God, you fill my whole life up with so many good things! Whenever I'm tempted to doubt whether or not you'll take care of me, remind me that giving is your joy. Teach me to give with that same kind of joy. Amen.

DECEMBER

Oh, the depth of the riches both of
the wisdom and knowledge of God!
How unsearchable are His judgments
and unfathomable His ways!

ROMANS 11:33 NASB

HAPPY ENDINGS

God himself will be with them. He will wipe every tear from their eyes, and there will be no more death or sorrow or crying or pain. All these things are gone forever."
REVELATION 21:3-4 NLT

One night Piper accidentally left her cocker spaniel Gio out in the winter cold. When she woke up the next morning, she missed the feel of his warm tongue licking her face good morning.

"Gio!" she said and sat straight up in bed. *Please be okay. Please be okay*, she whispered as she ran down the stairs. She threw open the back door. There was Gio curled up next to a bush.

"Gio!" Piper said and wrapped her arms around him even as he started licking her face. "I'm so sorry. I'll never leave you outside again."

We love stories that have happy endings. Boy gets girl, bad guy gets caught, and people who argue make up and become friends. That's the way things should be, right? Not all stories have happy endings though. Some dogs get lost and aren't ever found. Some people get cancer and don't get better. Some friends never make up.

When we're discouraged, it can help to remember that God gives us a forever happy ending. When Jesus comes back to rule as King, he'll wipe away every trace of sadness. Crying, pain, and even death will be gone. In their place, he'll bring peace and a lot of joy.

Dear God, thanks that there will be a happy ending even though I don't see one now. Amen.

CINNAMON ROLLS

"Do you give me orders about the work of my hands? I am the one who made the earth and created people to live on it. With my hands I stretched out the heavens."
ISAIAH 45:11-12 NLT

Every Christmas Luana goes to her grandma's house and they make cinnamon rolls together. They're big and fluffy and filled with cinnamon and sugar then glazed with powdered sugar.

Luana's grandma dissolves yeast in warm water and sprinkles in sugar and salt. She adds an egg, milk, flour, and stirs. Next she presses the heel of her hand into the dough, punching it down and pulling it back and forth, until the dough is shiny and smooth. Luana's grandma knows just how long to knead the dough, just how long to let the dough rise, and just how wide and long and thick to roll it. She knows what she's doing.

God knows what he's doing—in your life, your family, your school, and your city. He's kneading in all that happens to make something beautiful. He's totally in control.

It wouldn't make sense to say, "God, you don't know what you're doing" any more than it would be for the cinnamon roll dough to pop up off the counter and start to complain, "You're doing it all wrong!"

So relax, take a deep breath, and trust the big, big God you have.

Dear God, I trust you. Not everything I see and hear makes sense, but I know that you are in control. I pray that you'd keep working everything for good. Amen.

MAKING IT BIG

Anyone who wants to be important among you must be your servant.
MATTHEW 20:26 NIRV

If you want to make it big in the film industry, Hollywood is the place to be. If you want to make it big in the country music world, Nashville is the place to go. If you wanted to make it big in Bible times, Nazareth was definitely *not* the place to go.

Nazareth was small and unimportant and no one who was anybody lived there. "Nazareth nobodies" pretty much described the people who lived there. "Can anything good come out of Nazareth?" people said.

But someone in Nazareth caught God's attention. He sent his top angel, Gabriel, to pay a visit to a simple girl who was "highly favored" (which is saying something when you're talking about God). Mary had a servant's heart. She wasn't out to impress anyone or convince them how important she was.

If you want to build a career in God's kingdom, it won't take intelligence or power or riches. If you want to be great, it'll take a servant heart to impress him.

Dear God, I do want to be great in your kingdom. Teach me to have a humble heart. Instead of trying to get ahead and be important, help me put others first. Amen.

CHINESE TAKEOUT

Take delight in the LORD,
and he will give you the desires of your heart.
PSALM 37:4 NIV

For Brandy, Thursday nights meant one thing—Chinese takeout. And that meant her favorite—sesame chicken. Brandy and her mom walked into the restaurant and stood behind another couple about to order. The lady's phone started to ring.

"I need to take this call," she said.

"Well, what do you want?" the man asked. "What should I order for you?"

"You pick," she said, covering the phone and stepping outside.

Five minutes later she was back. "So what did you get?"

"Kung pao chicken with extra peanuts," he said.

"My favorite. I just knew I loved you."

A little mushy, Brandy thought. *But actually kind of cute.*

When someone knows you really well and that someone loves you a whole lot, trusting them comes easily. They know what you like. They know just what to pick for you.

If you love God with all you are, you can be sure he'll choose something for you that you really love. Instead of pouring your energy into stressing out about something, spend your energy trusting God. He knows you inside out and loves you more than you can imagine.

Dear God, you know me better than anyone else. I trust your choices. I want you to pick what you want for me. Amen.

AN OUTSIDER

Keep on loving one another as brothers and sisters.
Don't forget to welcome outsiders.
HEBREWS 13:1-2 NIRV

Caroline knew what it was like to feel like an outsider. When she was eight and her brother was five, their family moved from America to France. People in France looked different, sounded different, and ate different food. After a while, Caroline discovered that the French didn't think *they* were different; they thought *she* was different. "Different" depended on which country you lived in.

The week before school, Caroline met Carla.

"You must be new here," Carla said. "Here, come and meet some of my friends." That day was the first time Caroline felt like she was turning from an outsider to an insider.

You can welcome someone from a different school, a different country, or someone from right in your neighborhood. Treating them with hospitality makes them feel like they belong. It's an invitation to be a part of your circle of friends.

When you think of practicing hospitality, you might think you have to invite someone over for dinner. But even being friendly and generous with your time can give someone the confidence they need to fit in.

What's something you could do to help someone feel like they belong?

Dear God, thanks for welcoming me into your family. I'm happy to have a place to belong. Show me how I can make someone else feel welcome and at home. Amen.

UNDER THE SEA

Lord, you have made many things;
with your wisdom you made them all.
The earth is full of your riches. Look at the sea,
so big and wide, with creatures large and small
that cannot be counted.
PSALM 104:24-25 NCV

People said that Divya was born in the Caribbean Sea. She could dive under the salty sea and swim for two full minutes without coming up for air. She loved discovering the big, wide world under the sea: parrot fish that made a munching-crunching sound, fire coral that stung if you touched it, and giant conch whose pale pink shells inched across the ocean floor.

God filled the sea with unimaginable creatures. Each quirky, slippery, slimy, beautiful creature tells a story—a story about the wisdom of God. With sheer brilliance, he fit the whole marine ecosystem together in an amazing design. (And you thought putting together your science project was tough.) Nothing about it was an accident; God knew what he was doing. With wisdom he made it all!

Dear God, the whole earth and everything in it belongs to you. You made everything with wisdom and beauty. Thank you for the wonder of your creation. Amen.

FAMILY FIRST

Honor your father and your mother.
EXODUS 20:12 HCSB

If you had to choose between watching a movie with your mom or going to a friend's for a sleepover, which would you choose? If you had to choose between going out to eat with your friends, or heading to the mall with your dad, which would you choose?

You might be surprised to know that your answers don't tell whether you're putting family first or not. That's because family first isn't about what you want to do with whom. As you get older, you'll naturally want to spend more time with friends. That natural desire is God's way of preparing you for adulthood and independence.

Putting family first is more about giving family top priority in things that matter. You protect your time, so family doesn't get crowded out. You consider family first when you make a decision. You honor your dad or mom. You stick together with family through tough times and good times.

What would your life look like if you put family first? Would it look any different than it does now?

Dear God, thanks for my family. Show me how you want me to put family first. Amen.

BOY CRAZY

Has not the one God made you?
You belong to him in body and spirit.
MALACHI 2:15 NIV

I wonder if he'll notice me?
What should I wear?
Will he talk to me? What if he doesn't? Then what will I do?

There's a difference between liking someone and being boy crazy. The first makes you excited and happy—you want to hang out with someone. The second means all you think about is *that* boy. If a boy is taking over your life, then something's got to change.

How can you tell if you are boy crazy?

- You're always concerned about what he'll think.
- You decide what to wear based on what he'll think.
- You decide where you'll go based on if he will or won't be there.
- You start to change who you are so he will notice or like you.
- When you get together with friends, you always talk about boys.

No person should have that much power over what you think and do. You are *God's* creation; you belong to him. So put him first. Trust him to show you what to do through his Word and through the caring adults in your life. When you put God first, everything will fall into place.

Dear God, I want you to be first—always! If I'm getting caught up in what boys think or if they become too important, please let me know Amen.

BLESS HER HEART

"Now then, my children, listen to me;
blessed are those who keep my ways."
PROVERBS 8:32 NIV

"Now about John David," Amy heard Mrs. Ray say, "he's a little strange, bless his heart, but he's a sweet sort of boy. He tries hard enough but he gets a little mixed up, bless his heart."

"Well, God bless you for helping him out," Amy's mom said patting Mrs. Ray's arm.

Sounds like a whole lot of blessing to me, thought Amy.

"Bless" is a word people throw out all the time. "God bless America." *Achoo!* "Bless you!" "I just feel so blessed!"

But what does "bless" mean, and why should you care? A blessing is something that's good. When God blesses people, he gives them good things, like a home, a family, and good health.

But God has other blessings too: comfort for those who are sad, justice for those who long for what's right, the privilege of being called his children for those who work for peace, and the kingdom of heaven for those who suffer doing good. (See Matthew 5.)

Who do you know who would be encouraged to hear about these blessings?

Dear God, you give me so many things! You are so good. Help me to see and appreciate all that you do and all that you promise. Amen.

SECONDHAND STUFF

They share freely and give generously to those in need.
Their good deeds will be remembered forever.
PSALM 112:9 NLT

If you needed to shop at the thrift store, and only the thrift store, because money was that tight, what kind of clothes would you want to find? When you donate, give those kinds of clothes.

If you were shopping at the food shelf, and only the food shelf, because money was tight, what kind of food would you want to get? When you donate, give that kind of food.

If the Operation Christmas child shoebox was the only Christmas gift you got, what would you want to be in it? Fill it with those kinds of gifts.

God blesses those who care about the needy. When you give generously to the poor in your school, neighborhood, church, or even on your bus route, your good deeds will be remembered.

While giving someone clothes, food, and money is great, the most important thing you can give them is dignity. When you give someone dignity and respect, you give them the courtesy of being treated like an equal, not like someone inferior. You treat them like you'd want to be treated.

Dear God, you've given me so much. Thank you that I can bless others with a little bit of what you've given me. Take these gifts and multiply them times a hundred! Amen.

GREEN WITH ENVY

Love is kind. It does not want what belongs to others.
1 CORINTHIANS 13:4 NIRV

"Don't pay attention to her, Regina. She's just envious," said Juana as she looped her arm through Regina's.

Juana sighed. "I know I was chosen for student council and she wasn't. But does she have to be so mean about it?"

If you've ever been on the receiving end of envy, you know it can be miserable. You want to enjoy what you have but someone is making you feel miserable for it. On the other hand, who hasn't felt just a little envious? After all, don't you deserve a nice vacation or new pair of jeans too?

When someone is envious of you—Don't feel bad or apologize for what you have. Be thankful for whatever God has given you. Be strong and secure in who you are and pair that with kindness. (No one wants you looking down your nose at them.)

When you're feeling envious—Realize that life isn't about getting what you think you deserve. Thank God *out loud* for what you do have and for who he made you to be. Nothing chases envy away like thank-you words. Then find someone you respect to pray with you.

The bottom line is that God has no place in his kingdom for envy—at all.

Dear God, thank you for what I have and who I am. Please take away all envy and fill me with your love. Amen.

REDEFINED

I bow in prayer before the Father from whom every family in heaven and on earth gets its true name.
EPHESIANS 3:14-15 NCV

Nerd. Loser. Lame. Ugly.

Has anyone ever called you one of these names? Ouch.

If you belong to Jesus, he calls you his own. He removes old names, peels off old labels, and gives you his family name. That family name both fits you perfectly and gives you something to aspire to. He wraps you up in his big, loving arms and says, "You are…"

beautiful,

beloved,

precious,

My child.

Have you ever thought of yourself as beautiful, beloved, and precious?

Dear God, thank you for making me a part of your family. Thank you for redefining me because of your great name. Amen.

IMPERFECT PEOPLE

The high and lofty one who lives in eternity,
the Holy One, says this: "I live in the high and holy place
with those whose spirits are contrite and humble."
ISAIAH 57:15 NLT

If you flip through the pages of the Bible, you'll read about a whole lot of imperfect people. Jacob lied to his dad. Gideon was afraid. Moses was terrified of public speaking and had an anger problem. Jonah ignored God and ran away. Yet God still used them.

God uses imperfect people. That doesn't mean he's cool with sin, just that he doesn't expect perfection before he can use us. What touches his heart is humility.

You don't have to be perfect either before God can use you. When you make a mistake, get back up. When you do something wrong, ask for forgiveness and keep moving forward. Just keep a humble heart and focus on looking to God.

Dear God, you rule the whole earth but you still reach out to someone like me. Teach me to have a humble heart and to be quick to ask forgiveness when I do wrong. Amen.

LETTING GO OF BAGGAGE

Work at living in peace with everyone. Watch out that no poisonous root of bitterness grows up to trouble you, corrupting many.

HEBREWS 12:14-15 NLT

Peter was the kind of guy who liked to keep score. You know, an eye for an eye and a tooth for a tooth kind of person. What you give, you get. Mess with me, and I'll mess with you.

So he was feeling pretty generous when he asked Jesus, "How many times should I forgive someone? Up to seven times?"

Jesus wasn't impressed. He told Peter there wasn't a limit to forgiveness. No seven count. *Always* forgive.

That's because if you hold on to a hurt and don't forgive, it's like throwing it into a suitcase and hauling it around with you. The more unforgiveness you add to the bag, the heavier it becomes. If someone does you wrong and you forgive, you live absolutely free—free of bitterness and heaviness.

No matter what someone's done—called you a name, treated you differently because of the color of your skin, accused you of something you didn't do—forgive, then let it go. Show them the same undeserved grace God showed you and you'll live free.

Dear God, help me forgive even when it hurts a lot. Help me to think about what you've done for me instead of what they've done to me. Amen.

A BIRTH ANNOUNCEMENT

To us a child is born, to us a son is given....
And he will be called Wonderful Counselor,
Mighty God, Everlasting Father, Prince of Peace.
ISAIAH 9:6 NIV

"We just got a birth announcement from the Stevens."
Mrs. Cantrell began to read: "*Amelia Kate Stevens—such a
cute name!—was born December 1 and weighed 8 lb. 2 oz.
and is 22 inches long.* Oh, I'm so happy for them!"

"Mom, you're so funny," Anne said and smiled. Her mom
was goofy about babies.

When the angels made Jesus's birth announcement, they
said:

*Glory to God in the highest heaven, and on earth peace to
those on whom his favor rests.*

Their announcement included peace because Jesus is the
Prince of Peace. You can't have true peace—peace with God,
peace between other people, or even world peace—without
Jesus. Talking about having peace without talking about Jesus
is like trying to breathe without oxygen or do math without
numbers. Jesus *is* peace!

If you could ask Jesus to bring peace to anyone or any
situation (and you can!), what would you ask him to do?

**Dear Jesus, what people need the most is you. You are the Prince
of Peace. I pray that you'd use me to bring your peace to those I
know. Amen.**

I WISH

He satisfies your desires with good things
so that your youth is renewed like the eagle's.
PSALM 103:5 NIV

I wish I may, I wish I might
Have the wish I wish tonight.
I wish…

When you're soaping up in the shower or staring out the window at the moon at night, what do you secretly wish for? To be tall or funny or good at softball? To have a best friend or a bedroom of your own or a brother or sister?

Everything you long for is something that God sees and knows. You don't have to tell him what you wish for; he already knows. But he likes it when you tell him just the same. He likes talking with you, and he likes answering.

God isn't a make-a-wish kind of God. He doesn't wave a magic wand over us and give us three wishes. But he does care and he does answer prayer. Not always in the way we expect, but in a way that satisfies.

Dear God, you search me and know me. You know what I'm thinking and what I secretly long for. Thanks that I can talk to you about anything. Amen.

YOU ARE ENOUGH

We praise God for the glorious grace he has poured out on us who belong to his dear Son.
EPHESIANS 1:6 NLT

More than anything Janna wanted to know she mattered. She tried to matter by working hard and hoping someone would notice. *Maybe if I do something special or important, people will notice me. Then I'll matter,* she thought.

But no matter what Janna did, or how hard she did it, or who she did it for, it was never enough. Janna still didn't feel like she mattered.

One day God spoke to Janna. He said, "Janna, you are enough." It wasn't because of how hard she tried or how much people liked her. She was enough because of God. Because he loved her, she mattered.

Your sense of worth comes from God. It can't come from people because people aren't perfect. Parents will let you down; friends will let you down. But God is perfect and his perfect love will love you always. Nothing can separate you from his forever love.

Getting good grades doesn't give you value. Getting a spot on the softball team doesn't give you value. Volunteering at church doesn't mean you matter. You matter because God says, "You are enough."

Dear God, thank you that I am enough. I still struggle to believe that sometimes, but help me know more every day that my value comes from you. Amen.

CRUSHING IT

Since you excel in everything—in faith, in speech, in knowledge, in complete earnestness and in the love we have kindled in you—see that you also excel in this grace of giving.
2 CORINTHIANS 8:7 NIV

When Sophie's mom and dad were out on a date one night, Sophie decided to surprise her mom and wash the dishes—something her mom always appreciated.

She washed all the dishes and then thought, *Mom is always telling me, "If you're going to do something, do it well," so I will.* So Sophie cleaned the sink, wiped down the counter, and swept the kitchen floor.

When her parents came back, her mom said, "Wow! This is so nice to come home to. Everything is so clean. It looks great!" She gave Sophie a big hug.

The older you get, the more responsibility you'll have around the house, in school, and in the decisions you make. When you do something, you can do just the bare minimum, or you can go above and beyond. When you give your best, you can take pride knowing you've done things with excellence.

Do whatever you're given well and excel!

Dear God, I want to give you and others my very best. Show me different ways I can go above and beyond. Amen.

JEALOUS FOR YOU

*The LORD, whose very name is Jealous,
is a God who is jealous about his relationship with you.*
EXODUS 34:14 NLT

Lian thought it was a little strange. She'd invited eight girls over for her birthday party. All of them had brought gifts—but none of them were for her. One friend brought a bouquet of flowers for Lian's mom. Another brought a book for her little sister. No one said "Happy Birthday" to Lian; they treated her like they did any other day of the week. Lian tried not to feel hurt, but couldn't help but thinking that it was *her* birthday, after all.

Lian's story is something that would never really happen, of course. But it shows us how God feels when we give praise and attention to things other than him. He's jealous for our attention. He wants our praise.

God wants to be your focus. If you crowd him out with busyness, if you make going to church a last priority, if you forget about spending time with him, God gets jealous. You're giving attention and time to other things and other people that really belongs to him. God loves you so much, he doesn't want to share you with anyone else.

Dear God, I never realized you were a jealous God. I want you to be first in my life. Please show me if anything is taking my attention away from you. Amen.

ACCEPTED

God's grace has saved you because of your faith in Christ.
Your salvation doesn't come from anything you do.
It is God's gift. It is not based on anything you have done.
No one can brag about earning it.
EPHESIANS 2:8-9 NIRV

When she was eight years old, Amy told her dad she wanted to be baptized. Amy's dad wasn't sure that was such a good idea. "Maybe you should wait a year," he suggested.

Amy knew why. She didn't always listen. She was stubborn and outspoken and sometimes talked back, and she wasn't nearly as good as her brother, Matt.

"I know I am not as good as Matt," she told her dad. But in her heart she knew that wasn't true. God accepted her into his family and he loved her, even though she wasn't where she wanted to be on the outside yet.

In the end, Amy's dad changed his mind. When Amy stood up on the day of her baptism and started to talk, she began to cry. She couldn't explain it but she just *knew* God was saying, "You're my daughter and I accept you."

You can't earn God's love. He doesn't accept you because you're good enough or perfect enough. He accepts you just because you believe him. He gives you salvation happily as a gift.

Dear God, thanks for accepting me with all my imperfections.
I'm a work in progress and I'm excited to see what you do. Amen.

CHRISTMAS COOKIES

Do not be shaped by this world;
instead be changed within by a new way of thinking.
Then you will be able to decide what God wants for you;
you will know what is good and pleasing
to him and what is perfect.

ROMANS 12:2 NCV

Who doesn't like making Christmas cookies? Especially gingerbread people and sugar cookies shaped like Christmas trees, stars, and candy canes. A little frosting (or a lot of frosting), red and green sprinkles, some creativity and voila! Christmas!

Before the cookies are baked, you roll out the dough on the kitchen counter. Then you dip the cookie cutter into flour so it doesn't stick to the dough and press it into the dough to create your shape.

People, places, and things all around you are trying to shape what you think and what you do. Magazines, tv, social media, and even your friends are all telling you what you should think and buy and what's important in life. Whatever or whoever you actually listen to is what's creating the shape of your life.

Make sure your life is being shaped by God's Word not others!

Dear God, I pray that I wouldn't get caught up in everything around me—what people think, what I see, where I go. Instead help my thinking to be shaped by you and your Word. Amen.

ALL WRAPPED UP

It is surely true that I find my rest in God.
PSALM 62:1 NIRV

"Mom, where's the hot chocolate. I'm freezing!"

After an hour of hockey practice on outdoor ice, Jamie's insides and outsides were frozen. Her mom fixed a cup of hot chocolate, and Jamie plopped down on the sofa. She tugged on the quilt draped over the back and wrapped it around her. She sat shivering for a few minutes, all wrapped up with only her eyes peeking over the top of the quilt. Finally she started to relax.

Sometimes our insides need to relax—because we're tired or upset or frustrated or starting to worry. When our thoughts are in a jumble, being wrapped up in the love of someone who understands us best can help us sort things out. A hug from a friend, a smile from your mom, or some good advice from your dad helps. But God wants us to know that more than anything we need him.

How would things be different if you let God be your rest?

Dear God, help me to know what it is to find my rest in you. Amen.

A TINY GIFT

Never let loyalty and kindness leave you!
Tie them around your neck as a reminder.
Write them deep within your heart.
PROVERBS 3:3 NLT

The week before Christmas all the kids in Penelope's neighborhood got together to exchange gifts. When they passed out the gifts, Penelope thought her friends' gifts seemed so big; hers looked so small. Maybe the gift she got wasn't quite as special.

When Penelope opened her tiny gift, it took her breath away. A silver necklace engraved with her name lay in a velvety box. It was the best present of all. She put it on and that's where it stayed. She never went anywhere without it.

Loyalty and kindness are like a necklace that God tells you to place around your neck. Never take them off; wear them wherever you go. Build your reputation as someone who is always caring and trustworthy.

Here's an idea you might consider: Design a necklace or bracelet with a single "K" charm for kindness or "L" for loyalty. When your friend insists a math problem is right when you know it's wrong, or your sister borrows your sweater without asking (again!), reach up and touch your necklace. Remember to be kind. Remember to be loyal.

Dear God, I know that being kind and loyal are things I won't ever regret. Remind me to wear them wherever I go. Amen.

JINGLE BELLS

The grass withers, the flower fades,
but the word of our God stands forever.

ISAIAH 40:8 NASB

Jingle bells,
Jingle bells,
Jingle all the way!

Every year we sing this Christmas song: a song your parents probably taught you when you were little. That song has been around a lot longer than when you were born. Actually it's been around a lot longer than when your mom or even her mom were born.

Children in Massachusetts were singing this song in 1850—a long, long time ago! It's lasted over a hundred and sixty years, and maybe it'll last that many more.

The words in the Bible have been around even longer. They'll last more than a long time—they'll last forever.

Because God never changes, you can read his Word and know that it won't change either. It never gets outdated or needs an upgrade. And that means you can build your life on something that lasts.

Dear God, your Word lasts forever. I can count on it like I can count on you. It's never going to change. Thank you. Amen.

A CHRISTMAS GIFT

Today your Savior was born in the town of David.
He is Christ, the Lord.
LUKE 2:11 NCV

Most kids liked to sleep in but not Gabriella. Her favorite time was early in the morning when the house was still and her three brothers and sisters were still quiet. She went into the kitchen to make some hot cocoa and then padded out to the living room to plug in the Christmas tree lights.

The tree was covered from top to bottom with bright-colored ornaments, and bright-colored packages tied up with ribbons and bows. Long packages, small packages. Fat boxes, flat boxes. She couldn't wait to open gifts. But she knew the best gift wasn't under that tree. *It's here inside,* she thought and put her hand on her heart.

The best Christmas gift is Jesus and the salvation he brings. The creator of the snow and trees came as a baby so you could have the gift of forever life. It's a gift that he holds out to you. You can't earn it or buy it. It's a present. There's only one thing to do—receive it. Just believe.

Dear Jesus, thank you for the gift of your life, for coming to earth to live and showing me what God is like. To die on the cross so that my sins could be gone and I could have life. I want the gift of salvation. I believe that you are Jesus, Savior of the world! Amen.

A LADY NAMED LORRAINE

One who loves a pure heart and who speaks with grace will have the king for a friend.
PROVERBS 22:11 NIV

Fun. Funny. Loyal. Loud. Smiley. Caring. That's how people describe Lorraine: a youth pastor on the East Coast. Lorraine wraps people up in her big smile and grace-filled words. She's always busy—helping people, making them laugh, looking for the good in them, helping them succeed and feel better about themselves.

Jesus was like Lorraine times 100. He always had compassion on people. He always stopped to show them love and give them hope and he wants us to do the same.

Other people love it when we are busy seeing…

How far they've come, not how far they have to go.

What they do well, not what they do not-so-well.

What they do right, not what they do wrong.

What they have going for them, not what they have against them.

Who they really are, not who everyone expects them to be.

When we love people like that, it makes them relax on the inside. Love on people like Jesus did and wrap someone up with a kind word and a smile.

Dear God, thank you for the people you've put in my life. Open my eyes to see your image in them. Help me to be the kind of person that makes them comfortable being themselves. Amen.

LOST CHANCE, BIG GAIN

In humility value others above yourselves,
not looking to your own interests
but each of you to the interests of the others.
PHILIPPIANS 2:3-4 NIV

Abbey D'Agostino and Nikki Hamblin had never met before the 2016 Olympics, but both were running track with hopes for a gold medal. In qualifiers for the 5,000-meter run, Abbey accidentally clipped Nikki. Nikki fell and started to cry, knowing she'd just lost her chance at a medal.

Instead of running on, Abbey crouched down beside Nikki and helped her up. Even though it cost her time, Abbey looked out for Nikki. Both finished the race but well behind the leaders.

Jesus was always looking out for others. Though he was God, he came as a baby and grew up into a man who died on a cross—all because he loved the world, and that includes you.

You can follow Jesus' lead and look out for others. Instead of being wrapped up in yourself, invest in someone else. Think about others and what's best for them.

- You don't have money to go to soccer camp, but you help work a fundraiser with a friend so she can go.
- You're chosen for the volleyball team and your first thought is to reach out to your friend who didn't.
- You're tired from school but you help your dad with dinner because he's had a long day too.

Dear God, it's so easy for me to think about myself, about what I need to do to get ahead and be noticed. Help me think of others and look out for what's best for them. Amen.

ONE KID, TWO WORLDS

"Come to me, all of you who are tired and have heavy loads, and I will give you rest....The burden that I ask you to accept is easy; the load I give you to carry is light."

MATTHEW 11:28, 30 NCV

Gabriela lived in two worlds. Every Monday through Wednesday she lived with her dad, stepmom, and two stepsisters. Every Thursday through Sunday she lived with her mom, stepdad, a chocolate lab, and Hazel—a guinea pig who liked to snuggle. Gabriela spent Christmas Eve and Thanksgiving with her mom and Christmas Day and Easter with her dad.

Sometimes it was hard to keep track. Honestly, Gabriela wished she didn't need to keep track. She wished all her favorite things and favorite people were together.

Going between two worlds can be tough. If that's you, Jesus invites you to come to him. "I will give you rest," he says. You can express your feelings. Not by yelling, or slamming doors, or huddling up in your room, or taking it out on your family. Go to him and dump it all out. Be real, be raw, be honest. He'll listen.

Then, find someone you can trust and be real with them too. Most importantly, don't get all worked up and stressed out, just rest.

Dear Jesus, I need rest. I need a break from the back and forth and trying to keep things straight. Fill me with your peace. Fill me with your joy. Show me that you're with me. Amen.

LOADED

"Don't store up treasures here on earth,
where moths eat them and rust destroys them,
and where thieves break in and steal.
Store your treasures in heaven."

MATTHEW 6:20-21 NLT

If you traveled to London, England, you might come across a store called Asprey, a luxury store where people from around the world shop for exclusive jewelry and accessories. A designer handbag might run $4,000, a pair of earrings might cost $22,000. One time, a beautiful necklace and bracelet set sold for $166,000!

You probably don't have that kind of money. But if you did…would it be wrong? Should you feel guilty? Jesus did say that those who are rich can have a very hard time following God. The temptation is to make money more important than God. But having wealth can also be a gift, not just for you, but for others.

If you do have money, share your gift in way that pleases God. Here's what he says:

- Be generous. God loves a cheerful giver.
- Be fair. Give people what you owe them.
- Don't hoard your money. When you see someone in need, help them out.
- Don't go overboard spending it on yourself.

If you're generous with money and rich in doing good deeds, you'll be storing up treasure in heaven.

Dear God, remind me to guard my heart so you're first and nothing else. And no matter if I have a little or a lot, give me a strong desire to be generous. Amen.

DEAR MOM

Listen to your father, who gave you life,
and do not forget your mother when she is old.
PROVERBS 23:22 NCV

Dear Mom,

When you were a kid, I know things were different. You didn't have stuff like smartphones or laptops or PS3s. But I know you had a first day of middle school. You had your first crush (I'm curious. Who was it?) You probably had an argument with your mom, something she didn't want you doing but you really wanted to anyway. (What did you disagree about?) Maybe you tried out for something and didn't make it....

So much has changed since your mom was your age, but a lot is still the same—parent relationships, sibling rivalry, teacher tensions, etc. Why don't you ask your mom about what her life was like? It would be fun to know…

What was her favorite subject? Why?

Did she ever go to the prom? Who did she go with? What did she wear?

What did her parents do if she disagreed with them? What kinds of things did she disagree about?

Dear God, thanks for my mom. Thanks for what she does. Show her every day how much you love her. Show her what your plan is for her life. Amen.

WORRY-BUSTER

Good planning and hard work lead to prosperity,
but hasty shortcuts lead to poverty.
PROVERBS 21:5 NLT

"There! I'm done," said Nicole standing back to admire her science fair entry. "The axis on the globe is a little crooked, but I still like it!"

"Lucky you," said Gabriela, twirling a loose curl of her hair. "I don't even know what I'm going to do yet. And it's due in three days!"

Worry is never fun. It eats you up inside, keeps you distracted at school, and awake at night. You can bust worry if you just plan ahead. "Good planning and hard work lead to prosperity," says Proverbs. (Not to mention a good night's sleep and a day that's worry free.) Shortcuts just stress you out.

Instead of worrying about what you didn't do or what has to be done, take control and bust that worry with a calendar, a pen, and a plan.

Who could you ask to help you with some planning-ahead tips?

Dear God, could you help me learn to plan ahead? Especially as this year closes and a new one begins. Please give me someone who could be my planning-ahead coach. Amen.

A Little God Time for
Mothers (Hardcover)
978-1-4245-4985-6

A Little God Time for
Women (Hardcover)
978-1-4245-5047-0

A Little God Time for
Teens (Hardcover)
978-1-4245-5207-8

A Little God Time for
Teachers (Hardcover)
978-1-4245-5281-8

A Little God Time for
Couples (Hardcover)
978-1-4245-5368-6

A Little God Time for
Girls (Hardcover)
978-1-4245-5391-4

A Little God Time for
Women (Faux)
978-1-4245-5229-0

A Little God Time
Coloring Devotional
Hardcover
978-1-4245-5284-9
Softcover
978-1-4245-5255-9

A Little God Time
Devotional Journal
Hardcover
978-1-4245-4923-8

A Little God Time
for Mothers (Journal)
Hardcover
978-1-4245-5148-4